THE PLOT TO SCAPEGOAT RUSSIA

How the CIA and the Deep State Have Conspired to Vilify Russia

DAN KOVALIK, ESQ.

FOREWORD BY DAVID TALBOT

Founder of *Salon* and *New York Times* bestselling author
of *The Devil's Chessboard: Allen Dulles, The CIA,* and
The Rise of America's Secret Government

Hot Books

Hot Books may be purchased in bulk at special discounts for sales promotion, corporate gifts, fund-raising, or educational purposes. Special editions can also be created to specifications. For details, contact the Special Sales Department, Skyhorse Publishing, 307 West 36th Street, 11th Floor, New York, NY 10018 or info@skyhorsepublishing.com.

Hot Books® and Skyhorse Publishing® are registered trademarks of Skyhorse Publishing, Inc.®, a Delaware corporation.

Visit our website at www.skyhorsepublishing.com.

10 9 8 7 6 5 4 3

Library of Congress Cataloging-in-Publication Data is available on file.

Cover design by Brian Peterson

Print ISBN: 978-1-5107-3032-8
Ebook ISBN: 978-1-5107-3033-5

Printed in the United States of America

CONTENTS

"Too often we judge other groups by their worst examples while judging ourselves by our best intentions."

— George W. Bush, July 2016

FOREWORD

THE RUSSIANS ARE COMING . . . again. It seems that al-Qaeda, ISIS, North Koreans, Mexican "bad hombres," and various other bogeymen were insufficient to the task of terrifying Americans. So now the US war machine—that vast complex of weapons manufacturers, Wall Street speculators, saber-rattling Washington politicians, armchair generals, and the media industry that thrives on boom and bang (or the "beautiful pictures of our fearsome armaments" in the unforgettable words of MSNBC's Brian Williams)—has revived the tried and true Red Scare. Day after day, night after night, the US citizenry is bombarded with scare stories about the evil machinations of Vladimir Putin and his Kremlin henchmen. How they stole our democracy and are scheming to conquer the entire NATO alliance. How they are building a military machine and nuclear arsenal that threaten to eclipse our own. How they are subverting the global free press with its low-ratings Russia Today network and army of hackers and trolls. How they are blocking peace in the Middle East with their machinations in Syria.

This massive anti-Russian propaganda campaign is one of the biggest fake news operations in US history. And we've had some colossal ones, dating back to the days of the Spanish American War, when newspaper magnate William Randolph Hearst instructed artist Frederic Remington to help him fabricate a clash of forces that did not exist: "You furnish the pictures and I'll furnish the war."

Ever since World War I, war has been America's lucrative "racket," in the mordant observation of Major General Smedley Darlington Butler, the most decorated marine of his day. The country's economic engine runs on blood and oil. Without the constant specter of a foreign enemy, there is no American prosperity. President Donald Trump couldn't find the money to rebuild our collapsing infrastructure, but he could burn through $93 million to hurl fifty-nine Tomahawk missiles at a Syrian airfield to send a message that he was no Putin puppet.

Trump promised to ease growing East-West tensions by finding common ground with Moscow. But the US national security state—and its numerous media assets—soon convinced him of the folly of peace. Putin is doomed to become the baddest hombre in the Trump shooting gallery.

I have no desire to live or work in Putin's Russia. Independent journalists and dissident leaders are constantly at risk there. But while the Kremlin casts a shadow over Russia's own freedom and democracy, its ability to project power and influence abroad is wildly overstated by the US war lobby. Russia's economy has shrunk so much that its GDP is roughly that of Spain. The US military budget is bigger than that of the next seven countries combined, while Russia spends less than Saudi Arabia on defense.

Russia's intervention in the sovereign affairs of other nations pales in comparison to the massive intrusions of the US security juggernaut. Over the past century, the US military and the CIA have overthrown democratically elected governments in Guatemala, Iran, Congo, Chile, and Indonesia; assassinated, jailed, or exiled leaders in these and other countries; subverted governments and elections in even allied countries like France and Italy; and hacked the phones of friendly leaders in Germany and Brazil. When US covert operations prove unable to impose our will on foreign affairs, Washington puts boots on the ground, invading and occupying nations from Vietnam to Afghanistan. Accusations of Russian interference from a country that routinely

big-foots the rest of the world surely rank as some of the biggest displays of chutzpah in history.

Despite its diminished stature in recent years, Russia (along with China) is the only country capable of even marginally standing in the way of Washington's vast imperial ventures. Therefore, it must be turned into a pariah state by the dependable media servants of the US security complex. It's the so-called liberal media—including the *New York Times*, *Washington Post*, CNN, and MSNBC—that is taking the lead in demonizing Russia, just as it did during the first Cold War when CIA spymasters like Allen Dulles wined and dined the Washington press corps and fed them their headlines and talking points.

The deep state crowed when Trump abandoned his flirtation with Putin. "This was inevitable," opined Philip H. Gordon, a former NSC apparatchik now embedded at the Council on Foreign Relations, a national security bastion since the days of Dulles. "Trump's early let's-be-friends initiative was incompatible with our interests, and you knew it would end in tears." Whose interests was Gordon referring to? Certainly not the interests of the American people, who are sick and tired of endless war and foreign intrigue and yearn for a leader who will truly put their well-beings first.

Unlike our war-obsessed media, human rights lawyer Dan Kovalik does understand that peace and diplomacy are in the best interests of the American and Russian peoples. His book is an urgently needed counterassault against the propaganda forces that are trying to push us over a precipice that is too terrifying to even contemplate. It's time for all of us to speak truth to power before it's too late.

—David Talbot
April 2017

INTRODUCTION

THIS BOOK GREW OUT OF AN article I wrote for *Huffington Post* entitled "Listen Liberals: Russia Is Not Our Enemy," which was written in response to what I view as the bizarre hysteria over Russia—a hysteria that has been reignited in the past several years and which is most recently being manifested in the current frenzy over what some are now calling, "Russia-gate." The hubbub relates to allegations that Vladimir Putin somehow attempted—though no one really thinks to great effect—to influence the outcome of the 2016 elections in support of his "friend" or "dupe" or "puppet," Donald J. Trump.

This harkens back to the 1962 film (re-made in 2004), *The Manchurian Candidate*, in which a man unwittingly becomes an assassin for the communists who have brain-washed him. Some currently pushing the anti-Russia conspiracy theory are even referring to Trump as "the Manchurian candidate." As the synopsis for the film on Wikipedia explains, "[t]he film was released in the United States on October 24, 1962, at the height of the Cuban Missile Crisis," which is universally viewed as the tensest and most dangerous moment of the (old) Cold War.

Of course, the current invocation of *The Manchurian Candidate* makes perfect sense given that we are now in the throes of a new, and I would argue equally dangerous, Cold War. As for how dangerous it is, Senator John McCain has ominously stated that, in considering the

Russian hacking issue, we need to consider "what constitutes an act of war or aggression in cyberspace that would merit a military response."[1] There are also Democrats, like Congressperson Bonnie Watson Coleman, who are likewise opining that what the Russians did, or were alleged to do, "is a form of war, a form of war on our fundamental democratic principles."

A curious, but I believe relevant note about *The Manchurian Candidate,* was that it starred none other than Frank Sinatra. Sinatra had once been a solid leftist, famously doing a ten-minute anti-racist short in 1945 called "The House I Live In," in which he sang a song by the same name written by Earl Robinson (music) and Abel Meeropol (lyrics).[2] Earl Robinson was a Communist who was later blacklisted during the McCarthy period. For his part, Abel, who most famously wrote "Strange Fruit" for Billie Holiday, was also persecuted during the McCarthy period and went on to adopt the two sons of Julius and Ethel Rosenberg after they were executed for alleged Soviet espionage in 1953. It is generally-accepted today that Ethel, maybe the most emblematic victim of the McCarthy period, was certainly innocent of the charges against her, was prosecuted to put pressure on Julius to talk, and was put to death anyway. Indeed, her two sons are still trying to pursue justice for Ethel to this day.[3]

Sinatra had befriended a number of blacklisted writers during the McCarthy period, and even openly dined with them to publically show his support for them. He went on to aggressively campaign for John F. Kennedy for president, and indeed his song, "High Hopes" became Kennedy's campaign anthem. By the time he starred in *The Manchurian Candidate,* however, Sinatra had turned his back on the left, resentful of how the Kennedys had turned their back on him over his ostensible ties to the Mafia. Sinatra would become an arch-conservative, as many from that era did, ultimately supporting Ronald Reagan for President. I guess this goes to show that you just didn't cross 'Ole Blue Eyes.

But more importantly, the early career of Frank Sinatra, one of the greatest American entertainers ever, shows how influential the left in

general, and the Communist Party in particular, were in this society at one point, and, I would argue, for the good. The McCarthy trials effectively diminished the influence that the left, both Communist and otherwise, had on our society, and that was of course their intent.

What is shaping up to be a new McCarthy period, in which people are accused of being dupes for Russia for simply questioning the prevailing anti-Russian discourse, is obviously different from the old one, but with essentially the same intention and effect—to curb dissent, particularly in regard to US foreign policy, which, by any rational measure, is incredibly destructive for our country and the world at large. It is also intended to distract Americans from the real crimes that its own country is committing. I will give but one example of this for now.

According to the United Nations, the greatest humanitarian crisis in the world today is happening in Yemen. I doubt that you would know this from the mainstream media because they do not talk about it very much, and certainly not with the frequency with which it deserves. Simply put, Yemen, one of the poorest nations on earth, is being brought to the brink of famine by a one-sided war which Saudi Arabia and other Gulf countries are waging against the largely Shia population there. Now into its third year, the war has left "over 10,000 dead, 40,000 wounded, 2.5 million internally displaced, 2.2 million children suffering from malnutrition and over 90 percent of civilians in need of humanitarian aid."[4] What's more, the US has been supporting this war with billions of dollars of armaments, including cluster bombs; logistical support, including mid-flight refueling of Saudi coalition bomber planes; and with intelligence and location-tracking support. The support for the Saudi war effort began under Obama and seems to be intensifying under Trump. The result is that the civilian population is being killed in great numbers, and there is a great risk, according to the UN again, that in this already food-insecure country, over 7 million people could perish from starvation, and over 18 million will die without immediate humanitarian assistance.[5]

And yet there is near-silence about this conflict and the US role in

it from our mainstream press. Instead, the press would have you spend all of your emotional energy worrying about what Vladimir Putin may be up to in Ukraine, or in Syria or, allegedly, in Trump's White House. At the same time, there appears to be little concern over the bizarre hold that the retrograde, repressive monarchy of Saudi Arabia has over US foreign policy, or even that Hillary Clinton, as Secretary of State, approved a $29 billion shipment of fighters to Saudi Arabia—some of these jets are certainly being used against Yemen right now—after both Saudi Arabia and the maker of the jets (Boeing) made donations to the Clinton Foundation.[6]

Meanwhile, reminiscent of the old Cold War and the McCarthyite witch hunt that was one of the more shameful aspects of it, my *Huffington Post* article provoked much vitriol. Thus, for arguing that maybe we should re-consider whether Russia and Vladimir Putin are truly threats to our democracy and freedom as some are arguing, I was accused by some of being a Russian "agent" or at least a "useful idiot" of the Kremlin—the latter slur deriving from a quote usually attributed to Joseph Stalin.

I expect such attacks, and worse, after this book is published, as it is now quite fashionable to go around accusing people of working in the interests of Vladimir Putin and Moscow. Indeed, just the other day, Senator John McCain, on the floor of the Senate, accused a fellow Republican legislator, Rand Paul, of "working for Vladimir Putin" because Paul had the temerity to suggest that the US start reconsidering its current levels of funding for NATO. It is indeed the silly season. However, not all the reactions to my piece were bad. Indeed, some were quite validating. For example, I received an email from Ray McGovern, a man I had never spoken with before, but who I discovered had served as an analyst for the CIA from 1963 to 1990, chaired National Intelligence Estimates in the 1980s and received the Intelligence Commendation Medal upon retirement. McGovern is now an outspoken critic of many of the CIA's practices, including torture, and is very skeptical of the current claims about Russia hacking. In any

case, Mr. McGovern emailed me a simple message. Under the subject line, "MANY THANKS," he wrote the following message: "from Jerusalem w Veterans For Peace group doing solidarity w Palestinians your piece is good; i've asked son/webmeister joseph to post on raymcgovern. Keep em coming! r."

For me, this message was very rich in meaning. First of all, the fact that a long-time CIA analyst turned critic thought I was on track with my message, and bothered telling me while he was on a trip half way around the world, gave me great encouragement. Truth be told, it has been others just like Ray—others who left the CIA in disgust and became activists against the war machine—who have played probably the biggest role in helping me to view the world as I do today.

Thus, at the University of Dayton in the late 1980s, my activist friends and I spent a lot of time studying the crimes of the CIA, most of which were revealed by former agents. There was a veritable cottage industry of these guys writing and speaking at that time, and we couldn't get enough. Our interest was sparked at that time by what was a pretty big national movement to protest CIA recruitment on college campuses, and the CIA did indeed recruit at our school every year. We thought this was particularly inappropriate at a Catholic school like ours.

Probably the most famous of the CIA exiles was Phil Agee, who is universally regarded as the first CIA officer to blow the whistle on "the Company," as he and others called the CIA. I myself was particularly interested in Agee because his background was a lot like mine—he was a devout Catholic who went to Catholic schools his whole life, eventually graduating from Notre Dame in 1956. He actually overlapped with my dad, who also went to Notre Dame and graduated shortly after Agee. Just to give a little context here, my dad used to gleefully recount how a priest at Notre Dame would organize football players to go out and beat up Communists on campus. Or, at least, the victims were accused of being Communists. This was, after all, in the 1950's, during the McCarthy Period, when a Communist was seen lurking in

every closet. Maybe, in fact, these "Communists" were merely unionists or civil rights activists or Democrats, or others who represented the
main evil Senator McCarthy was trying to wipe out—President Roo-
sevelt's New Deal. In any case, whomever these poor folks were, they
got a good ass-whooping.

After several years of training, Agee worked as undercover agent
for eight years in Latin America—in Ecuador, Uruguay and Mexico,
in particular.[7] While he joined the Company, as I assume most people
do, out of a sincere belief that it was an institution necessary to protect
the US from various evils around the globe, most notably from those
inspired and/or supported by the USSR, he soon became disillusioned
by the evils that he and his fellow agents perpetrated.

In particular, Agee became quite upset by his being a party to the
torture of people in Uruguay, some of whom, as the agents were quite
aware, knew nothing and had done nothing. Rather, they were simply
guinea pigs taken off the street at random to try various torture techniques out on. As Agee would say later, these people couldn't even say
anything to stop the torture because they had no information to give
to stop it. Agee left the CIA in disgust, saying, "'[a]fter 12 years with
the agency I finally understood how much suffering it was causing,
that millions of people all over the world had been killed or had their
lives destroyed by the CIA and the institutions it supports.'"[8]

Meanwhile, John Stockwell was another former CIA agent who
made a huge impression on me. I don't remember how we came into
possession of it, but my friend Jon and I listened over and over to a
cassette tape which contained a speech by Stockwell. It was incredibly revelatory. Stockwell too tells how he joined the CIA for all the
right reasons and then became disillusioned by what he witnessed in
Angola, where he was stationed. At that time, the US and South Africa
were supporting the UNITA counter-revolutionary forces against the
revolutionary Angolan government, which in turn was being bolstered
by Cuban ground forces.

Stockwell explained how the CIA manipulated the news about the

Angolan conflict. He related that it was in fact easy to do so because the press, both gullible and lazy, was willing to publish any story they put out, no matter how outlandish. For example, Stockwell explained how he and his CIA team submitted fake stories about one particular Cuban military unit, all of which were dutifully published in the papers. In this instance, they stated that a Cuban unit raped Angolan women. This unit was attacked and wiped out by UNITA forces, only to then miraculously return from the dead to continue more mayhem. He assured the listener that such CIA tales continue to be passed along as news by the media. He also explained how he ended up deciding that it was the Cubans who were the good guys in the Angolan conflict.

Armed with such knowledge, my activist friends and I ended up taking over the University President's office for three days in protest of CIA recruitment on campus. While we were not able to prevail upon the University to end this recruitment, we were allowed to help plan a speaker series on the CIA which included, at our urging, a talk by Phil Agee. Agee at that time was travelling under Cuban and Nicaraguan passports, his US passport having been stripped from him long before. Soon after we met Agee, he would go into self-exile in Cuba, where he would peacefully die at the age of 72.

I guess this is a long way to explain why Ray McGovern's email message about my Russia piece meant so much to me, and also triggered long-held feelings about the evils of US foreign policy, the lies told to make us go along with this policy, and the particular role the CIA has in both the policy and the lies. All of this is quite relevant to the current discussion about alleged Russian hacking and the greater story being weaved about Vladimir Putin.

Of course, the character of Vladimir Putin, and I call it "the character," or really "the caricature" of Putin that the press is feeding us, is important because he is being thrust before us as a symbol or proxy for a revived Russia, which we are being encouraged to hate and fear again, just as we did during the first Cold War. This process of fear-mongering has been going on for some time, but is now being

even further exaggerated by the Democrats, who are desperately looking for anyone but themselves to blame for their seemingly impossible
loss to Donald Trump in the 2016 elections.

And the press is more than happy to go along with this Putin/
Russia bashing based upon facts which are exaggerated, invented and
sometimes just plain false. I'll give an example: I was listening to NPR,
and I heard David Greene, a fellow Pittsburgher, do a story about the
2008 Russia-Georgia conflict.[9]

First of all, what immediately struck me about the story was that
NPR was transparently seizing on an event which happened almost a
decade ago to fan the flames of anti-Russian sentiment. Indeed, here is
how Greene sets up the piece:

> You know, one thing you can say about Russia's president, Vlad-
> imir Putin—when he spots an opportunity, he grabs it. I mean, here's
> just a list—alleged cybermeddling in last year's US presidential elec-
> tion; sending his military into Syria, into Crimea, into Ukraine. And
> now here's another story that is not so well-known. And it takes us to
> the former Soviet Republic of Georgia and a renegade province called
> South Ossetia, which sits right on Russia's southern border. This Putin
> opportunity came in 2008 when Georgia tried to put down South
> Ossetia's drive for independence. Russia's military moved right in.

At least to me, the way this story was framed was so obviously
meant to keep the NPR listenership wariness about Putin at a fever
pitch. Greene is obviously just trying to stack up as many of Putin's
misdeeds as he can, for example stretching Crimea and Ukraine into
two conflicts when they are arguably one given that Crimea is a disputed territory between Ukraine and Russia. The problem for people
like Greene, of course, is that as bad as Putin might be, he just isn't
involved in that many conflicts beyond Russia's borders, certainly
not when compared with the US, which certainly outdoes him in this
respect by leaps and bounds.

Moreover, the simplistic way in which "journalists" like Greene paint such conflicts as the 2008 Russia-Georgia conflict—with clear good guys and bad guys—simply does not fairly take into account the reality that the countries and peoples of the former Soviet Union are still suffering the growing pains (or really, shrinking pains) of the tumultuous collapse of the USSR in 1991. To lay this all of this on the feet of Vladimir Putin is overly simplistic, one-sided and simply bad journalism, again, if you could even call what people like David Greene do journalism.

This brings us to the most glaring problem with this piece: in order to tag Putin with as many ostensible crimes as possible, Greene simply invents one. Thus, Putin was not President at the time that Russian troops were sent into South Ossetia, and he consequently did not order this invasion. Rather, the Russian President who ordered that invasion was a leader whom the US (though apparently not the Russian people so much) actually likes—Dmitry Medvedev.[10] The reason I know this is that I paid very close attention to this conflict at the time, given that the leader on the other side of the conflict—then-Georgia President Mikheil Saakashvili—graduated from Columbia Law School just one year after me in 1994.

So, just to connect the dots here, Greene pulls out an event from nearly a decade ago to try to tarnish Putin with, and it turns out that Putin wasn't even behind this event. What we have here, then, is propaganda, pure and simple. And not from *Fox & Friends*, but really from the *Fox & Friends* for liberals—National Public Radio, which must be trustworthy, because they talk in a soft voice and play jazz and classical music between news segments.

Still, their apparently liberal bona fides do not prevent the good folks at NPR from cheerleading every US intervention, threatened or ongoing; minimizing the cruelties of these interventions and over-emphasizing the misdeeds of our adversaries. As just one example of this, I recall vividly listening to NPR's Scott Simon when he gave a whole monologue on how the US "shock and awe" campaign against Iraq in

2003—a campaign which, of course, was wholly premised on lies—constituted a "humane bombing."[11] Our bombs just don't hurt as much, apparently, because of the loving intentions behind them. George Orwell is rolling in his grave.

To analyze the current anti-Putin/Russia hysteria, we must do what the mainstream press will not. First and foremost, we must honestly analyze our own role in the world. This is more difficult than it may seem at first blush, given our seemingly unshakeable belief in the myth of "American Exceptionalism"—that is, the belief that the US is a uniquely benign actor in the world, spreading peace and democracy wherever we go. I think when we objectively look at the US's actions—even when compared to Russia's over the past fifty or so years—and the reasonably foreseeable results of those actions, we shall see that this belief is wholly unwarranted.

Of course, that this is true, as I believe, would certainly not excuse any meddling by Putin in our democratic process. But I think when one analyzes the "meddling" allegations being made at this point, they largely boil down to the claim that Russia attempted to undermine Americans' faith in their own democratic system through the spreading of "fake news." My answer to this would be that the spreading of "fake news" has been much more effectively done by those in our own country (most notably the CIA itself, which is pushing the "Russia-gate" issue so hard) who are so invested in the waging of eternal war, and by the subservient press which is complicit in this. I would also say that the "fake news" component of the Russia-baiting is much more damning of us than the Russians. Thus, if the US democratic system is so fragile and brittle that it could be impacted by the machinations of "internet trolls" (which the Senate Intelligence Committee spent a whole day talking about) or by RT News broadcasters, this says volumes about the poor state of our own democratic institutions. And indeed, these institutions are in a poor state, and this has many reasons, none of which can be blamed on Russia, though it may make us feel better to do so.

A final, related issue before we dive in is whether, by writing this book, I am somehow apologizing for the misdeeds of Vladimir Putin. In the end, others will have to, and I'm sure will, be the judge of that, but I would submit that what I am trying to do is not to apologize for Putin or to deny his own wrongdoings, but to explain them; to put them in some context, particularly in the context of US conduct, which has been seen, many times quite reasonably, as hostile to Russia and its interests, and which have helped bring us to the point where our two countries now stand in relation to each other.

I think what often happens when we talk about the types of issues raised in this book—for example, human rights, or the rightness of military action—there is a very strong tendency to focus on the failures of others rather than of ourselves. While this may be comforting, it is largely useless, because we have much more control over the conduct of our own country (at least to the extent it is truly democratic) than we do over others. In addition, it is the essence of morality to meditate on one's own wrongdoing, to try to find ways to make up for it and to be resolved not to repeat it. That is, as the Bible tells us, we are called to refrain from picking a speck from our brother's or sister's eye when we have a plank in our own. In that spirit, this book focuses on the sizeable plank in our own eye with the hope that we can pull it out ourselves.

1

COLD WAR KID

Since childhood, I have been fascinated by Russia. In my early years, I was, like many in this country during those Cold War days, quite fearful of Russia—then the USSR—and viewed it as the greatest threat in the world to democracy, freedom, and "our way of life." I vividly remember thinking, as I enjoyed a day riding the roller coasters at the amusement park or watching my favorite television shows, "I bet they don't have these kinds of things in Russia." Such thoughts gave me a very warm feeling of comfort and moral superiority.

My fear of Russia at this time was indeed religious. As with many fellow conservative Roman Catholics at that time, it was my wont to say the Rosary for the purpose of asking Our Lady of Fatima for the "conversion of Russia." Of course, what this meant was praying for Russia to be "converted" from its then-current state as the Communist Soviet Union to some type of "free," "democratic" and free-market nation, like the United States. If this conversion took place, I certainly believed, the world would find itself at peace, and free from the threat of a nuclear holocaust which I was otherwise certain was forthcoming.

As I grew older, I came to find that life and geo-politics were much more complicated than originally thought. The war in Central America in the 1980's was a huge eye-opener for me. It began to gnaw at me that the US was arming and training quite repressive military forces, in the

case of El Salvador, Guatemala and Honduras, against the peoples of much weaker and poorer countries than ourselves.

My interest in Central America began in the fall of 1979, when two new students entered my small, and hitherto all-white middle school of St. Andrew's in Milford, Ohio, about a 30-minute drive to downtown Cincinnati. The two students were named Juan and Carlos Garcia. And, they had just moved to town from Managua, Nicaragua.

Juan and Carlos were huge kids, much taller and heavier than any other student at the school. Indeed, Juan ended up playing center for our middle school's basketball team. As anyone who has visited Nicaragua would tell you, the large size of these two boys was quite unusual for a country which, especially back then, was so poor and undernourished. However, Juan and Carlos claimed to be special: they were the grandsons of the President of Nicaragua who had just been toppled over the summer (on July 19 to be exact) by a rag-tag group of insurgents known as the Sandinistas.

Now, even I knew that the leader toppled in Nicaragua was named Somoza—Anastasio Somoza. However, it is certainly possible that Juan and Carlos had taken on different, and quite common, names to hide their notorious identity. Was it possible that these two affable boys were related to the famous dictator? This seems to me even today to be far-fetched, and my research has not borne fruit on this topic. In any case, the presence of these ostensible Somocistas at my school triggered a life-long curiosity about Central America.

Then, one evening at the age of 12, I was sitting alone in my parents' room with their tiny TV, watching one of my favorite shows—*60 Minutes*. On this particular night, *60 Minutes* focused on the rape and murder of four Catholic Church women in El Salvador and on the subsequent murder of the Salvadoran Catholic Archbishop, Oscar Romero. Shockingly, the gist of this segment was that those responsible for these crimes were not in fact the left-wing guerillas in El Salvador the US was fighting, but rather, right-wing forces, known as "death squads," aligned with the government and military which the US was

funding and arming. There must have been some sort of mistake or accident, I thought, as I squirmed at this revelation.

This *60 Minutes* episode caused me great cognitive dissonance. Why would the US—the most noble, righteous nation in the world, as I believed at the time—be supporting the killing of nuns and bishops? This was quite troubling to me, though I tried to slough it off, excusing our possible excesses as an unfortunate and accidental consequence of our otherwise righteous fight against Communism. But the damage was done. A seed of doubt was starting to germinate within me. And, when I studied the case of El Salvador further, as I did at that time for a school paper, my doubts only grew.

From my reading of history, the US appeared to be on the wrong side of every conflict in El Salvador dating back to 1932—supporting the few rich landowners over the vast poor who were struggling for what seemed to be a fair share of the land and resources.

And, the US's support of the rich and powerful in that country had disastrous consequences, with mass killings by the US-backed Salvadoran Army, such as in the case of the El Mozote massacre in 1981 which claimed 800 victims, mostly landless peasants and indigenous people.

As Noam Chomksy explains in his introduction to the book *Colombia: The Genocidal Democracy*, by Father Javier Giraldo (now out of print), the violence inflicted against the Salvadoran population by the army trained and funded by the US was "religious" in nature—many of us would say, though he does not, satanic—but was hardly ever covered in the US press. As Chomsky explains:

> The record of horrors is all too full. In the Jesuit *America*, Rev. Daniel Santiago, a priest working in El Salvador, reported in 1990 the story of a peasant woman who returned home one day to find her mother, sister and three children sitting around the table, the decapitated head of each person placed on the table in front of the body, the hands arranged on top 'as if each body was stroking its own head' The

assassins, from the Salvadoran National Guard, had found it hard to keep the head of an 18-month-old baby in place, so they nailed the hands to it. A large plastic bowl filled with blood stood in the center of the table.

Two years earlier, the Salvadoran human rights group that continued to function despite the assassination of its founders and directors reported that 13 bodies had been found in the preceding two weeks, most showing signs of torture, including two women who had been hanged from a tree by their hair, their breasts cut off and their faces painted red. The discoveries were familiar, but the timing is significant, just as Washington was successfully completing the cynical exercise of exempting its murderous clients from the terms of the Central America peace accords that called for 'justice, freedom and democracy,' 'respect for human rights,' and guarantees for 'the endless inviolability of all forms of life and liberty.' The record is endless, and endlessly shocking.

Such macabre scenes, which rarely reached the mainstream in the United States, are designed for intimidation. Father Santiago writes that "People are not just killed by death squads in El Salvador—they are decapitated and then their heads are placed on pikes and used to dot the landscape. Men are not just disemboweled by Salvadoran Treasury Police; their severed genitalia are stuffed in their mouths. Salvadoran women are not just raped by the national guard; their wombs are cut from the bodies and used to cover their faces. It is not enough to kill the children; they are dragged over barbed wire until the flesh falls from their bones while parents are forced to watch."

When confronted with the fact that my own government was behind such horrors, my response was muddled. I concluded that though possibly mistaken in its historical support for those who oppressed the poor in El Salvador, the US nonetheless had to stay the course against the greatest evil in the world—the Communist menace which, as I recognized, was awakened in El Salvador as a direct consequence of the

US's prior bad policies. In other words, I openly advocated the continuation of a wrong policy to confront a threat created by that policy to begin with—a natural position for a child desperately clinging to a dogma that didn't make sense (though also a common position for adults trying to justify the worst types of crimes).

My complete and final break with my once-held belief in the inherent goodness of American foreign policy came with the realities I learned about the war in another Central American country—Nicaragua. During my freshman year of College, still under the sway of my anti-Communist ideology, I had very mixed views about Nicaragua. On the one hand, I understood that the Contras were filled with ex-members of the brutal Somoza regime, and that, true to their roots, they were gross human rights abusers. At the same time, I was skeptical of the Sandinistas for what I was told was their strong ties to the Soviet Union and its "client state," Cuba, and for what I was led to believe was its own human rights abuses.

At the beginning of the summer of 1987, I was reading *The Nation* magazine when I saw a small ad which caught my eye: "Travel to Nicaragua. Learn about the realities of the revolution while helping Nicaragua grow on a reforestation brigade." This was an ad placed by the Nicaragua Network which hosted regular delegations to Nicaragua.

I thought to myself that joining such a trip was what I needed to deal with my ambivalence over Nicaragua. I had to see for myself what was happening in that country. Reading opposing narratives of the Nicaraguan experience was simply not helping to resolve the conflict I was having within me over the war in Central America as well as the greater question of the real role of the United States in the world. So, I resolved to travel to Nicaragua in September—the first month of my sophomore year at the University of Dayton.

Professor Pat Donnelly, Chair of the Sociology Department, gently warned me before my trip that the enthusiasm which was motivating my adventure, though admirable in some ways, was also potentially dangerous. He strongly suggested that my enthusiasm

bordered on gullibility (which was probably true to some extent) and cautioned me to be careful lest I fall under the sway of the Sandinistas too easily.

It is said of the ground-breaking rock and roll band The Velvet Underground that while they only sold 25,000 albums in their career, everyone who bought an album started their own band as a result. A similar thing can be said of the relatively few who travelled to Nicaragua during the 1980s—they would carry the impression of Nicaragua and the revolution for the rest of their lives and would be life-long activists against US intervention abroad. This was certainly true of me.

For a guy whose only foreign trip was to the Canadian-side of Niagara Falls, Nicaragua was a jarring experience. The first night my delegation of about 12 landed in Managua, there was a black-out in the part of town where we were staying. This was a part of the daily rolling blackouts which were a consequence of the Contra war. While the Contras never controlled one centimeter in Nicaragua, and never gained anything but the most marginal support amongst the population, they were able to succeed at their chief mission—they wreaked havoc in Nicaragua, completely undermining the economy and sewing seeds of fear among the population.

Pretty early on into the war on Vietnam, the US determined that it could not "win" the war by vanquishing the liberation forces, so it instead adopted a program through which the US would bomb Vietnam back to the Stone Age, leaving the liberation forces with a pile of rubble to govern over. Similarly, the US determined that in Nicaragua, the only realistic option was that of terrorism. The goal was not to overthrow the Sandinistas—they were simply too popular and too organized to allow for that. Instead, the US would try to turn Nicaragua into an economic and social basket case—as an example of what other would-be revolutionaries in the region and around the world had to look forward to should they prevail.

Speaking to us in a small restaurant by candle-light, the Nicaragua Network representative based in Managua gave us an introduction

to our journey. She explained to us that we would be travelling by bus to Ocotal, a small town on the border with Honduras. While this was technically a "war zone," the Sandinistas had things well in hand. Therefore, we would be safe.

She gave us a bit of background on the revolution and what the Sandinistas were trying to accomplish—including battling the huge illiteracy problem they inherited from the Somoza years, as well as bringing health care and a better standard of living to the remotest parts of the country. She explained how, in trying to accomplish these goals, the Sandinistas had made mistakes. For example, they had tried to bring development to the Mosquito coast of Nicaragua, inhabited by English-speaking members of the Mosquito Indian tribe, where they met resistance by the residents who believed that they were unduly interfering with their region and culture. The Sandinistas reacted in a heavy-handed way, which ended up backfiring. A number of those in the region ended up supporting the Contras in reaction, though the Contras proved to be so violent and abusive that much of this support had, by then, dissipated.

She also told a wonderful anecdote about Sandinista leader Tomas Borge, who was simply called "Tomas" in Nicaragua, just as Fidel Castro was known as simply, "Fidel." Tomas was infamous in the US at that time, labeled as enemy number one by President Reagan who portrayed him as a hard-line Marxist-Leninist who would usher Communist reign into Central America if not stopped. You could say that Tomas served the same role, though on a smaller scale, as Putin does today—as the bogeyman under the bed we needed to be afraid of. In truth, he was a communist, but a Christian as well, and he was also one of the founding members of the Sandinistas back in 1962, earning his credentials as a life-long fighter against the Somoza dictatorship which the US supported until the bitter end.

Tomas was also, as I learned, "the most tortured man alive" according to Amnesty International. During the Somoza years, Tomas had been caught and captured, along with his wife, by the notorious

National Guard. As they were wont to do, either as National Guardsmen or as their later incarnation as the Contras, the soldiers raped and
killed Tomas's wife in front of his eyes. They then turned to physically
torturing Tomas himself, castrating him in the end. However, they
made the mistake of leaving Tomas, who vowed vengeance against
these soldiers, alive.

Tomas not only survived, he went on to help topple the Somoza
regime in 1979. And, now, as he vowed, it was time for revenge. Shortly
after the "triumph" over Somoza, Tomas learned that some of his torturers had been captured and were in prison. Tomas himself told what
happened next in his book, *Christianity and Revolution: Tomas Borge's
Theology of Life*: "[a]fter having been brutally tortured as a prisoner,
after having a hood placed over my head for nine months, after having
been handcuffed for seven months, I remember that when we captured
these torturers I told them: 'The hour of my revenge has come: we will
not do you even the slightest harm. You did not believe us beforehand;
now you will believe us.' That is our philosophy, our way of being."

Borge then approached the man and hugged him, telling him that,
for his punishment for torturing not only he and his family, but many
of his fellow Nicaraguans, he was to be let free—free to see the Nicaraguans he had kept down for so many years learn to read and write
and prosper. With tears streaming down his face, as well as that of the
prisoner, Borge swung the gate of the cell open and ushered the man
to walk out free into the streets.

It was this act of forgiveness and humanity by the "hardliner"
Tomas Borge which characterized the Sandinista revolution. The Sandinistas, having studied and learned from the lessons and mistakes of
the Soviet, Chinese and Cuban revolutions, and being motivated by
the radical Christianity of Liberation Theology, were resolved to be different. No firing squads would they set up for the Somocistas. Rather,
one of the first acts of the Sandinistas was to abolish the death penalty
altogether.

The US would take advantage of the decency and benevolence of

the Sandinistas to undermine them. Right after the fall of the Somoza dictatorship, then-President Jimmy Carter airlifted hundreds of National Guardsmen to Honduras. These would later be organized by the CIA under Reagan as the Contras, a terrorist organization which would plague Nicaragua for years to come.

While I was in Octotal, a young man in the town was ambushed and murdered by the Contras, and my delegation was invited to the funeral. I stood by the father of the slain man near his grave, and as we put our arms around each other, I apologized for his son's death, which was just as surely the fault of my country as anyone's. I knew then that I would never think of the world quite in the same way again.

Meanwhile, even in a war zone, I saw very few soldiers of any kind. The few Sandinsta soldiers I did see were armed with guitars as they serenaded the community from a balcony in the town square. I did see one Cuban soldier. He stood out as a towering, handsome figure. I also recall after seeing him, I asked a Nicaraguan in a community meeting we attended in Ocotal, "Aren't you afraid of the Cubans taking over Nicaragua; of the 'Cubanization' of Nicaragua," as Reagan termed it. This question was not only prompted by my encounter with the Cuban soldier but also what I had been taught by my dad and my government to fear in Nicaragua.

The answer to my question, though, was as direct as it was simple: "No, we are not worried about that. The Cubans are sending us teachers and doctors to help us. They don't try to influence our country; they just give us aid that we otherwise would not have. They are our brothers." This made a huge impression on me, and I began to wonder if in fact I had been hoodwinked about the true nature of my country's role in the world. And, indeed, the much-maligned Cuba continues to offer its "brotherhood" throughout the world, providing medical assistance to over 70 countries.

Sandinista guerrilla Omar Cabezas, in his memoir *Fire From The Mountain*, a book many of us were reading in the 1980's, recounts one of the galvanizing events of the revolutionary insurgency—an event,

as he notes, which was foolishly broadcast on nation-wide TV. As the whole nation watched, the repressive National Guard—a force created by the US to keep the Somoza dictatorship in power—surrounded the hideout of a group of top-level Sandinista insurgents, including the legendary Comandante Julio Buitrago. Cabezas, in a wonderful passage which deserves quoting, especially since his book is no longer in print, recounts how Comandante Julio wowed the nation by holding off the Guard single-handedly from a small house he was trapped in:

> We couldn't take our eyes off the screen . . . . We saw the barrel of Julio's submachine gun at the balcony window, and the smoke of the gun bursts when he fired back. Then he was at the basement window, or at another window on the first floor, or at the door of the second floor that opened onto the street. Then suddenly Julio wasn't anywhere to be seen, and the Guard wasn't moving, and nobody was firing. The officers of the Guard were conferring outside. The Guard started advancing on the house. Then, Julio suddenly appeared, shooting from one of those placed I mentioned, and the Guardsmen turned tail and shot off running in the other direction. . . .
>
> There was a long silence . . . then the tank opened fire. Our eyes practically popped out of our heads when the tank shattered the wall, exploding it to pieces. 'Maybe they haven't hit him,' we said, 'maybe they haven't . . . ' When the tank stopped firing you could see the officers screaming for their men to advance on the house. Nobody answered from inside, and when the Guardsmen got really close, Julio started shooting. And the Guardsmen turned tail again, and the tank opened fire again, and it was the same thing all over. An endless silence followed. A small plane appeared. Then all hell broke loose—the whole Guard started shooting, and the tank, and the plane, almost grazing the roof, and in a matter of seconds the house was a pile of rubble. . . . We couldn't imagine how Julio could possibly be alive. But the Guardsmen were ducking; Julio's bullets were zinging past them; they fell down wounded; and then suddenly

something happened that moved us very much: we saw Julio come bursting through the front door, running and firing his submachine gun, and seconds later he started to double over; still firing he doubled over a little more, firing and doubling over until he fell to the ground. We felt like crying, but at the same time we felt that we had an indestructible force. . . .

You can bet that every last person in Nicaragua with a TV set saw it. And people without a set saw it too, because Somoza was stupid enough to keep showing it for several days on television. People went over to their neighbors' to see it. They saw the Guardsmen shaking in their boots; they heard them screaming through megaphones for Julio to surrender. They saw the tanks—I remember now, there were two tanks. One plane and two helicopters. And Julio, all by himself.

It was such a heroic act, a true example of David versus Goliath, that helped to galvanize the Nicaraguan people against the Somoza dictatorship—a dictatorship which the US had installed and supported even beyond the dictatorship's end.

The David/Goliath myth is maybe one of the most over-used and misused myths, especially by the United States. I cannot emphasize too much how the US, despite its many times claiming to be a David fighting in the face of Goliath, has, with very few and quite remote exceptions, never in fact been, or even supported, the David in biblical battles.

Rather, as in the case of Nicaragua, it was clear to me that the US, which always portrays itself as the underdog in a world of bullies set upon its destruction, has been the Goliath trying to crush David by sheer, overpowering violence. Sometimes the US is the Goliath wielding the club, and other times, it is supporting mini-Goliaths, like Somoza, in attempting to vanquish the Davids. In Nicaragua, David, in the form of everyday people, sometimes wielding only bricks and stones against National Guardsmen armed by the US with machine guns and tanks and airplanes, was the victor. And the US

simply could not tolerate such a result—thus, its support of the murderous Contras.

It was just such a realization, which Nicaragua gave me in spades, that led me to the realization, as Malcolm X famously stated, in words he could have said to me: "You've been hood-winked, you've been tricked, you've been bamboozled." I would never be the same. It now dawned on me that, as Martin Luther King said much better than I could in denouncing the US war in Vietnam, "The US is on the wrong side of the world-wide revolution." Daniel Ellsberg, the former RAND Corporation analyst who leaked the Pentagon Papers in 1971, went even further, saying, "The US is not on the wrong side; it is the wrong side."

Of course, the strong implication being that the Soviet Union, which was supporting the liberation struggles we were trying to suppress, was on the right side. Indeed, King said in the same speech, without actually endorsing communism, that, nonetheless, "Communism is a judgment against the US way of life; against its materialism, against the poverty it tolerates in the face of great wealth, against its constant insistence on war, and against our failure to make democracy real and follow through on the revolutions that we initiated." As he explained, "[I]t is a sad fact that because of comfort, complacency, a morbid fear of communism, our proneness to adjust to injustice, the Western nations that initiated so much of the revolutionary spirit of the modern world have now become the anti-revolutionaries." This is undeniably true. A speech that I heard Hugo Chavez give at a meeting in Caracas in July of 2010 comes to mind. He said something that seemed quite profound to me and which has stuck with me ever since: that the 20th Century was not "The American Century" at all as the US claims, but it was indeed the Century of Revolution—for example, the Mexican, Russian, Chinese, Cuban, Vietnamese and Nicaraguan Revolutions—and the US violently opposed every single one of these.

I would soon come to realize that the Cold War, at least from the vantage point of the US, had little to do with fighting "Communism,"

and more to do with making the world safe for corporate plunder. As I describe further below, the US would, for example, destroy democracy in Guatemala in order to protect United Fruit's interests there; overthrow a secular, democratic government in Iran to protect Western oil interests; and overthrow the oldest Constitutional democracy in Latin America—Chile—in the interest of numerous corporate interests there, such as the International Telephone & Telegraph Company (ITT). And, the US would do so all in the name of fighting communism and protecting democracy.

One bit of evidence that the *casus belli* of the Cold War was mere pretext was that the US was up to the very same type of Third World interventions even before Russia's 1917 Revolution. As Major Smedley Butler, the commander of a Marine unit landing in Nicaragua in 1909 and 1912, opined after his years of US military service,

> I spent years being a high class muscle man for big business, for Wall Street and the bankers. In short, I was a racketeer for capitalism. I helped purify Nicaragua for the international banking house of Brown Brothers in 1902-1912. I helped make Mexico safe for American oil interests in 1916. I brought light to the Dominican Republic for American sugar interests in 1916. I helped make Haiti and Cuba a decent place for National City (Bank) boys to collect revenue in. I helped in the rape of a half a dozen Central American republics for the benefit of Wall Street.

This struggle to make the world safe for American business predated communism and has continued well after it—the "enemies" justifying this struggle have shifted and changed, but the goal has always remained constant. John Perkins, in his book *Confessions of An Economic Hit Man*, would indeed reiterate almost an identical story to Smedley Butler's in his modern recounting of his years working for the consulting firm of Chas T. Main, acting jointly with the National Security Agency. He explains how he and other Economic Hit Men helped pave

the way for corporate penetration of the Third World through all sorts of chicanery, including financial manipulation, rigged elections, sexual extortion and even murder. As Perkins relates, if such tactics failed, it was then up to the "jackals" of the CIA to come in and actually forcibly overthrow the target government.

I began to seriously question which side I should be rooting for in the Cold War struggle. I was impressed with the Soviet support of Nicaragua, for example its sending huge ships of humanitarian aid and then leaving the ships as well for the Nicaraguans. Of course, the Soviet support of Nicaragua would come at a huge price, for it would be just the justification the US needed to support a counter-revolutionary war there. And, indeed, Fidel Castro had warned Daniel Ortega of just this problem shortly after the Sandinistas took power. He told Ortega, from his own very difficult experience, not to cozy up too close to the Soviets. While Ortega tried at first, it became impossible at some point, for, as was the case in Vietnam, the US began to destabilize Nicaragua—mining its harbors, engaging in targeted assassinations, and cutting it off internationally—even before Nicaragua turned to the Soviets for help.

And the US continued such destabilization efforts well after the Soviets cared anymore about such far-flung nations. As I learned later from reading Chomsky, this was a common tactic of the US: while claiming it wanted to keep countries out of the sphere of influence of the Soviet Union, it actually pushed newly liberated countries into the Soviet camp in order to justify violent retaliation against them. A classic case of this was Vietnam which, as I detail further below, would have gladly partnered with the US in lieu of the Soviet Union to throw off French Colonialism, but was unpleasantly surprised when the US, true to MLK's words, intervened on the side of the French, and then took over for the French, to prevent Vietnamese independence.

In the end, the Contras managed to do much damage to the Nicaraguan people, with around 50,000 Nicaraguans killed during the Contra war (out of a population then of less than 3 million), along with

much civilian infrastructure—which the Contras specifically targeted—
destroyed. Just to give you a bit of flavor of what the Contras—whom
Reagan termed "freedom fighters"—were up to in Nicaragua, here is
a quote from former CIA agent John Stockwell, which I listened to
many times on that old cassette tape I mentioned above:

> I don't mean to abuse you with verbal violence, but you have to
> understand what your government and its agents are doing. They [the
> Contras] go into villages, they haul out families. With the children
> forced to watch they castrate the father, they peel the skin off his face,
> they put a grenade in his mouth and pull the pin. With the children
> forced to watch they gang-rape the mother, and slash her breasts off.
> And sometimes for variety, they make the parents watch while they do
> these things to the children.[12]

President Reagan justified supporting these terrorists based upon
his claim that we could not allow a Soviet beachhead a mere two-day
drive (it's actually about a five-day drive, as I know from having driven
there in 1988) from the Texas border. Reagan was even willing—after
Congress pulled the plug on funding to the Contras through passage
of the Boland Amendment in 1982, and then again in 1984, based upon
concerns over the Contras' horrible human rights practices—to continue funding them illegally. His Administration hatched the brilliant
plan of selling arms to Iran in return for cash which could then be used
to fund the Contras. This was a particularly cynical move given that
Reagan claimed Iran was a terrorist state and a threat to national security. Moreover, during the period in which this exchange took place,
Iran was at war with our ally Iraq, under Saddam Hussein, whom we
were also arming. In other words, the US ended up arming both sides
of a brutal armed conflict for the purpose of supplying arms for another
brutal armed conflict in Central America. And for what reason?

Certainly by the time I was in Nicaragua, the Soviet Union under
Mikhail Gorbachev was pulling far back from foreign interventions

and calling for nuclear disarmament and détente with the US. By 1988, the USSR began withdrawing from Afghanistan.

The USSR had even abandoned the Brezhnev Doctrine by the early 1980s. Pursuant to this Doctrine, the USSR took the position that it had the prerogative to intervene militarily in any Communist bloc country in order to keep the government in power, and consequently, to preserve the security of the Warsaw Pact countries as well as the Soviet Union. This Doctrine was most famously put into action in 1968, when Brezhnev sent troops into Czechoslovakia to put down the reform government there and to nip the "Prague Spring" in the bud. The "Prague Spring" was a reform movement that aspired to continue socialism, but with a "human face." Brezhnev feared that if this sentiment spread, the whole East Bloc might fall. In the end, the Soviet invasion of 1968 probably did more to quicken the end of the East Bloc than it did to prevent it. Given that I am Slovak and happened to be born in 1968, these events were always of great interest to me.

To this day, it should be emphasized, the US continues to reaffirm the Monroe Doctrine, pursuant to which it views Latin America as its "backyard," in which it can intervene at any time to protect what it views as its interests.[13] It also continues to abide by the (Jimmy) Carter Doctrine—indeed with reckless abandon—pursuant to which the US maintains the right to intervene in the Middle East at any time to protect its access to, or even control over, world oil supplies.

In the end, Poland, Hungary and East Germany peacefully left the Soviet orbit entirely by 1989, with Gorbachev making no move to keep them in. In light of the fact that the Soviet Union would not even intervene to protect its interests in Eastern Europe, it was obvious that they would not do so in Central America either. Therefore, the whole basis for the Contra War—fighting international Soviet aggression—seemed to be just a mere pretext for a cruel policy of keeping a poor country from pursuing its own path to liberation and development.

I should note that my feelings about the Nicaraguan conflict have

now been validated, as the Sandinistas whom we were fighting are now in power, and we get along with them just fine. Indeed, Nicaragua under the Sandinistas is the most stable and peaceful country in Central America, and is therefore not a source of refugees fleeing to the US, as El Salvador, Guatemala and Honduras are.[14]

Meanwhile, the US has never made reparations to Nicaragua for its terrorist war, and also for its mining of the Nicaraguan harbors (which, by the way, the US never even warned its allies about), as ordered by the International Court of Justice (ICJ).[15] One might recall that Nicaragua brought a case against the US before the ICJ—also known as the World Court, and created by the UN Charter for the peaceful resolution of international disputes—in the mid-1980s. The US, believing that international law is only for the weak and not for great countries like itself, did not even deign to show up to defend itself. The ICJ therefore proceeded with a hearing and rendered a judgment against the US *in absentia,* finding that the US had engaged in an unlawful act of aggression against Nicaragua, without any valid claim to self-defense or any other proper justification. The ICJ therefore found the US in violation of international law, including its bi-lateral treaty obligations with Nicaragua itself.

Soon after the judgment against it, the US withdrew from the jurisdiction of the ICJ altogether, making it clear to the world that while it would enforce its own version of justice throughout the world, and violently when it decided to do so, it would not be subject to any form of justice itself. Recall also that the US is not a party to the International Criminal Court (ICC)[16]—which, at least from experience so far, appears to only prosecute African countries—for the very same reasons.

While it may not seem so at first blush, the Nicaraguan Contra War is very relevant to many aspects of the current discussion of the Russian hacking claims, which has now blossomed into a full-blown scandal.

First of all, the Contra War demonstrated how much US government

officials—particularly in the CIA, which is one of the chief protagonists in the current "Russia-gate" saga—are willing to debase themselves, to lie and to undermine the security and well-being of American citizens, to pursue their own agenda. In the case of the Contra War, this agenda was greatly motivated by the old Cold War, while the current claims about Russian hacking are motivated by the new Cold War.

And so, in the case of the old Contra War, what we have known for a long time is that, to support terrorists in order to undermine a tiny, poor country in Central America, the US government was willing not only to illegally sell weapons to Iran, but was also willing to play a role in selling drugs to our fellow citizens, particularly poor and Black citizens. As Greg Grandin in The Nation recently wrote, "the Contras, backed by Ronald Reagan's White House [and CIA], were turning Central America into a transshipment point for Colombian cocaine, using the drug revenues to fund their war on the Sandinistas" after the US Congress cut off funding due to human rights concerns.[17] This cocaine was then sold in the US and "helped kick off South Central Los Angeles' crack epidemic."

Many will remember—and a recent Hollywood movie called *Kill The Messenger*, made by and starring everyone's least favorite Avenger, Jeremy Renner, reminds us—that this Contra cocaine scandal was most famously brought to light by the very brave journalist Garry Webb in his 1996 series, *Dark Alliance*. However, as Greg Grandin points out, Webb was not the first person to reveal these allegations. Earlier, in the 1980s, Robert Parry and Brian Berger reported on the story for the AP, and the allegations were then picked up by then-freshman Senator John Kerry, who in 1988 released an "extensively documented committee report" which demonstrated the truthfulness of these allegations. However, despite such strong, independent support for Webb's claims, the mainstream press, led by the *New York Times*, went after Garry Webb in an aggressive campaign to try to debunk his story and assassinate his character, ultimately driving Mr. Webb to suicide.[18]

In the end, Webb was right, even more right than he knew, but

even to this day, the job done on him by the mainstream media lingers in the public's mind, leading many to believe that the Contra cocaine story was not true.

This is a relevant part of the story as well, for the new Cold War—or Red Scare (without the reds, of course)—and the Russian hacking story that is a small part of it, is being pushed hard, and nearly unanimously, by the mainstream press, which, for reasons that I do not fully grasp, is heavily invested in it. There is no room for debate on this issue. There is only one side of the story: Vladimir Putin is a demon; Russia is a rising giant set out to dominate the globe; Hillary Clinton lost the election because of Putin; and the US—the eternal victim of Russia (and now China too)—is just doing its level best to spread freedom and democracy around the world despite the best efforts of countries like Russia to stop it.

None of this story is true, and indeed, it is demonstrably false. But again, like the Contra cocaine story, the truth has been so submerged in lies that it is hard for it to see the light of day.

And, as in the greater Nicaraguan Contra story, it is Russia that is again assigned its typecast role as the bad guy in this story, and the foil on whom we can feel free to blame all of our collective failings. By raising the specter of Russia and the new Cold War, the government and media are tapping into deep-seated feelings that were hammered into us during the first Cold War, and that is why it is so easy to get people on board the latest Russia-baiting campaign. And that is why the old Cold War must be scrutinized as well.

I came to the understanding at a pretty young age that the old Cold War fears and hatred allowed the US to get away with the worst of crimes. Thus, after WWII, the US decided that, in order to gain advantage in its struggle against the Soviet Union and the East Block, it would partner with the most unsavory forces in the world—right-wing dictatorships, terrorist groups, and even neo-Nazis.

And, of course, the US courted the possibility of nuclear conflagration in this struggle as well, continuing to press forward with planning

and building the capacity to launch a nuclear first strike against the USSR while still being able to "win" the war. Reagan's "Star Wars" program—the idea for which apparently came from the Death Star in the Star Wars films—was greatly feared as, in fact, a means to have such first strike capability. This program, which was developed by Edward Teller, the father of the hydrogen bomb and one of the inspirations for Stanley Kubrick's Dr. Strangelove character,[19] was hoped to be able to allow the US to be shielded from oncoming nuclear missiles from the USSR while allowing the US to have a free shot at Russia with its weapons. Of course, even if such a project worked, the US would still suffer great casualties. But, as a recent article on recently-declassified documents shows, US officials were willing to take this risk. Thus, these documents reveal that, again reminiscent of the movie *Dr. Strangelove*, top US officials believed that a nuclear war that resulted in the deaths of 200 million Americans would still be a "victory," for we would still have as many Americans as we did at the time of the Civil War.[20]

The current demonization of Russia under Vladimir Putin, which has now broken out into a revived Cold War, is again putting the US and the world at equally great risk. Indeed, this is not just my belief. As was widely reported earlier this year, the Bulletin of the Atomic Scientists moved the "Doomsday Clock," the symbol created in 1947 to illustrate the danger of nuclear annihilation, ahead to two-and-a-half minutes to midnight.[21] This is the closest to midnight we have been since 1953. In addition to the climate change crisis, the Bulletin cited increased tensions between Russia and the US, which together possess 90% of the world's nuclear weapons, as the reason it was moving the clock ahead. In short, the Bulletin "says we are at the most dangerous moment since the height of the Cold War."[22]

Such alarm is certainly warranted. As investigative journalist Robert Parry explains, "[o]fficial Washington's Russia hysteria has reached such proportions that *New York Times* columnist Thomas L. Friedman has even compared the alleged Russian hacking of Democratic emails

to Pearl Harbor and 9/11, two incidents that led the United States into violent warfare."[23]

This is obviously quite alarming, and it is of course meant to be.

Given the high stakes implicated by the new Cold War, and the subsidiary Russian hacking story, some rational thought on these issues, which I at least hope to give here, is certainly in order.

2

THE NEW COLD WAR (NOT) THE SAME AS THE OLD ONE

IT SHOULD GO WITHOUT SAYING THAT the old Cold War and the new are not seamless events, and are not the same, for the nature of one of the players has indeed changed in profound ways. However, this fact seems to be lost on many.

Thus, as Tony Wood, writing for the *London Review of Books*, points out, "[t]he rhetoric emanating from US politicians and media commentators . . . seems to be drawn from another era. . . . In January, Fox News rolled back the years by announcing there was 'no Soviet Source' for the DNC leaks, and the title of a piece in the *New York Times Review of Books* asked: 'Was Snowden a Soviet Agent?'"[24]

Of course, the Soviet Union is long gone, having dissolved in 1991, and leaving in its stead a Russia, standing alone, and in the throes of unfettered capitalism. Even more importantly, Russia is a much-weakened nation post-Soviet collapse, and, as I shall detail more below, the US, particularly under the Clinton Administration, did much to help weaken it.

As Wood explains, "[i]n terms of military might, economic weight

and ideological reach, Russia is no match for any of the larger NATO member states," with a GDP still smaller than Portugal's and a military budget 8% of NATO's.

For his part, Dmitri Trenin explains in his must-read *Should We Fear Russia* (a book that Wood reviews in his piece), Russia has neither the resources nor will to re-create its former empire or to militarily challenge NATO member states. Indeed, he mocks the US's fear of Russia, stating, quite correctly,

[i]t is truly an irony of history that the United States should be overtly challenged by a party such as today's Russia—a country whose GDP is a small fraction of America's, whose share in global trade is a mere 1 percent, and even whose defense budget is a tenth of the Pentagon's.

As for the smallness of Russia's military budget compared to that of the US, I note that, as I write this book, *the mere increase* in the annual military budget that Trump is proposing ($54 billion) is equal to over 80% of Russia's *total* annual military budget.[25]

Trenin scolds the US for being threatened by Russia, stating that "[t]o most educated Americans, Russia is the day before yesterday's news, a country on the long and irreversible trajectory of decline. It is a third- or fourth-tier actor in a remote corner of the globe, with a contemptible leadership mired in corruption, which can be a nuisance at best." In a recent interview in *Counterpunch*, Noam Chomsky echoes such sentiments, saying that "most of the world is collapsing in laughter" at the very notion that Russia could have effectively intervened in the US's elections.

Trenin does hit the nub of the problem that Russia does pose for the US—it is unique in its open aversion and resistance to "domination of the international system by any one power." Of course, given that it is the US which is the "one power" trying to dominate the world, this puts Russia at natural odds with the US.

However, I believe history shows that Russia is correct in opposing the US's attempt at a unipolar world, in which the US is able, and quite willing, to run wild on all sorts of military adventures which are harmful both to the US and the world at large.

And indeed, my view is very much in line with the rest of the world, which, according to a recent poll of 66,000 people in 65 countries, believes the US is by far the greatest threat to world peace, with "just under a quarter nam[ing] Uncle Sam as the greatest threat to world peace. Other menaces didn't even come close: 8 percent named Pakistan, putting that country in second place, while 6 percent named China. A mere 4 percent found Iran threatening—which tied it with Israel."[26] Russia didn't even make the top 5. Again, historian Eric Hobsbawm explains, in words even more true today, "[p]robably for the first time in history, an internationally almost isolated America is unpopular among most governments and peoples. . . . [as] the most obvious danger of war today arises from the global ambitions and apparently irrational government in Washington."[27]

In addition to its relative economic and military weakness, Trenin makes another point which should be obvious to any honest observer— that Russia does not now, and never had the ability to penetrate Western culture the way that Western culture (e.g., through movies, popular music, blue jeans, McDonald's, Starbucks, etc.) has been and continues to be able to penetrate Russia.

Indeed, I heard Keith Richards once take credit for helping bring down the Berlin Wall, and he was probably not too far off on that point. Francis Fukuyama, in his famous piece, "The End of History?", explained this phenomenon well back in 1989 as the Soviet Union was quickly declining, and it at least appeared, to observers like him, that Western liberal values would be forever triumphant: "This phenomenon extends beyond high politics and it can be seen also in the ineluctable spread of consumerist Western culture in such diverse contexts as the peasants' markets and color television sets now omnipresent throughout China, the cooperative restaurants and clothing stores in

the past year in Moscow, the Beethoven piped into Japanese department stores, and the rock music enjoyed alike in Prague, Rangoon,
and Tehran."

Russia simply has no analogous cultural influence in the West,
though, of course, this doesn't stop some US pundits from trying to
claim that it does. For example, I was listening to Steve Inskeep in an
NPR segment in which he interviewed the CEO of Voice of America
(VOA), John Lansing, about the continuing need of VOA as a news
source to counter what was termed in the interview as "Russian propaganda."[28] Lansing claimed in the interview, with Inskeep hanging on
his every word:

> Well Russia has a very, very well-financed media conglomerate.
> You can see RT, Russia Today, here in the United States. And some-
> times it's much more subtle and nuanced than you might think. It's
> a way of twisting a narrative or questioning a narrative that puts the
> United States at a disadvantage on an important issue.

This is just nonsense. As Lansing points out, RT stands for Russia Today. Everyone knows this, and everyone knows that the news
coming from it is from the Russian point of view (which, by the way, I
think is healthy for Americans to hear). There is in fact nothing "subtle" or "nuanced" about this, and I truly doubt that RT has much real
influence in the US as a consequence.

While Lansing tried to claim that the US is somehow being outgunned because it is not funding the VOA anywhere near the level at
which the Russians are financing RT, it is this type of claim which is
in fact pure propaganda. The truth is that we don't need a VOA at all
because mainstream news outlets like NPR, the *New York Times*, and
nearly all others, do a much better job propagandizing, and "manufacturing consent," if I might borrow a phrase from the book of the same
name by Noam Chomsky and Edward Herman, in which they describe
the subtle ways in which we are manipulated by our own press—for

example, by its selective focus on the "crimes" of others (such as Russia) to the near exclusion of our own.

I recall an apt quote I heard one time from someone from who had been an activist in the Polish Solidarity movement of the 1980s. He was asked, after Solidarity was successful in ousting the Communist government there, how they were able to hold together for so many years and finally prevail given the fact that the press had been so tightly controlled by the state. His response was that this was precisely how they were able to succeed. They did not believe what the press was saying BECAUSE it was state-run, so they relied on communications between themselves to know what was really happening.

He then had a pointed comment for his American questioner: the problem with you Americans is that you are being lied to by your press too, but you believe them. Indeed!

As I try to detail herein, it is the NPRs and the *New York Times* of the world that have sold the public on wars in Iraq and Libya, for example, which have been based on lies. They also continue to stir up fear and distrust of countries like Russia and China. We don't need an official government voice or organ to do that when we have outlets like these that will do it for free, and do it much better precisely because they pose as news outlets independent of the government.

Finally, while Russia, as the Soviet Union, did wield sizable political and ideological influence in the world for some time, due to the appeal of its socialist message as well as its critical role in winning WWII, Russia is no longer socialist and the memory of its role in WWII has greatly subsided.

However, it was the USSR's socialist system and message that the US claimed to despise and to be fighting against during the first Cold War. Where is the ideological justification for the new Cold War? There really isn't one. And that is the reason the US has had to focus so much on the personality of Vladimir Putin, imbuing him with a level of power, reach and craziness that he just doesn't have.

And so the hand-wringing continues over a perceived foe whose

bite is certainly much less than its bark. I am not one wringing his hands about Russia. Rather, I wring my hands over my own country, which seems more out of control and dangerous than any other in the world, and which is tapping into old Cold War fears to justify its permanent war footing.

Possibly, if we saw ourselves as the rest of the world does, we would stop being taken in by another manufactured scare story designed to manipulate us, and we'd actually have a chance of making much needed change in our own country.

3

BACK IN THE USSR

VLADIMIR PUTIN ONCE FAMOUSLY SAID, "ANYONE who doesn't regret the passing of the Soviet Union has no heart. Anyone who wants it restored has no brains."

This is a statement rich in meaning, and deserves some analysis. As an initial matter, if taken at face value, this is strongly suggestive of Putin's lack of desire to reconstruct the USSR. He indeed mocks the very idea, which certainly would be a poor tactic if he wanted to convince others to go along with a project of reconstruction. And, as indicated above, he could not do so even if he wanted. The current chaos reigning in the Ukraine, which I shall detail later, would certainly preclude that, in any case. And Putin is smart enough to see reality for what it is.

This brings us to the first part of this quote, which I find more interesting—as I write this book during the Centennial year of the Russian Revolution—and frankly more persuasive. I certainly endorse the view that the passing of the Soviet Union was a sad event. I was sad when it was clear, in August of 1991, that the Soviet Union was going away, and I grieve its passing still. I go so far as to agree with Putin who, in 2005, told the Russian Parliament that the USSR's collapse was "the major geopolitical disaster of the [last] century."[29] And I am not alone in this view.

First of all, while we are currently being urged to fear a return of the Iron Curtain, many of those who lived in the USSR, and even in many of the Soviet-dominated East Bloc nations stretching from East Germany to the Russian frontier, really don't share our fear. Indeed, a recent poll showed that a majority of Russians (56%) view the fall of the USSR negatively, and that an even stronger majority (58%) dream of its restoration.[30] Truth be told, the vast majority of Soviet citizens (76.4%) just several months before the collapse of the USSR expressed their desire in a non-binding referendum for the preservation of the Soviet Union.[31] This sentiment was particularly strong in Russia (with 71.4% approval), Ukraine (70.3%), Belarus (82.7%), and in Azerbaijan and each of the Central Asian Republics (with over 90%).

Similarly, in Hungary, Bulgaria, the former Yugoslavia and even in the former East Germany, the majority of the people pine for the good old days of communism.[32]

As Reuters has reported, "Capitalism's failure to lift living standards, impose the rule of law and tame flourishing corruption and nepotism have given way to fond memories of the times when the jobless rate was zero, food was cheap and social safety was high."[33]

Writer Stephen Gowans notes:

> While at the time the demise of socialism in the Soviet Union and Eastern Europe was proclaimed as a great victory for humanity, not least by leftist intellectuals in the United States, two decades later there's little to celebrate. The dismantling of socialism has, in a word, been a catastrophe, a great swindle that has not only delivered none of what it promised, but has wreaked irreparable harm, not only in the former socialist countries, but throughout the Western world, as well. Countless millions have been plunged deep into poverty, imperialism has been given a free hand, and wages and benefits in the West have bowed under the pressure of intensified competition for jobs and industry unleashed by a flood of jobless from the former socialist countries, where joblessness once, rightly, was considered an

obscenity. Numberless voices in Russia, Romania, East Germany and elsewhere lament what has been stolen from them—and from humanity as a whole: "We lived better under communism. We had jobs. We had security."[34]

As for the losses that the working class of the West suffered due to the loss of the USSR and the East Bloc, former Assistant Secretary of the Treasury under President Reagan, Paul Craig Roberts, has this to say, and he has said it often:

> The collapse of the Soviet Union was the worst thing that ever happened to the United States. The two main consequences of the Soviet collapse have been devastating. One consequence was the rise of the neoconservative hubris of US world hegemony, which has resulted in 14 years of wars that have cost $6 trillion. The other consequence was a change of mind in socialist India and communist China, large countries that responded to "the end of history" by opening their vast under-utilized labor forces to Western capital, which resulted in the American economic decline that this article describes, leaving a struggling economy to bear the enormous war debt.[35]

Poverty skyrocketed after the collapse of the Soviet Union, with the number of people living in poverty rising by 150 million persons.[36] Of course, on this score, a major impact of the USSR's disappearance was the pretty swift disappearance of social democracies throughout the world, including the US's own social democracy lite. The truth is that many Western countries reacted to the Russian Revolution, and the gains that workers had in the Soviet Union in terms of social benefits, by feeling compelled to grant their own workers some of these concessions.

Once the Soviet Union was gone, these governments no longer felt such pressure. In our own country, it was Democrat Bill Clinton, elected just after the Soviet collapse, who quickly destroyed "welfare

as we know it," even though it was the Democrats who had created the modern welfare system which had helped lift millions out of poverty. Clinton ended the entitlement to cash benefits which the poor had been given by prior legislation (Aid to Families with Dependent Children) and replaced it with legislation (called, quite appropriately, Temporary Aid to Needy Families) that put a 5-year lifetime federal limit on cash aid to the poor and allowed states to set even shorter limits.[37] The new legislation also required a certain number of people in a recipient home to either be working or volunteering, and paid out benefits to states in block grants which allowed the states to use the money for something entirely other than benefits to the poor. Clinton's "reforms" have ended up knocking around 10 million people off the welfare rolls, many of them children, and have been particularly disastrous for the poor during economic crises such as the 2008 Great Recession.

As Roberts alludes to, Clinton would also take advantage of the disappearance of the Socialist Bloc to enter into horrible trade deals— for example, the infamous NAFTA of 1994 and the PNTR agreement with China in 2000—which allowed major capital flight away from the US and therefore a massive loss of jobs in this country, while also creating a general downward pressure on wages world-wide. As historian Eric Hobsbawm explains, "the currently fashionable free-market globalization has brought about a dramatic growth in economic and social inequalities both within states and internationally. . . . This surge of inequality, especially in the conditions of extreme economic instability such as those created by the global free market of the 1990s, is at the roots of the major social and political tensions of the new century."[38]

With NAFTA, for example, the US lost around one million good manufacturing jobs to Mexico for its much lower labor costs.[39] Meanwhile, this process had the effect of depressing wages in the US—by 20% for 2/3 of the displaced manufacturing workers. And, for its part, Mexico suffered greatly from the agricultural provisions of NAFTA, which allowed the US to dump cheap food into Mexico, thereby

destroying the livelihoods of 2 million small farmers, who were forced to move to the cities and compete for low-paying, dangerous jobs, or to migrate to the US altogether. While the US's shining examples of NAFTA are hollowed-out cities like Detroit, the city which was to be Mexico's model NAFTA city—Ciudad Juarez—became famous for crime rates at war zone levels and rampant "femicide" in which hundreds of women and young girls were raped and murdered.[40]

Of course, NAFTA and the loss of manufacturing jobs became a huge issue in the 2016 elections. Hillary Clinton, who was not only associated with Bill Clinton's policies by name and marriage, but also aggressively lobbied for NAFTA herself, simply had no credible position on this issue. To the contrary, showing her utter disdain for the very people whose lives were ruined by Clinton's cruel, neo-liberal policies, she referred to them in a moment of candor as a "basket of deplorables." This did not go down so well, especially in places like the former mining communities of Appalachia, which have suffered so much under neo-liberalism, and which feel alienated by a culture that seems to be laughing at them and their plight. It is a telling fact that the welfare system which was created in the Kennedy/Johnson years— the very one dismantled by Bill Clinton—was created in response to a book by socialist Michael Harrington entitled, "The Other America," that detailed the suffering of the Appalachian poor. The left, which at one time thought about issues of class and poverty, actually cared about these people once, but seemingly no more.

Trump, on the other hand, capturing the desperate spirit of large swaths of de-industrialized America, was able to take great advantage of this issue, and most likely won the key swing states of Ohio, Michigan, Wisconsin and Pennsylvania as a consequence of this. While I have no doubt that these voters will be greatly disappointed by the actual policies of Trump, any autopsy of the Clinton loss has to take this reality into account, rather than wasting time pointing fingers at Vladimir Putin.

Meanwhile, as Paul Craig Roberts touches upon, the counterweight

to US foreign policy initiatives disappeared with the collapse of the USSR, and this was not good in many ways. As just one example, history shows that the US, though trying to claim otherwise now, supported and protected apartheid in South Africa for decades—including, of course, during some of the period of the US's own apartheid (Jim Crow) system—while the USSR consistently opposed this system, both diplomatically and eventually militarily.

As for the military effort, the Soviet Union supported the efforts of the Cubans in Angola against counter-revolutionaries in that country, who were being backed both by the US and Apartheid South Africa, with the Cubans eventually confronting and routing the South African military in the legendary battle of Cuito Cuanavale.

Nelson Mandela, whom the CIA helped capture and imprison in 1962[42] and who remained on the US terrorist list until 2008, credits the victory at Cuito Cuanavale for bringing the South African government to the bargaining table, and leading eventually to the end of apartheid.[43] This is a little inconvenient episode that you will rarely study in school.

Finally, there were intangible benefits that "real existing socialism" brought with it. One big benefit, as Stephen F. Cohen has documented, was friendship. The citizens of the USSR and former East Bloc felt a much closer kinship with one another, and, if you'll forgive me, comradeship, than they do now.

In the end, while the Russian Revolution and the USSR certainly fell short on many of the goals they had promised, and while they were marked by periods of great repression which undermined the project they claimed to be building, they delivered on many of their promises, and against great odds. And, they helped force a rise in the standard of living of all working people, even in the West, in the process.

In any case, the goals of the Russian Revolution—equality, worker control of the economy, universal health care and social security—were laudable ones, even if not fully realized. And it was sad when the people of the USSR seemed to have given up on these goals, only

to trade them in for the handful of magic beans that the capitalists offered them.

It has been equally sad for me to see the West, and particularly the US, so gleefully dance on the grave of the lofty hopes of the Russian people in particular. One of the reasons that the West continues to dance on the grave of the Soviet Union, and to emphasize the worst parts of that society and downplay its achievements, is to make sure that, as the world-wide economy worsens, and as the suffering of working people around the world deepens, they don't get any notions in their head to organize some new socialist revolution with such ideals.

Even when the US seemed to realize its chief goal of the USSR's demise, this was not enough. Instead, it decided to force the worst economic policies down the throats of Russia, making the transition to capitalism certainly much worse than it had to be; to encircle it with troops and military bases even after promising not to; and to insist that it take this awful medicine with a smile.

And now, to add insult to injury, we angrily begrudge the Russian people every attempt their country makes to stand on its feet again and to reclaim some of its former self-esteem, and maybe even a little of its past glory.

Now that we appear to own the whole world, we resent the Russians (and Chinese too) for striving for security and say-so in the little slice of the world they live in.

I suspect that a lot of the anti-Russian sentiment in this country is motivated by such sentiments, and I simply cannot jump on that bandwagon.

4

OUR KILLERS AND THEIRS

PROBABLY THE BIGGEST OBSTACLE TO AMERICANS' ability to perceive our own actions in the world, and our own place relative to other countries like Russia, is our deep-seated belief in "American Exceptionalism"—that is, the belief that our country is uniquely good, democratic and freedom-loving, and that anything we do in the world, no matter how incidentally harmful, is motivated by the purest and best motives. Every other country, especially adversaries like Russia, are motivated by the worst and most selfish motives, the philosophy goes, and therefore are inherently more dangerous than the US

The truth is, however, that "American Exceptionalism" is a false religion and is not borne out by even a cursory examination of US history, particularly post-WWII, and even compared with Russia for the past half a century.

Indeed, President Trump, much to the chagrin of many, especially members of the liberal establishment, dared to touch upon this fact when he queried, in response to the suggestion by Bill O'Reilly on *Fox News Sunday* (Feb. 5, 2017) that Putin is a killer, "There are a lot of killers. We've got a lot of killers. What, you think our country's so innocent?"

The mainstream press could not believe that Trump would have the temerity—especially on our most hallowed of days (Super Bowl Sunday)—to stray so far from the required script for American presidents. However, what Trump said in response to O'Reilly's statement was undeniably true.

Let's start with the easier premise—that the US has its own killers. A good place to begin is with the only President we have ever had (with the possible exception of Lincoln) who is also apparently viewed as a saint by many, and that is Barack Obama. Those who now believe in the holiness of Obama—who himself deported 2.5 million people (as of 2015, that is)[44] with barely a whisper of protest from anyone—simply were not paying attention. In addition to being the Deporter-In-Chief, Obama was also a killer, and an avowed one at that.

I think it is fair to say that Obama was also the Bomber-In-Chief, greatly expanding the US's heroic campaign of bombing poor villagers safely from above. Indeed, during Obama's first weekend in office, he got busy killing people, ordering two drone strikes on two villages in Pakistan which killed nearly 20 innocents, including women and children.[45] Meeting with one of my liberal lawyer friends after this massacre, I remarked how Obama killed more people than Charles Manson before his first full week in office. Her quite testy response was, "Well, that's harsh." Of course, what she meant was that my statement was "harsh"—not that Obama's wanton murder was harsh. This just illustrates how inured we have become in this country to the horrible crimes of state, especially if we happen to like the person occupying the highest office at the time.

All told, Obama's bombing spree greatly exceeded that of George W. Bush. As Medea Benjamin, writing for *The Guardian*, explains[46]:

> [H]e dramatically expanded the air wars and the use of special operations forces around the globe. In 2016, US special operators could be found in 70% of the world's nations, 138 countries—a staggering jump of 130% since the days of the Bush administration.

Looking back at President Obama's legacy, the Council on For-eign Relation's Micah Zenko added up the defense department's data on airstrikes and made a startling revelation: in 2016 alone, the Obama administration dropped at least 26,171 bombs. This means that every day last year, the US military blasted combatants or civilians overseas with 72 bombs; that's three bombs every hour, 24 hours a day.

While most of these air attacks were in Syria and Iraq, US bombs also rained down on people in Afghanistan, Libya, Yemen, Somalia and Pakistan. That's seven majority-Muslim countries.

As people rightly protest Trump's attempts to ban immigrants from six to seven Muslim nations—and, by the way, I have participated in such protests—it is worth recalling the near-silence which greeted Obama's manic bombing of seven Muslim nations.

Recall that Obama even turned these bombings into a fun weekly ritual on Tuesdays—dubbed something like "Terror Tuesdays" appar-ently because that's when Obama got to inflict terror on others—in which Obama would personally order drone attacks upon unsuspect-ing people. I say simply "people," because Obama did not only target militants, but indeed all males of a certain age in certain regions of the world. As The *New York Times* explained,[47]

> Mr. Obama embraced a disputed method for counting civilian casualties that did little to box him in. It in effect counts all mili-tary-age males in a strike zone as combatants, according to several administration officials, unless there is explicit intelligence *posthu-mously* proving them innocent.

(emphasis added). Literally, this was a case of killing first and asking questions later, and this was a method that even George W. Bush refused to embrace. In addition, Obama became well-known for his "signature strike" in which he would target areas for drone attack based upon "suspicious activity" there without even knowing the

identity of the individuals there.[48] Under his watch, the tactic of "double tapping," in which an area is bombed twice in quick succession to hit first responders to the area, was oft used as well.[49] Such attacks clearly violated the Geneva Conventions which requires warring states to take all necessary measures to protect civilian non-combatants, and certainly made Obama a war criminal many times over.

Moreover, Obama's policy of treating every male over a certain age in some areas as legitimate military targets may even have amounted to genocide, at least as judged by another event which is considered genocide and which was used as a justification for NATO's seventy-eight-day bombing of Serbia. This event was of course the notorious Srebrenica massacre in which the Bosnian Serbs killed "Bosnian Muslim Men of Military Age" in the small town of Srebrenica after first busing "all the women, children, and the elderly men to safety . . . ."[50]

Obama didn't even have women, children and elderly bused away before targeting all men of a certain age for death in an area, thus ensuring that some women, children and elderly, and of course the occasional wedding party,[51] were indeed killed. Indeed, one study showed that 90% of the victims of drone strikes in Afghanistan were not militants at all or even the intended target of the attack, and that this awful rate was probably even greater in Yemen and Somalia.[52] One Administration official explained, "[a]nyone caught in the vicinity is guilty by association."[53]

As just one example, Obama ordered the successful drone killing of 16-year-old Abdulrahman al-Awlaki, an American citizen, as well as another innocent American citizen named Samir Kahn. This particular drone strike followed by two weeks the Obama-ordered drone strike which killed the 16-year-old boy's father, American citizen Anwar al-Awlaki, for his alleged activities in terrorism (though he had never been tried, much less convicted for such). No valid reason has ever been given for the second drone strike which killed a child. And, when asked about the strike that killed the 16-year old boy, White House

Press Secretary Robert Gibbs could only say that "he should've 'had a more responsible father.'"[54]

As I said, Obama was proud of being a killer, telling staff that he's "really good at killing people."[55] And, in all fairness, he was very good, with his drone strikes responsible for "hundreds of dead innocents" in just his first four years of office.[56] All told, as of 2013, Obama's drone strikes had already killed upwards of 4,000 people, and he still had three more years to go.[57] Given his method of counting militant kills, which cast too wide a net over who was a militant, we will certainly never know how many innocents he actually killed. What we do know is that whatever numbers the Administration gave for civilians killed were way too low. Well, I guess one man's psychopath is another man's saint.

Not to be outdone in the "killer" category, Trump has gotten his bombing campaign off with killing nearly 300 civilians in Iraq in just one bombing raid.[58] He also decimated a school, killing 33 innocents in Raqqa, Syria. Trump is also greatly increasing ground forces in Syria, from "a couple hundred to at least 1,000" at the time of this writing.[59]

As a *Truthout* piece correctly complains,[60] the Democrats, who long ago ceded to Obama the right to kill at will abroad, and who are fixated on Russia-gate to the exclusion of almost anything else, are shamefully raising no opposition to any of this, and neither does the press seem to be.

Meanwhile, as commentator Keith Gessen in *The Guardian* explains, "[a]t no time in history have people with less knowledge, and greater outrage, opined on the subject of Russia's president."[61] Indeed! And I agree wholeheartedly with Gessen's assertion that "the Russia card is not just bad politics, it is intellectual and moral bankruptcy. It is an attempt to blame the deep and abiding problems of our country on a foreign power."

What's more, the Russia card is being played with more fury than possibly ever, even during the height of the old Cold War. Professor Stephen F. Cohen, who taught Russian studies at Princeton and New

York University, was an adviser to and is still a friend of Mikhail Gorbachev, and who travelled to the USSR and then post-Soviet Russia many times, told me in an interview during the summer of 2015 that he does not recall a Soviet leader being vilified in the mainstream press the way that Putin is now. Moreover, he explained that he himself, and other intellectuals like himself, have never been so maligned and marginalized for urging rationality about Russian discourse as he is now. And yet, in spite of being oft ridiculed as some type of "pawn of the Kremlin," Cohen persists, arguing forcefully for a peace with Russia which he believes, and I agree whole-heartedly, is long overdue.

As Cohen, a man I greatly respect for his willingness to tell the truth at great cost to himself in terms of reputation, told me:

> I entered public debate about American-Soviet Russian policy in the 1970s, during the preceding Cold War. . . . I don't ever recall, in a systematic, mainstream, un-dissenting way, such vilification of a Russian leader of the person who sits in the Kremlin. . . . Quite to the contrary, I mean we saw Eisenhower and Krushchev, two veterans of World War II, meet warmly with each other. We saw Kennedy and Kruschev, we saw . . . Nixon and Brezhnev develop a kind of warm, personal relationship.

Meanwhile, Cohen explained, the vilification of Putin has "become an actual political institution in the United States. And it blocks, makes almost impossible, any rational, factual analysis of the dangerous, new Cold War that we're in." Indeed, when you watch Cohen in an interview or debate—no longer on major networks but on some fringe news program—he looks haggard and beaten down, himself labeled some type of Russian (or, in a case of anachronism, a Soviet) agent because he won't jump on the anti-Putin bandwagon.

So, with that, let's analyze the claim that Putin is a killer, or at least more of a killer than any US President, including Obama. That is a very high bar indeed.

As an initial matter, a commentary in the *Chicago Tribune* noted from the outset in trying to answer this question that we must at least start from the premise that "Putin is not a bloodthirsty, Stalin-like dictator. He has stubbornly resisted calls for the reinstitution of the death penalty in Russia,"[62] for example, which puts him ahead of the US, which still carries out the death penalty in a number of states. As the commentary explains, Putin takes this position against the death penalty on the grounds that there is no proof that the death penalty is a deterrent of crime. Hmm, sounds pretty reasonable to me.

For his part, Keith Gessen, writing for *The Guardian*[63], explains that the accusation that Putin is a killer, "like most Putinology," is simply "sloppy." As he notes, those with any familiarity with the famous cases of Russian "'journalists and political opponents'" being killed—notably Boris Nemtsov in 2015 and Anna Politkosvskaya in 2016—believe they were most likely killed upon the orders of "the violent dictator of Chechnya," Ramzan Kadryrov.

Indeed, one might recall the case of Anna Politkosvskaya, who wrote critically of both the Russian and Chechen governments in their prosecution of the Chechen war. Five men, including four from the same Chechen family, were convicted and sentenced for the shooting that killed her.[64] And, interestingly, Putin, in denying that the Kremlin was somehow behind Anna's murder, stated that her death was "more damaging to the current authorities, both in Russia and the Chechen Republic, than her activities."[65] Again, this may not exonerate Putin, but it does show that he possesses some awareness of how killing an opposition journalist may not be in his or Russia's best interest, and why, therefore, he might not be inclined to order such a killing.

Five Chechens are also being tried for the killing of Nemstov, an opposition leader shot dead in Moscow while he was working on an expose of what he claimed to be Putin's involvement in the Ukrainian separatist movement.[66] These suspects were arrested very quickly after the killing, and Putin has at least vowed to prosecute those responsible.

And, for what it's worth, "though both Politkovskaya and Nemtsov

were outspoken critics of Putin, friends, colleagues and family have not accused him of ordering the assassinations." [67]

Gessen does not believe the fact that the Chechen leader Kadryrov may have ordered the killings of Politkovskaya and Nemtsov totally lets Putin off the hook, for the Chechen leader Kadryrov ultimately works for Putin, but still, this does not make Putin a "killer" in the way that he is being accused of. Or, as the *Chicago Tribune* commentary states, "[i]t would, however, be unfair to ascribe crimes Kadyrov may have ordered or committed directly to Putin. The Russian leader is himself a hostage to the scheme he chose to end a decade-long war of secession in Chechnya."

And while, as Gessen points out, there is reason to believe that Putin "probably approved of the assassination" of Alexander Litvinenko—the "former operative" of the KGB and then its successor, the FSB, who was famously killed with a radioactive isotope in London—this is not the type of operation "that will get you kicked out of the international community."

Maybe more importantly, this is not the type of action that should cause Americans to lose one ounce of sleep for fear that the Russians are coming.

Indeed, how the approval of the murder of a former KGB agent who went into exile, and who is at least fairly viewed as a traitor of his country, is worse than Obama ordering the drone killing of a 16 year-old boy whose only sin was having the wrong father, is simply beyond me.

Moreover, while not successfully killing whistleblowers like Bradley (now Chelsea) Manning—the individual who supplied the lion's share of Wikileaks's very first trove of documents—Obama did aggressively pursue prosecution of her for blowing the whistle on horrible crimes like the murder of innocents in Iraq and Afghanistan. This prosecution led to her being placed in such horrible prison conditions, which included solitary confinement, that she was driven to twice attempt suicide. And while Obama did commute Manning's

sentence as he was leaving office, Manning is not set to be freed until May 2017—which leaves more than ample time for her to be tortured, possibly to death.

In any case, Manning's incarceration was "part of President Obama's war on whistle blowers that has led to his administration arresting more people under the 1917 Espionage Act than all of the previous governments put together."[68] That this "war" also included the persecution of John Kiriakou, a former CIA intelligence analyst, who was sentenced to two and half years in prison for exposing torture as official US policy, sums up the attitude of Obama's government."

In light of the foregoing, it is hard to see how Putin, at least with respect to allegedly being a "killer," is worse, or even as bad, as our beloved Barack Obama.

The other significant allegation against Putin is that he has waged "aggressive wars," specifically in Ukraine and Syria. (He has also waged such a war in Chechnya, but no one seems to care much about that, quite possibly because our buddy Boris Yeltsin did the same).

Much more on this later, but suffice it to say that if we assume the very worst of Putin in regard to these wars (which I do not think the facts warrant), they pale in comparison to the wars of aggression that the US has and continues to wage in many more countries throughout the planet. To name just some, the US has recently been involved in major wars in Iraq, Afghanistan and Libya, and has also been in major military efforts in Syria, Yemen and Somalia. All told, under Obama alone, the US had Special Forces deployed in about 138 countries,[69] and I have no doubt that Trump will have them deployed in at least as many. Still, these undeniable truths did not stop the *New York Times* editorial board from condemning Trump for not "endorsing American exceptionalism," when he somehow suggested to Bill O'Reilly that America is as equally brutal in its foreign policy and in its treatment of dissidents at home.[70] As the *New York Times* explained, Trump just doesn't understand that "[a]t least in recent decades, American presidents who took military action have been driven by the desire

to promote freedom and democracy, sometimes with extraordinary results, as when Germany and Japan evolved after World War II from vanquished enemies into trusted, prosperous allies."[71]

Of course, Russia—which bore the brunt of WWII, losing over 25 million people in the war, and having slain over 80% of the Nazis killed in the war—also deserves credit, if not most of the credit, for its noble intentions in liberating Europe from Nazism.[72] The Red Army was the real hero of WWII, having driven the Nazis back in the great battles of Stalingrad and Moscow, and driving them all the way to Berlin, at great cost to themselves. I still get goose bumps when I see the famous photo of the Russian soldier raising the Soviet flag over the Reichstag in Berlin.

The last time I was in Paris (in 1998), there was still a Metro Stop called "Stalingrad," in honor of the heroic battle that took place there and which all regard as the positive turning point of the war. The Red Army would go on to liberate death camps, most notably Auschwitz, "the largest killing center and concentration camp," as well as the concentration camps of Stutthof, Sachsenhausen and Ravensbrueck.[73]

For a great movie on the Red Army liberation of Auschwitz, check out *Truce*, with John Turturro, which is based upon the memoirs of Primo Levi, who was, in fact, liberated and treated quite kindly by the Soviets.

Moreover, it is quite telling that the *New York Times* had to reach back over 70 years to WWII to cite an event in "recent decades" revealing the US's benign intentions, for there is absolutely no evidence since then which proves such intentions. Indeed, one cannot even truthfully say that the US has been more benign than Russia, at least in the past 50+ years.

As Noam Chomsky has so eloquently pointed out:

> It is not seriously in question, as John Coatsworth writes in the recently published Cambridge University *History of the Cold War*, that from 1960 to "the Soviet collapse in 1990, the numbers of political

prisoners, torture victims, and executions of nonviolent political dis-
senters in Latin America vastly exceeded those in the Soviet Union
and its East European satellites." Among the executed were many
religious martyrs, and there were mass slaughters as well, consistently
supported or initiated by Washington.[74]

Washington justified such repression, not just in Latin America,
but throughout the globe, on the grounds that it was necessary to keep
the world safe from the threat of Soviet totalitarianism, whether the
threat in a particular case was real, imagined or just made up. The truth
is that the US escalated its cruel foreign policies as Russia, beginning
with Nikita Khrushchev's soul-searching 1956 "Secret Speech" about
the crimes committed during Stalinism, was ending its worst forms
of repression. The US continued such policies, moreover, even while
Mikhail Gorbachev was further democratizing Russia through *Glas-
nost* in the mid-1980's, and well after the collapse of the USSR.

To truly understand the US's policies, we need look no further
than the US's own post-WWII policy statements, as well-articulated by
George Kennan, serving as the State Department's Director of Policy
Planning, in 1948:

> [W]e have about 50% of the world's wealth but only 6.3 of its
> population. This disparity is particularly great as between ourselves
> and the peoples of Asia. In this situation, we cannot fail to be the
> object of envy and resentment. Our real task in the coming period is
> to devise a pattern of relationships, which will permit us to maintain
> this position of disparity without positive detriment to our national
> security. . . . We need not deceive ourselves that we can afford today
> the luxury of altruism and world benefaction. . . .
>
> In the face of this situation we would be better off to . . . cease
> to talk about vague—and for the Far East—unreal objectives such
> as human rights, the raising of the living standards, and democra-
> tization. The day is not far off when we are going to have to deal in

straight power concepts. The less we are hampered by idealistic slo-
gans, the better.[75]

And the US's "straight power" plays since WWII have succeeded in
allowing itself, with only 5% of the world's population, to monopolize
about 25% of its resources.[76] In other words, far from advancing the
"lofty" and "benign" goals of freedom and democracy, as the *New York
Times*'s editorial would have us believe, the US has been waging war
around the globe to protect its own unjust share of resources. However, the US has needed the perceived threat of the USSR, or other
like enemy, to justify this. Kennan recognized this fact as well, when
he said: "Were the Soviet Union to sink tomorrow under the waters of
the ocean, the American military-industrial establishment would have
to go on, substantially unchanged, until some other adversary could
be invented. Anything else would be an unacceptable shock to the
American economy."

Indeed, even when the Soviet Union existed, its threat had to be
exaggerated in order to justify the unjustifiable. As just one example of
this, 42-year CIA veteran Melvin A. Goodman, examining a declassified study by a Pentagon defense contractor, explains that policymak-
ers in the US intentionally exaggerated both Soviet nuclear weapons
capacity as well as their desire to use it, willfully ignoring evidence,
particularly during the Brezhnev years of the 1970s and thereafter, that
the USSR was scaling back its military preparedness, deathly feared a
nuclear war, and had no plans for a first strike. As Goodman writes:

> The Pentagon study demonstrates that the Soviet military high
> command "understood the devastating consequences of nuclear war"
> and believed that the use of nuclear weapons had to be avoided at "all
> costs." Nevertheless, in 1975, presidential chief of staff Dick Cheney
> and secretary of defense Donald Rumsfeld introduced a group of neo-
> conservatives, led by Harvard professor Richard Pipes, to the CIA in
> order to make sure that future NIEs [National Intelligence Estimates]

would falsely conclude that the Soviet Union rejected nuclear parity, were bent on fighting and winning a nuclear war, and were radically increasing their military spending.[77]

Further, "[t]he CIA ignored the Soviet slowdown in the growth of military procurement, exaggerated the capabilities of important strategic systems, and distorted the military and economic power of the Warsaw Pact states."

As Goodman notes quite correctly in this piece from 2009, this Pentagon study begs serious questions about the current US exaggeration of 'threats' emanating from Iran, North Korea, and Afghanistan," and, I would argue now, Russia as well. Indeed, given the CIA's unreliability about threats emanating from other countries—its claims about Iraq's non-existent WMDs comes to mind—its current crusade against Putin and Russia must be looked at with great skepticism.

Now that the USSR is gone, the US has to continue to invent enemies in order to justify its bloated military—by far the biggest in the world. Thus, the US, which spends just shy of $600 billion per year on defense, spends more on its military than the next 7 nations (which includes Russia at the #4 spot) *combined*.[78] Meanwhile, the disparity between the US and Russian military budgets will grow by leaps and bounds, as Trump is going for a huge increase in military spending this year, while Russia has announced its largest military budget cut since the 1990's, saying that it will decrease its military budget by 25.5% in 2017.[79] If Trump is truly the "Manchurian Candidate," he certainly doesn't appear to be acting like one.

The US's outsized military exists not only to ensure the US's quite unjust share of the world's riches, but also to ensure that those riches are not shared with the poor huddled masses in this country through annoying things such as social programs and works projects. Instead, a disproportionate amount of tax revenue (about 54% of the US's discretionary budget[80]) is sucked right back into the military-industrial complex, a form of welfare for the rich, while the working class

and poor are left on their own to suffer. One commentator correctly described this as "Redistributive Militarism"—that is, the process by which income is redistributed from bottom to top through the escalation of military spending.[81]And so, the need to vilify countries like Russia and leaders like Vladimir Putin, conflating them with our former Soviet nemeses, is so critical to the social order which our leaders have so carefully constructed over decades.

The blindness of Americans, particularly of liberals who claim to care and to know better, to the evil of US wars abroad may equal or exceed the irrationality of their hatred for Vladimir Putin and Russia. And indeed, their hatred of Putin is a distraction from what they should be focusing on—the unjustifiable reach of their own military in ways that no other country in the history of the world, even the greatest of empires, has even attempted.

5

THE US DRAWS FIRST BLOOD

GIVEN THAT KENNAN SAW THE "FAR East" as the area in the world which had the most to resent about the US and therefore would have to be dealt with "in straight power concepts," it is quite fitting that the US fired the first shots of the Cold War there. While there are differing views as to when the Cold War actually began, it is fair to say that it began in 1945 when the US decided to drop two atomic bombs upon Japan.

William Blum, former State Department employee as well as former anti-communist, explains this well, quoting, amongst others, General Dwight D. Eisenhower in support of the proposition that, contrary to popular belief even today, Japan was thoroughly defeated by the time the bombs were dropped and was actually trying hard, but unsuccessfully, to surrender.[82] As Blum explains:

> [D]ropping of the atomic bombs was not so much the last military act of the Second World War as the first act of the Cold War. Although Japan was targeted, the weapons were aimed straight to the red heart of the USSR. For more than 70 years, the determining element of US foreign policy, virtually its *sine qua non*, has been "the communist

factor." World War II and a battlefield alliance with the Soviet Union did not bring about an ideological change in the anti-communists who owned and ran America. It merely provided a partial breather in a struggle that had begun with the US invasion of Russia in 1918 [intended to strangle the fledgling revolution in its crib].

As Blum relates, "quoting Manhattan Project scientist Leo Szilard, Secretary of State Byrnes had said that the bomb's biggest benefit was not its effect on Japan but its power to 'make Russia more manageable in Europe.'" Imagine the cynicism of deciding to vaporize tens of thousands of innocent souls in Japan to send a message to Russia.

Of course, the next shots of the Cold War, which still reverberate today, as so many do, is the Korean war, or "police action" as it has been called. Some have described the Korean conflict as the "forgotten war." And, the truth is that most in the US would like to forget the Korean war because the US conducted itself in an unforgivable way during that conflict, carrying out what a number of scholars believe was genocide against Korean civilians.

To begin thinking about the US's misdeeds in Korea, a good place to start is a paper written by Dong Choon Kim, a Professor of Sociology at Sungkonghoe University in Seoul, South Korea, and former Standing Commissioner of the Truth and Reconciliation Commission of Korea. This paper, published in the *Journal of Genocide Research*, and entitled, "Forgotten War, forgotten massacres—the Korea War (1950-1953) as licensed mass killings," challenges long-held beliefs in the US that the Korean War was somehow a good and righteous war that the US fought. As Dong Choon Kim shows, it was anything but.

Professor Kim illuminates forgotten truths about the Korean War. Thus, he explains that (1) the war was greatly inspired by the US's efforts in Korea from 1945 to 1950 to restore fascist and dictatorial military leaders who had been trained by the Japanese, just as the US had supported fascist restoration in Greece after World War II; (2)

the US provided critical military support to these rightist leaders in South Korea to carry out a "white terror" which included the murder of at least 100,000 Koreans between 1945 and the outbreak of the war in 1950, and the jailing of about 20,000 more who were later summarily killed; and (3) the US, fueled by anti-Asian racism, engaged in the indiscriminate slaughter of thousands of Korean civilians, numerous rapes of Korean women and the wholesale destruction of major Korean cities through massive aerial bombardment which included the large-scale use of napalm and incendiary bombs.

As Professor Kim explains:

> According to the witnesses, US air and ground forces shot at children, women and aged people who were easily distinguishable as unarmed civilians. North Korean authorities have long accused American troops of 'criminal acts' before and after the outbreak of the Korean War. They maintained that the US army killed more than a million innocent civilians by bombing, shooting, and the use of napalm and chemical weapons. . . . [And] the facts on the ground force us not to discount their veracity.

Professor Kim further notes that "the US soldiers killed civilian refugees lacking even a modicum of self-defense, including women and children, even when no North Korean soldiers or grass-root guerilla forces threatened them." And, he emphasizes *"that the number of unarmed civilians killed under ROK [South Korean] and US command overwhelms those killed at the hands of North Korean command, contrary to the public knowledge about the Korean War atrocities."*

Professor Kim quite rightly concludes that the wholesale atrocities committed by the US during the Korean War foreshadowed, and help us to understand, the US's countless atrocities in later wars, such as in Vietnam and in Latin America as well.

A recent book by Korean scholar Bruce Cummings, entitled *The*

Korean War: A History, fully supports the conclusions of Professor Kim, and opines that the US was engaged in a racist, genocidal campaign in Korea. As Cummings poignantly notes,

> What hardly any Americans know or remember . . . is that we carpet-bombed the North for three years with next to no concern for civilian casualties. Even fewer will feel any connection to this. Yet when foreigners visit North Korea, this is the first thing they hear about the war. The air assaults ranged from the widespread and continual use of firebombing to threats to use nuclear and chemical weapons, finally to the destruction of huge North Korean dams in the last stages of the war. It was an application of the air campaigns against Japan and Germany, except that North Korea was a small Third World country that lost control of the air to the United States within days of the war's start.

In light of this history, it is hard for me to feel anything but sorrow and sympathy for North Korea. While it is fashionable to mock that country, and while the Trump Administration seems to be considering bombing it off the map, I cannot join in this chorus either.

* * *

The next great conflict of the Cold War, which looked much like the Korean War, was the US war on Vietnam, the memory of which the US has been trying desperately to shake to this day. The wounds of this war, however, have been harder to forget than those of Korea.

When I drove to Nicaragua in 1988 from Dayton, Ohio, I travelled with the Veterans for Peace, which, at least at that time, was made up mostly of Vietnam War veterans who, regretting what they had seen and what they had done in Vietnam, had become some of the best peace activists our country has ever seen. The Veterans for Peace organized the convoy I participated in to bring humanitarian aid to the

Nicaraguan people, who were suffering from the US-backed Contra War at the time.

Many of these vets ended up risking more for peace than they had in waging war, but monuments are very rarely erected in this country to peace-makers. It is not an exaggeration to say that I fell in love with those guys, and probably learned more on that trip from them than I learned in all of college. I think of that trip nearly every day.

One veteran I met on that trip was dying of cancer from the war that, unbeknownst to he and his fellow US servicemen at the time, was waged by the US against them in the interest of testing out nuclear weapons. As he explained, he was an Atomic Veteran of Bikini Atoll.[83] The Atomic Veterans were on, or in the waters near, Bikini Atoll when the US, without prior warning to them or proper explanation afterward, detonated nuclear weapons to test them both on the indigenous population, who ended up having to leave the island for good because it was made uninhabitable by these tests, as well as on the US soldiers themselves. These nuclear tests, 23 detonations in all, were done periodically over the period from 1946 to 1958. As The *New York Times* reported much later, "[b]y Pentagon estimates, between 250,000 and 500,000 service and civilian personnel were exposed to the atmospheric tests," with thousands dying prematurely of cancer and other horrible diseases.[84] These were some of the unsung victims of the US's prosecution of the Cold War which, as you might have noticed by now, seems to have been waged against everyone (including our own soldiers) but the Russians themselves.

Another Vietnam veteran I met on the trip was S. Brian Willson (not of The Beach Boys), who, by then, had lost his legs lying down on train tracks to stop a shipment of arms bound for the US war in Central America. What I didn't know until later was that Willson had written about the connection between the American war on Vietnam and the early days of the US Republic.

I learned of this from John Marciano's book *The American War In Vietnam, Crime or Commemoration* (Monthly Review, 2016). Marciano

cites Willson's work, in which he "writes that [George] Washington's direct orders to General Sullivan 'established imperial US military principles for centuries to come,'" including "'total war/genocide targeting all inhabitants for elimination; (2) preventing peace; (3) pre-emptive war; (4) terror; (5) crime of self-defense; (6) revenge.'"

Specifically, as both Willson and Marciano relate, our founding father, General George Washington, ordered Major General John Sullivan in 1789 to "lay waste to all [indigenous] settlements around . . . that the country may not be merely overrun but destroyed . . . You will not by any means listen to any overtures of peace before the total ruin of their settlements. . . . Our future security will be in their inability to injury us . . . and in the terror which the severity of the chastisement they receive will inspire them." In the end, General Sullivan followed Washington's orders faithfully, as did many US military leaders to come, committing possibly one of the greatest genocides in history, certainly involving the slaying of tens of millions of indigenous persons.[85]

While Americans obsess over the numbers killed under the Stalin Terror, few care to consider the most-likely greater numbers killed in the US genocide of Native Americans. It is always more convenient, of course, to pull the speck from your brother's eye than the plank from your own.

In any case, all of these elements of the slaughter of the Native Americans were surely an integral part of the US war in Vietnam, as Willson and the other vets knew all too well.

Before getting to the conduct of the war in Vietnam, it is important to consider the actual reasons the US was there, as contrasted with the stated goals. Thus, the US did not send tens of thousands of US soldiers to kill and die in Vietnam in order to defend democracy and freedom, as we are meant to believe. Rather, after World War II (in which the US had received significant help from Ho Chi Minh and his Viet Minh guerilla fighters to fight off Japan) the US initially entered the fray in Vietnam in order to defend French colonialism there.

And, as has been quite typical of the US's willing collaboration with fascists and even Nazis after WWII, the US allied with recently-defeated Japan in helping to defeat the Vietnamese independence effort against the French. As John Marciano explains, "[i]n a stunning shift in history, US vessels brought French troops [many of themselves who had just fought on the side of Vichy France] so they could join recently released Japanese troops to support France's attempt to crush the Vietnamese independence movement." Marciano notes that this aroused the very first anti-war protests against the American intervention in Vietnam—this time by US sailors who could not stomach the hypocrisy of what the US was doing and whom they were doing it with.

Ultimately, of course, the Viet Minh triumphed against the French in the heroic battle of Diem Bien Phu on May 7, 1954. As Marciano relates, the Viet Minh "'had organized and inspired a poor, untrained, ill-equipped population to fight and ultimately win against a far better equipped and trained army." One might believe (and Ho Chi Minh in fact did at one point) that the US, in the Spirit of '76, would welcome and support such an independence victory. Indeed, Ho Chi Minh cited the American Declaration of Independence in declaring the independence of Vietnam from France.

Of course, the painful reality is that the US, despite its lofty rhetoric, has been quite consistent in its conviction that colonial independence is only for itself, and that other peoples must be punished for seeking an independent path to development.

And so, in 1956, as elections scheduled pursuant to the Geneva Accords to unify Vietnam approached—elections which the US government knew would be won handily by the popular Ho Chi Minh with an anticipated 80% of the vote—the US acted quickly and decisively to scuttle these elections and to support the Diem dictatorship it had installed in South Vietnam to brutally repress, through murder and imprisonment, thousands of Vietnamese who sympathized with the Viet Minh. In other words, far from supporting democracy in

Vietnam, the US effort at this point, and for the next 20 years, would be to prevent it by any and all means necessary. The American War in Vietnam had now begun in earnest, and it was not pretty.

The gruesomeness of the US war effort in Vietnam is best typified by the My Lai Massacre, which Obama has recently tried to white-wash as the "My Lai Incident." In case the reader never heard of this incident, or possibly forgot about it, here is a little summary of that event, which is described in detail in Nick Turse's recent *Kill Anything That Moves: The Real American War in Vietnam.*

On the evening of March 15, 1968, US soldiers from Company C, or, "Charlie Company" entered the village of My Lai, where they were ordered to "kill everything in the village"; "to kill everything that breathed." This admonition included women and children. Indeed, Charlie Company met no armed adversaries that day—just women, children and the elderly. And so, the Americans "gunned down old men sitting in their homes and children as they ran for cover. Tossed grenades into homes. Shot women and babies at close range." For good measure, "they raped women and young girls, mutilated the dead, systematically burned homes, and fouled the area's drinking water." General Westmoreland congratulated these brave soldiers for their "heavy blows" against the enemy, and their "aggressiveness." All told, over 500 civilians were killed in this massacre.

As Turse explains, there were many My Lai's during the war. Indeed, he cites a January 21, 1971 letter from a Vietnam veteran named Charles McDuff to President Nixon in which he expressed his disgust over the war in Southeast Asia, saying that My Lai was merely the tip of the iceberg. Indeed, My Lai-type incidents were encouraged by the US military's designation of "free fire zones" in which "everyone, men, women, children, could be considered [a fair target]; you could not be held responsible for firing on innocent civilians since by definition there were none there."

One other notable example of such crimes is the operation for which the baby-faced Bob Kerrey, who would later become Democratic

Governor and then Senator of Nebraska, would be awarded the Bronze Star.[86] The operation—which was part and parcel of the CIA's Phoenix Program—took place in the tiny village of Thanh Phong, which the Navy Seal unit under Lt. Kerrey's command had surveilled the night before, finding no Viet Minh combatants. The day of the action, the unit predictably encountered no resistance, and so decided to fire at the only living targets they could find—namely, twenty civilians, including women and children. For good measure, they slit the throats of some of these civilians and even heroically located and killed children hiding in a drain pipe—a drain pipe now forever remembered in a war museum in Vietnam.

Kerrey would later be awarded the Medal of Honor for his exceptional service in Vietnam, and go on to have a stellar political career. And, while the later revelation of his atrocities in Vietnam did present a bump in the road for him for a time, Obama helped him land on his feet by appointing him to head the Fulbright University in Vietnam. Incredibly, this stirred a bit of controversy in Vietnam where some have the audacity to believe that Kerrey, rather than being given an academic sinecure, should be rotting in jail or even brought before a firing squad. But, as we all know, our war criminals are never held to account for their crimes. We instead obsess on everyone else's misdeeds, real or imagined, to help us sleep better at night.

In addition to such atrocities, the US subjected Vietnam to the equivalent of 640 Hiroshima-sized atomic bombs—*the lion's share on South Vietnam, which was the US's ally.* The US even bombed Catholic Churches throughout South Vietnam.

All told, according to Nick Turse, the US, with its superior air and fire power, killed approximated 3.8 million Vietnamese (8% of its total population), and created over 14 million refugees. Meanwhile, Vietnam continues to feel the effects, in terms of environmental degradation and horrible birth defects, from the "millions of gallons of chemical defoliants, millions of pounds of chemical gases, [and] endless canisters of napalm" which the US dumped on that country.

Meanwhile, even as Obama was drawing "red lines" on Syria in regards to the use of chemical weapons, babies in Iraq were being born—and continue to be born—with horrifying birth defects from the white phosphorous used by the US there during the Second Gulf War.[87] In Syria itself, as has recently been confirmed, despite the Obama Administration's initial denials, the US has been firing munitions with depleted uranium, which is a toxic material likely to cause cancer and birth defects.[88] The US has also used depleted uranium in Iraq "thousands of times" since 2003,[89] and there have indeed been recorded spikes in both cancer rates and birth defects in areas where it was used.[90]

No wonder that Martin Luther King, who ultimately came out against the war on Vietnam, would be inspired by the brutality of this conflict to describe the US as "the greatest purveyor of violence in the world."

And MLK did not even live long enough to see Richard Nixon expand the war in Vietnam to neighboring Laos, reducing about a quarter of the population of about three million to refugees and subjecting another third of the population to the most intense bombardment in history.

The war was also expanded to the then-very peaceful country of Cambodia, creating one million refugees out of six million inhabitants, thereby radicalizing some of the population and leading directly to the "killing fields" of the Khmer Rouge—a force which the US would first oppose but then support when the Vietnamese, having defeated the US (after the French), invaded Cambodia, thus freeing the Cambodians from the vicious Khmer Rouge. As commentator Gregory Elich opined, the Vietnamese 1978 campaign against the Khmer Rouge "was one of history's great liberations."[91] Historian Eric Hobsbawm agrees, pointing to the general "consensus" that this was an "obvious" case of "justified intervention."[92] And so, of course, the US had to oppose it, and to support the one force that could continue to harass the Vietnamese and the new government in

Cambodia—the Khmer Rouge—and the US did so for many years to come.[93]

Despite the one-sided devastation to which the US subjected Vietnam, President Jimmy Carter, our "human rights President," "took the position that no apology is necessary and no obligation to rebuild Vietnam warranted given that, in his remarkable words, 'the destruction was mutual.'"[94]

Meanwhile, as the world quite rightly urges Japan to apologize for its exploitation of Korean "comfort women" during WWII, notice that no one suggests that the US, whose military raped Vietnamese women on a mass scale and had a brothel at nearly every base in Vietnam, is never asked to apologize for its exploitation of Vietnamese "comfort women."

Of course, as we well know, being the United States means never having to say you're sorry, even when you've visited horrendous atrocities against a country that has never, and could never, attack you. Then, to add insult to injury, we in the US, even after such an event, will find a way to paint ourselves as the victim. It is worthy of note that Russia, on the other hand, actually has apologized for many of its sins, including for the human rights abuses it committed against Polish civilians, and even "for foreign policy errors that 'heightened tension with the West'" during the first Cold War.[95]

In the end, the US war on Vietnam, at least from the point of view of national security and even fighting the Cold War, was entirely unnecessary. It is clear that Ho Chi Minh, who had worked with the US during WWII, and who looked to the Declaration of Independence for his inspiration, would have willingly worked with the US, allowed US investment—*as communist Vietnam, now an ally, allows now*—and most likely would not have entered the Soviet orbit. It was the US's decision to defend the French occupation of Vietnam, and then to bomb Vietnam to the Stone Age after the French were driven out by a popular uprising, which forced Vietnam to seek help from and to become dependent upon the USSR until its collapse. And, far from

promoting democracy in Vietnam, the US did everything it could, just short of nuking Vietnam off the map (though Nixon and Kissinger had considered that too), to prevent it.

And, because the pretexts for preventing Soviet expansion and defending democracy were so weak, another lie was needed to justify the intensification of the war effort in Vietnam. The Johnson administration, with the help as always of the compliant US media, found one in the "Gulf of Tonkin incident." Thus, in 1964, the Johnson Administration claimed that American ships had been preemptively fired upon by Viet Minh forces in international waters in two separate incidents, that this was an act of war and that the US must therefore attack Vietnam accordingly. As it turns out, much of this story was fabricated, with the truth being that the US ship had fired first—just warning shots—to scare off the Vietnamese boat in the first incident, while the second incident most likely did not occur at all. However, by the time the US press got around to questioning it, the US Congress had already authorized major military force against Vietnam based on this "fake news" in the Gulf of Tonkin Resolution.

As we now enter the new Cold War, it is important to judge the US's assertions about rivals such as Russia, and to judge the US's conduct abroad, by these experiences, which have been repeated time and time again.

6

OUR PRAYERS ARE ANSWERED, BUT STILL PEACE HAS NOT COME

As HISTORY HAS DEMONSTRATED, THE FERVENT prayers many of us Catholics had been making to Our Lady of Fatima were answered, and Russia was "converted"—quite abruptly, and with little bloodshed, in 1991, with the collapse of the Soviet Union. Moreover, even before this "conversion" or "collapse," the East Bloc had already disintegrated with the acquiescence of the USSR. This disintegration was best symbolized by the fall of the Berlin Wall on November 9, 1989.

However, the peace we had been promised upon Russia's "conversion" and the end of the Cold War did not come, nor did the promised "peace dividend"—the monies which were supposed to flow into education, medical care and other social programs once this war was won.

As Eric Hobsbawm succinctly explained, "[s]ince the fall of the Berlin Wall, we once again live in an era of genocide and compulsory mass population transfers, as in parts of Africa, southeastern Europe and Asia. It is estimated that at the end of 2003 there were perhaps thirty-eight million refugees inside and outside their country,"[96] and that figure has of course grown since. Meanwhile, as noted above, the UN

has announced that it is facing its worst crisis since WWII, with 20 million people in Africa now facing starvation. And this disaster is being presided over by the only superpower in the world, the United States, which is largely unchecked and unchallenged. Those who believed that a unipolar world with the US as that one power would usher in a new and better world order were wrong, which may call into question things about the nature of the US that few dare to contemplate.

For his part, Noam Chomsky has noted on a number of occasions that the fall of the Berlin Wall was followed just one week later by the murder in El Salvador of six Jesuit priests, along with their housekeeper and her daughter, by forces trained and backed by the US[97] All told, 75,000 Salvadorans lost their lives in this tiny nation[98] in a conflict that the US claimed was to stem the tide of Soviet-backed insurrection in Central America, despite the fact that the USSR had little to do with this home-grown conflict and despite the fact that the conflict continued until 1992, well after the collapse of both the East Bloc and the USSR.

Events like these made me start to wonder why we were not also praying for the "conversion" of the United States as well. I must also note the quite interesting fact that while the "secrets" of Our Lady of Fatima—who, it is claimed, visited three children in Portugal in 1917 (note the significance of this date)—were not revealed until 1942, there seemed to be a glaring omission from what these "secrets" called upon us to do. Thus, while we were told to say the Rosary to stop Russia from "spreading her errors," the main "error" Russia was spreading at the time was the liberation of Europe from the Nazis. And we were not asked, quite strangely, to pray for Nazi Germany's "conversion." Of course, as I found out later, the apparently skewed nature of these revelations could be explained by their source—Pope Pius XII, who played a critical role in helping the Nazis take power in Germany, and who famously remained silent during a critical moment about the persecution of the Jews and the Final Solution.[99] But I digress.

During the waning days of the Soviet Union in 1990, the US also

invaded Iraq in the First Gulf War, which was ostensibly carried out in retaliation for Saddam Hussein's invasion of Kuwait. This invasion was carried out, moreover, with the reluctant assent of the Soviet Union which—under Mikhail Gorbachev, who was, and remains, quite popular in the West, but not in Russia—voted in favor of the Security Council Resolution authorizing force to expel Iraq from Kuwait.

The ability of the US to carry out such an action in the Middle East would have been much more difficult during the days in which the USSR was stronger and more resolute—a time in which the Soviet Union would have certainly vetoed the UN Security Council authorization of force in such an instance. However, as CNN explained later, "the Soviet Union of January 1991—economically weakened and politically unstable—adopted the role of the middleman, condemning Baghdad's aggression against Kuwait while working feverishly to avert allied military action against Iraq."[100] In the end, though, the USSR, despite its best efforts, could not prevent the war from coming.

In the case of Iraq, the US had helped install and then backed Saddam Hussein even during his most brutal years, such as when he famously gassed the Kurds living in Iraq. By the time of the first Gulf War, the US had grown tired of Hussein, who had become less and less compliant. And though his invasion of Kuwait—in response to what he perceived to be economic warfare waged by Kuwait against Iraq, including Kuwait's stealing of Iraqi oil through "slant drilling" into Iraq's Rumala oil fields—was certainly unlawful and immoral, he appeared to have been given an advance green light for the invasion by US Ambassador April Glaspie.[101]

Moreover, it appeared that there was a chance to prevail upon Hussein to leave Kuwait short of an invasion, including through a possible Russia-brokered agreement with Hussein, but President George H.W. Bush shunned those opportunities, instead opting for what he believed would be a quick war to boost his anemic polling numbers.[102]

Apparently, Bush's 1989 invasion of Panama, which immediately preceded the First Gulf War, and which involved the one-sided

slaughter of hundreds, if not thousands, of defenseless, and mostly poor and working people in center city Panama City, was not enough to increase his popularity.[103]

Meanwhile, one of the critical claims justifying the Iraq invasion—that Iraqi troops in Kuwait were allegedly taking babies out of incubators and leaving them on the floor to die, turned out to be entirely fabricated.[104] Indeed, while the information was initially said to come from a crying, 15-year-old girl simply named, "Nayirah," to protect her and her family, it was later revealed that she was in fact the daughter of the Kuwaiti Ambassdor to the US who made up the story to spur on a US intervention.[105] And, it turned out that Democratic Congressman Tom Lantos was in on the ruse the entire time.

This was a case of "fake news" if there ever was one, and nearly every war we wage depends upon "fake news," willingly peddled by our "free press," to generate public approval.

In any case, the US did invade Iraq, and did prevail easily with its far superior air power, which it was able to use at will, and Iraq did leave Kuwait. However, regardless of how one viewed the rightness of the US's decision to attack Iraq, its prosecution of the war was brutal and unforgivable, though you wouldn't know it by watching the evening news at that time.

In short, the US violated the Geneva Conventions and the rules of war on a massive scale by targeting civilians and civilian infrastructure necessary to sustain human life. As Ramsey Clark, a former Attorney General under Lyndon Johnson who was radicalized by what he saw as the horrors of the Vietnam War, and who was an eye-witness to the carnage in Iraq, explains:

> Before the assault was over US planes flew more than 109,000 sorties, raining 88,000 tons of bombs, the equivalent of seven Hiroshimas, and killing indiscriminately across the country.
>
> What was visible was a nation with thousands of civilians dead; without water, hospitals, or health care; with no electricity,

communications, or public transportation; without gasoline, road and bridge repair capacity, or parts for essential equipment; and with a growing food crisis. Because of the nature of American weapons, Iraq was being crippled from afar and left to a painful struggle for survival. The bombing . . . was hardly surgical, but was clearly designated to break a whole country and its population for a long time to come.[106]

Moreover, strong evidence suggests the US murdered hundreds of Iraqi soldiers, and nearby civilians as well, with cluster bombs and napalm as they pulled out from Kuwait—in compliance with UN Resolution 660— on what came to be known as the "Highway of Death."[107] Our former ally, Osama bin Laden, was inspired by the carnage suffered by the Muslim nation of Iraq during the First Gulf War to start recruiting his new terrorist group, al-Qaeda, which would now be aimed at the US. As NPR would later report, this war "became a cause célèbre for Osama bin Laden and one of the factors that led to al-Qaeda's attacks against the US on September 11, 2001."[108]

The suffering inflicted upon the Iraqi people during the First Gulf War would continue to be exacerbated by President Clinton, who continued to bomb Iraq periodically (usually when he needed to distract the American public from some scandal), and who imposed sanctions upon Iraq which only increased their inability to feed themselves and obtain necessary medicines. The result would be the death, according to the UN, of about 576,000 Iraqi children.[109]

Recall that, when asked about these 500,000 dead Iraqi children, then Secretary of State Madeleine Albright responded, "The price is worth it."[110] Albright, known now for her fancy pin and broach collection, would later express regret for saying this, but she never expressed regret for aggressively supporting the policy which resulted in these deaths. Indeed, Albright did not even have the self-awareness to know how ironic it was when, campaigning for Hillary Clinton, she said that women who don't support Hillary have a "special place in hell"

reserved for them. [111] Of course, this led some to wonder if, quite possibly, Albright has a special place in hell reserved for her much more serious crimes.

When the US decided to attack Iraq again in 2003 based upon even more flimsy pretexts, Russia under Vladimir Putin would not go along with this second war, and that appears to be one of Putin's unforgiveable sins.

In any case, despite the fact that the end of the Cold War was supposed to usher in a new period of peace and prosperity for the US, it did not, and it did not because the US never wanted peace, nor did it really want prosperity, except for the very few on top. (He says as I-85 just collapsed in Atlanta) And so, based on fake news story after fake news story, it would continue to engage in wars throughout the globe with no other power to contest it. However, it has always needed a good alibi for its wars, and Vladimir Putin right now is a convenient one.

Meanwhile, the prosperity the West promised to Russia if it would only give up its silly notions of socialism did not come either, and Bill Clinton and his cronies made sure of that.

* * *

7

CLINTON MEDDLES IN RUSSIA WITH DISASTROUS CONSEQUENCES

MEANWHILE, BACK IN RUSSIA, ITS "CONVERSION" experience was quite exacting on the lives of average Russians, and the US made sure it was so.

As Russian Scholar Stephen F. Cohen explains in his important work *Soviet Fates And Lost Alternatives*,[112] post-Soviet Russia suffered a major economic collapse, with investment in the economy falling by 80%, and 75% of the population falling into poverty. As Cohen explains, Russia became "the first nation to ever undergo actual de-modernization in peacetime." Cohen relates that this led one Moscow philosopher to state, in regard to those who long wanted to destroy the Soviet Union, "They were aiming at Communism but hitting Russia."

As explained in a study conducted by the National Center for Biotechnology Information (NCBI), "[t]he changes in Russian mortality in the 1990s are unprecedented in a modern industrialized country in peacetime." In this study, the NCBI estimated that, between 1992-2001, there were approximately 2.5 to 3 million premature Russian deaths as a result of the combination of the economic and social dislocation

caused by the collapse of the USSR and the 1998 economic crisis which followed.[113] Other Western demographers have put the total excess deaths at between 5 and 6 million.[114]

This collapse in post-Soviet Russia was overseen and managed, or mismanaged to be more precise, by the drunkard and buffoon Boris Yeltsin. And, of course, Yeltsin was a darling of the US and the Clinton Administration which backed him to the hilt.

In a Congressional Research Service (CRS) Report, entitled, "Russian Political Turmoil,"[115] Russia's economic crisis of the 1992 to 1998 period "can be traced . . . ultimately to [Boris] Yeltsin . . . under whose stewardship the GDP has contracted by 50%, accompanied by economic distress worse than the Great Depression of the 1930s in the United States for most of the Russian population." And, as the CRS Report continues, when Yeltsin's administration "assembled a western-oriented economic team and pursued economic policies supported by the Clinton Administration, the G-7, and the IMF . . . economic conditions and the government's and Yeltsin's approval ratings continued to deteriorate."

The Report goes on to admit that "[s]ome critics of US policy toward Russia charge that it is too closely linked to Yeltsin and is seen by ordinary Russians as endorsing Yeltsin and the unpopular economic policies that they blame for leading the country to ruin." On the other hand, the Report states, "[d]efenders of US policy reply that Yeltsin has steered Russia on an essentially correct, *though painful*, course." (emphasis added). In other words, regardless which side one was on in this debate, there was no questioning the fact that the course supported by the US was "painful" for the Russian people. But, the argument went, the Russian people's pain was potentially our gain, given that "[a] weak and unstable Russia may be less likely to pose an aggressive military threat . . . ." And the man to continue Russia's pain and unraveling was Boris Yeltsin.

Therefore, as a July 15, 1996, *Time* magazine article entitled, "Rescuing Boris," detailed,[116] this meant sending in a team of US political consultants, who were paid $250,000, plus expenses, to secretly

manage and re-direct Yeltsin's failing 1996 Presidential campaign. Richard Dresner, who had helped with Bill Clinton's electoral victories for Arkansas Governor, was one of the chief consultants who aided Yeltsin. Dick Morris, who was then Clinton's chief Presidential campaign advisor, was also involved. Clinton was well aware of the consultant team's assistance to Yeltsin, though the extent of his knowledge about their work, and any possible input he may have given, remain shrouded in secrecy.[117] What is known is that the US under Clinton successfully prevailed upon the International Monetary Fund to give a $10.2 billion "emergency infusion" to Russia as further means to bolster Yeltsin's awful poll numbers.[118]

The Americans' help was absolutely critical, *Time* magazine explained, because Yeltsin was deeply unpopular with the Russian people given "his brutal misadventure in Chechnya; his increasing authoritarianism; and his economic reform program, which has brought about corruption and widespread suffering." Indeed, Yeltsin had a 6% approval rating at the time the American consultants intervened.[119]

Through the US consultants' help, however, Boris was in fact rescued. The *Time* magazine article concluded in a triumphant tone, explaining that, with Yeltsin's ultimate nail-biter of a win, "Democracy triumphed—and along with it came the tools of modern campaigns, including the trickery and slickery Americans know so well."

Examples of the American "trickery and slickery" which Yeltsin used to win re-election were "extensive 'black operations,' including disrupting opposition rallies and press conferences, spreading disinformation among Yeltsin supporters, and denying media access to the opposition.[120] The dirty tricks included such tactics as announcing false dates for opposition rallies and press conferences, disseminating alarming campaign materials that they deceitfully attributed to the [opposition] Zyuganov campaign, and cancelling hotel reservations for Zyuganov and his volunteers. Finally, widespread bribery, voter fraud, intimidation, and ballot stuffing assured Yeltsin's victory in the runoff election.

Meanwhile, buried in the *Time* magazine article was a reference to

"the Duma catastrophe," which the article also cited as an event that
made Yeltsin's re-election bid so difficult. It is worth re-visiting what
this "catastrophe" was, as it illustrates what kind of "democrat" Yeltsin
really was, and reveals just as much about the US, which continues to
hold Yeltsin up as a pillar of democracy.

In short, "the Duma catastrophe" began with a political stand-off
between the Duma—the Russian legislature, and at the time the most
powerful branch of Russian government—and Boris Yeltsin. The Duma,
which still had a large contingent of Communists who were resistant
to the market changes which were, by all accounts, wreaking havoc in
Russia, was refusing to approve Yeltsin's pick for Prime Minister, Yegor
Gaidar. As one publication explains, "Gaidar, who was the architect of
the economic shock therapy and Yeltsin, who backed the plan, were vastly
unpopular among the Russian public at the time, which encouraged the
decision of the Duma leaders to act against the executive branch." [121]

In other words, the legislators were being asked by their constit-
uents to resist an unpopular President, just as the Democrats are now
being urged to resist Trump.

In response, Yeltsin tried to dissolve the Duma, but the Duma
declared this action to be unconstitutional. They then proceeded to
remove Yeltsin from office and to install the Vice-President in his stead.
Yeltsin responded by shutting off electricity and water to the White
House, which then housed the Duma. And, when a number of Duma
lawmakers still refused to leave and supporters showed up to the White
House to protest Yeltsin's actions, Yeltsin did what any good, democratic leader would do: he shelled the White House, killing anywhere
between 200 and 2,000 people. [122] A new Constitution was then adopted
which gave more power to the Executive Branch. In the end, these
"events that took place on October 1993 secured the domination of the
executive branch over the legislative and judicial branches, effectively
prohibiting the country from being a parliamentary republic." [123]

As I remember quite vividly from that time, the actions of Yeltsin
in bombing his own legislative building and assuming greater power

was applauded by both Washington and the US media as a triumph for Russian democracy. In this event—reminiscent of the "Tiananmen Square massacre" in China just four years before, in which 300 to 3000 people were killed[124]–the West was rooting for the tanks.[125]

It is worth noting that the US also had no problem with a similar event which took place in the very same year as the Tiananmen Square massacre. This event, which the US media has entirely ignored, involved the state murder of hundreds (at least 300), if not thousands (possibly 3,000) of protestors in Venezuela.[126] In other words, the estimates of those protestors killed in Venezuela are identical to the estimates of those killed in Beijing, China. Of course, given that Venezuela has a tiny population (around 30 million) compared to that of China (over 1 billion), these numbers are proportionately much greater. But of course, the Caracazo massacre deserves no commemoration by the US government or media, because these killings were carried out by a government—that of President Carlos Andres Perez—that was aligned with the United States at the time, and because the Caracazo was an important factor in the rise of our perceived nemesis, Hugo Chavez, who stood up against this repression.

As Stephen F. Cohen explains, the Russian people, not surprisingly, characterized the deeply flawed reign of Yeltsin as "shit-ocracy," and they naturally welcomed a change in the person of Vladimir Putin who was, and is, viewed as being able to bring back order, stability and national pride to Russia.[127]

David Satter, writing for *The Wall Street Journal*, explained it succinctly: "Yeltsin . . . and the small group of economists who advised him, decided that the most urgent priority for Russia was putting property immediately into private hands, even if those hands were criminal. In this, they were fully supported by the US. The result was that the path was laid for the pillaging of the country and the rise in Russia" of Putin.

Meanwhile, it is worth remembering, as US officials and media fret about Vladimir Putin's conduct in the former Soviet Republic of

Ukraine, that the Clinton Administration also showed no tangible concern for Yeltsin's prosecution of a brutal war in the Chechnyaen Republic. As Helsinki Watch (now Human Rights Watch) reported at the time:

> Russian forces prosecuted a brutal war in the breakaway republic of Chechnya with total disregard for humanitarian law, causing thousands of needless civilian casualties. . . .
>
> Russian President Boris Yeltsin ordered 40,000 troops to Chechnya on December 11, 1994, to stop that republic's bid for independence. A December 17, 1994, government statement promised that "force [in Chechnya] will be employed with due consideration of the principle of humanity." But within one week Russian forces began bombing Grozny, Chechnya's capital, in a campaign unparalleled in the area since World War II for its scope and destructiveness, followed by months of indiscriminate and targeted fire against civilians. Russian Human Rights Commissioner Sergei Kovalyev, who remained in Grozny through much of the bombing, bore personal witness to the destruction of homes, hospitals, schools, orphanages and other civilian structures. Indiscriminate bombing and shelling killed civilians and destroyed civilian property not only in Grozny but also in other regions in Chechnya, especially in the southern mountain areas. [128]

Helsinki Watch complained that "[t]he Clinton administration responded sluggishly to the slaughter in Chechnya and failed to link Russian conduct with important concessions, such as the May summit with President Yeltsin or support for IMF loans." [129] To the contrary, as noted above, Clinton prevailed upon the IMF to give a massive infusion of money to Russia in the year this Helsinki Watch report was written in order to guarantee Boris Yeltsin's re-election.

In the end, there was nothing very democratic about the Yeltsin regime, and the US, beyond some lip service, did nothing to coax Yeltsin into being democratic. Indeed, given that the communists in the mid-1990's had much popular support, real democracy in Russia

was anathema to the US goal of making sure that Russia was subject to the cruelties of unfettered capitalism.

This is why the Clinton Administration even stood by as Yeltsin oversaw passage of "the Law on the Federal Security Service (or FSB, formerly the KGB), which permits the FSB to conduct searches without warrants, conduct their own investigations, arrest suspects, and run their own prisons, [and which] suspended fundamental civil rights and restored powers that were among the hallmarks of the Soviet era."[130] Helsinki Watch noted that "[t]his legislative carte blanche is especially alarming since the FSB increasingly has been involved in human rights violations."

The US's indifference to such measures proved once again that it is not repression *per se* which is a problem—not even Soviet-style repression—as long as the West's free market goals are advanced by the repression. Indeed, Yeltsin has been compared to another favorite of the US, Augusto Pinochet, the fascist leader the US installed in Chile in 1973 in order to make sure that social justice would not break out in that country.[131]

And, in the end, what galls the US the most about Vladimir Putin is not how authoritarian and un-democratic they view him to be (though polls do show that he is wildly popular in Russia), but that Putin has helped Russia rise from its knees and become an independent nation and world actor again. Indeed, as Paul Craig Roberts, former Assistant Secretary of the Treasury under President Ronald Reagan, explains:

> [D]uring the long Cold War, the Soviet Union, which is Russia in most people's minds, was demonized effectively. This demonization persists. Remember, the initial collapse of the USSR worked very much to the West's advantage. They could easily manipulate [Boris] Yeltsin, and various oligarchs were able to seize and plunder the resources of the country. Much Israeli and American money was part of that. When Putin came along and started stopping this and trying to put the country back in place, he was demonized.[132]

It is worth noting here that many of the Reaganites, like Paul Craig Roberts, and also Jack F. Matlock, Jr.—who served as US Ambassador to the Soviet Union from 1987-1991, and who also served as Senior Director for European and Soviet Affairs on President Reagan's National Security Council staff—are very much against the current vilification of Putin and Russia. They are proud of Ronald Reagan's contribution to ending the Cold War (probably giving him too much credit, in my view, over Gorbachev), and are very troubled about the rise of the new Cold War. One might think that their views should count for something, and yet their views are notably absent from the mainstream debate about current US-Russia relations.

Moreover, as the Democrats and the holdovers from the Hillary Clinton campaign aggressively push the Russia-gate issue, this issue must be considered in the context of Bill Clinton's meddling in Russia in the 1990's. Thus, even if we accept everything the Democrats are saying about alleged Russian meddling in the US election, it pales quite greatly in comparison to Bill Clinton's role in propping up the terribly unpopular Boris Yeltsin, with very real impacts on the Russian people, including widespread suffering and premature deaths due to the economic policies imposed upon them by Clinton's economic team. Forgive me if I find their current protestations particularly galling and hypocritical in light of this history. Indeed, while it is very true that the Clintons have been the victim of all sorts of untrue and vicious "fake news" hit pieces and conspiracy theories, I would submit that this is more than made up for by the conspiracy of silence around the very real misdeeds the Clintons have committed around the world. Much more on that below.

8

"OUR BACKYARD"

BEFORE EXAMINING THE UBIQUITOUS CONCERNS IN this country about Putin's conduct in Russia's neck of the woods, it might be worthwhile to examine the conduct of the US in what it still views, quite condescendingly, to be "our backyard"—Latin America.

One can start in a number of different places to analyze the nature of the US's foreign policy in Latin America, but I think a fine place to begin is with the U.S intervention in Guatemala in 1954.

It is now generally accepted that the US engineered the overthrow of the democratically-elected President, Jacobo Arbenz, in that year. This coup was carried out at the behest of the United Fruit Company (now Chiquita Brands International), which opposed Arbenz's land reform program, pursuant to which the government would buy United Fruit's land at the fair market rate as determined by their own tax records. The Dulles brothers—Allen, who was head of the CIA at the time, and John Foster, the Secretary of State—both had financial interests in United Fruit and were therefore happy to protect its interests in Guatemala from such an affront.

While many have written off the coup as simply dirty tricks by the CIA, the Guatemalans, thousands of whom lost their lives during and in the immediate aftermath of the coup, see this event quite differently. The US installed a military dictatorship in the place of President

Arbenz that would rule Guatemala, with support and funding from the US, for almost 40 years. This military dictatorship was responsible for the murder of approximately 200,000 civilians, many of whom were "disappeared" by the regime. Over 80% of the victims were indigenous Mayan Indians who were targeted by the military, which suspected the Mayans of sympathizing with left-wing insurgents who began to challenge the dictatorship in 1962.[133] The targeting and murder of the Mayans is now universally considered as an act of genocide[134] that Guatemala continues to feel the effects of to this very day, with Guatemalans continuing to flee the violence in their country which was unleashed long ago and which has not abated.

Indeed, as the US complains about migration from countries like Guatemala, and is even considering building a wall to keep refugees like them out of the country, it may behoove us to consider the ways in which our government's policies have created the violence and suffering they are now fleeing from. I would go so far as to say that we owe these people entrance to our country as some (small) measure of remediation for our crimes against them. Instead, we not only try mightily to keep such migrants, many of them unaccompanied children, out of the country, our ICE officials often subject them to sexual violence and other unmentionable abuses, victimizing them all over again. For example, in recent days it was reported that ICE officials sexually assaulted two migrant girls who waved them down for help, and another group of ICE officials forced a young migrant to consume the blue meth he was carrying with him, thereby killing him. Possibly, instead of worrying about what Putin is doing over there, we could begin thinking about the crimes our people are committing at our own borders. Charity starts at home, after all, though of course it is much more convenient and comforting to think of others' lack of charity.

As with many such interventions, the US claimed that it was fighting Communism in Guatemala, when in fact Arbenz was a social democrat, like Bernie Sanders. The Cold War gave continued cover for such actions, which were inherently undemocratic.

Meanwhile, in 1962, President Kennedy announced the National Security Doctrine which, as is generally true with US "national security" policies, had nothing at all to do with the security of the US homeland and its citizens, but rather with the goal of preserving the US's unjust hold over the world's resources by destroying social movements in the Third World that aimed at securing their countries' resources for their own people—an unforgivable aim.[135]

A key aspect of this doctrine was the creation of paramilitary death squads, and Colombia was chosen as the first testing ground for these forces.[136] I focus herein quite a bit on Colombia, not only because it is so critical to the story of US intervention in our sister countries, but also because it's the country I know most about, having travelled there more times than I can count, and throughout every region of that country. I must add that I began travelling there in 1999 as the Clinton Administration was pushing for Plan Colombia (known in Colombia as "Plan Washington"), the major military aid package pursuant to which we have provided the Colombian military with about $10 billion since Plan Colombia's passage in the year 2000.

The first city I visited was Barrancabermeja, an oil town which, at that time, was quite progressive in many ways, including being the site of the wonderful Popular Feminist Organization (OFP), which was so welcoming to me when I was there. At the time, the OFP was sponsoring a photo exhibit featuring Che Guevara. I'm not sure what is particularly feminist about Che, but then again, I find feminists in Colombia to have a much broader idea about what feminism means than folks in our country.

Shortly after I left Barranca, as it is known, the paramilitary death squads took over that town, and they have yet to leave at the time of this writing. The OFP, which tried to hold out for years despite the paramilitary threats, did end up leaving, along with a lot of other good people I met there. By the way, I don't recall any outcry in the US, which claims to be the protector of women's rights around the world, when the OFP was driven out of Barranca, but I guess that's how it goes.

I still have a small momento of my trip to Barranca—a replica of the "Oil Jesus" statue which stands in the Magdalena River near the oil refinery. I was told that it represents Jesus being crucified by the oil interests that govern much of Colombia. It is also an appropriate symbol for US policy in Colombia, which is aimed at controlling Colombia's ample resources, such as oil. As the great Latin American writer Eduardo Galeano once wrote about US intervention abroad, it is usually for three reasons: "petróleo, petróleo, petróleo" (oil, oil, oil). In Colombia, it is also about fresh water, gold, emeralds and rich soil for the planting of cash crops like bananas and palm oil.

Not surprisingly, a number of US companies have themselves sponsored paramilitaries to protect their interests in Colombia, most famously Chiquita Brands International (formerly United Fruit Company) which pled guilty to paying the paramilitaries $1.7 million between 1997 and 2004 and running them 3000 Kalashnikov rifles. As I wrote in the *Huffington Post* after he was nominated by President Obama to serve as US Attorney General, it was Eric Holder who defended Chiquita on these charges and got them a sweet plea deal in which they were fined a mere $25 million, which they were allowed to pay in installments over 5 years.[137] This was a particularly nice deal given that Chiquita's support of the paramilitaries resulted in the death of thousands in the Uruba region of Colombia and allowed the paramilitaries to take hold of other huge swaths of the country as well.

As for companies involved in growing and harvesting palm oil—which is used both for food as an alternative to trans-fats and as an allegedly eco-friendly fuel source—about half of these companies, some of which benefitted from monies given by the US. Agency for International Development (USAID), are actually owned and controlled by paramilitary forces which also make money through drug trafficking.[138]

On this note, let's delve into the nature of the paramilitary groups, the brainchildren of the US, which continue to haunt Barranca and other Colombian towns.

The idea behind the death squads, as articulated by their intellectual author, US General William Yarborough, was to have a force which could carry out dirty jobs, including human rights abuses, without tarnishing the reputation of the regular forces of the US or its allies. A report by Human Rights Watch explains[139] this well:

[Colombian] General Ruiz became army commander in 1960. By 1962, he had brought in US Special Forces to train Colombian officers in cold war counterinsurgency. Colombian officers also began training at US bases. That year, a US Army Special Warfare team visited Colombia to help refine Plan Lazo, a new counterinsurgency strategy General Ruiz was drafting. US advisors proposed that the United States "select civilian and military personnel for clandestine training in resistance operations in case they are needed later." Led by Gen. William P. Yarborough, the team further recommended that this structure "be used to perform counter-agent and counter-propaganda functions and as necessary execute paramilitary, sabotage and/or terrorist activities against known communist proponents. It should be backed by the United States."

Judging by the events that followed, the US recommendations were implemented enthusiastically through Plan Lazo, formally adopted by the Colombian military on July 1, 1962. While the military presented Plan Lazo to the public as a "hearts-and-minds" campaign to win support through public works and campaigns to improve the conditions that they believed fed armed subversion, privately it incorporated the Yarborough team's principal recommendations. Armed civilians—called "civil defense," "self-defense," or "population organization operations," among other terms—were expected to work directly with troops.

These paramilitary groups did go on to work with Colombian troops, as the US is quite aware, and they do so to this day. Though, true to their purpose of operating in the shadows to do the dirty work

that the US and Colombian armed forces are not supposed to do, their existence is now denied by both the US and Colombian governments. Indeed, when I visited the US Embassy in October of 2015 with my friend Marino Cordoba, an Afro-Colombian leader who has been threatened by the paramilitaries numerous times and who has lost a son and two other family members to paramilitary violence in recent months, the US Ambassador, Kevin Whitaker, had the gall to look us in the eyes and claim that the paramilitaries no longer exist. As I wrote this paragraph, I received an SOS from my friend, Father Sterlin, an Afro-Colombian priest in El Choco Department, who alerted us to the paramilitary incursion of an Afro-Colombian town. These paramilitaries, who we are told do not exist, killed several of the residents and "disappeared" a number of others.

For his part, Colombian human rights advocate and dear friend, Father Javier Giraldo, S.J., describes Colombia as "genocidal democracy." He explains that, as revealed by various journals of the armed forces, reports of high military commanders, as well as manuals from the School of the Americas, the US, and consequently Colombia, have equated trade unionists, the peasants, Liberation Theologians, human rights defenders and non-traditional political leaders with Communism, and, therefore, as legitimate military targets of the counter-insurgency.[140] The quite elderly Father Giraldo, who can't be five feet tall, and who probably barely weighs a hundred pounds sopping wet, is probably the bravest person I know, never stopping to defend the poor and the downtrodden even as his life has been threatened on numerous occasions by the paramilitaries.

As to the murder of Catholic priests advocating for the poor, Colombia's paramilitaries have done a quite thorough job of eliminating them, with over 80 Catholic priests, and 2 bishops murdered in Colombia since 1984.[141] And this is all according to design, for, as Father Javier Giraldo, Noam Chomsky and others have explained on numerous occasions, the National Security Doctrine, which the US paramilitary strategy was designed to advance, was quickly being

aimed at wiping out the doctrine of Liberation Theology and its "preferential treatment for the poor," which arose in response to the Roman Catholic Church's Second Vatican Council in 1962.[142]

The US has, in fact, trained more military leaders and personnel from Colombia than from any other country in the Western Hemisphere, and its trainees have had an abysmal human rights track record. For example, a report released by the Fellowship of Reconciliation (FOR) demonstrates a direct correlation between US military funding and training, particularly at the School of the Americas (SOA, or now, WHINSEC), and the incidence of egregious human rights abuses, including "false positive" killings in which over 5,000 civilians were killed and then passed off by the military as guerillas killed in battle. This is not ancient history, taking place in the early to late 2000s.

As to the "false positive" killings, the FOR report concluded that "[o]f the 25 Colombian WHINSEC instructors and graduates for which any subsequent information was available, 12 of them—48%—had either been charged with a serious crime or commanded units whose members had reportedly committed multiple extrajudicial killings." [143] Moreover, "[s]ome of the officers with the largest number of civilian killings committed under their command (Generals Lasprilla, Rodriguez Clavijo, and Montoya, and Colonel Mejia) . . . received significantly more US training, on average than other officers" during the high water mark of the "false positive" scandal.

Father Giraldo explains in his recent "The Origins of The Armed Conflict, its Persistence and its Impacts,"[144] that the single biggest factor behind the armed conflict in Colombia is land and its unequal distribution. As he relates, 4.2% of the land in Colombia remains in the hands of 67.6% of the population, while 46.5% of all land is in the hands of a mere .4% of the population. This unequal distribution of land, furthermore, has resulted in Colombia becoming one of the most unequal societies on earth, with a Gini coefficient of 53.5.

And of course, the US has contributed to the root cause of the conflict by siding for many decades with the small percent of the Colombia

population that owns most of Colombia's land, for it is this landed aristocracy who then allow this land to be penetrated and exploited by US transnational interests. If this land were left to peasants, indigenous and Afro-descendants, on the other hand, they would insist upon using the land communally and for their own subsistence—something which is simply anathema to the US and the logic of unfettered Capitalism.

The US—through various means, including through the DEA and CIA—have supported both the right-wing paramilitaries, as well as drug cartels aligned with these paramilitaries, in order to foster the unequal distribution of land in Colombia. For example, as I was writing this book, Pablo Escobar's son went public with his claim that his father sold drugs for the CIA to fund the CIA's anti-communist efforts in Latin America.[145] This would not be surprising given that Alvaro Uribe, who worked with Escobar's Medellin Cartel as a young man and was a drug dealer in his own right, as recognized by the US Defense Intelligence Agency (DIA), became President of Colombia and received strong backing by both Presidents George W. Bush and Obama.[146] As described further below, the civil conflict and the paramilitaries would reach their apex during Uribe's tenure as President from 2002 to 2010.

These narco-paramilitaries—which are rarely spoken of, as contrasted with the so-called "narco-guerillas"—began a massive land grab by massacres and mass displacements of the population since the 1980's, and continuing to the current time. During the same period, of course, the US supported the internal war on the side of these groups carrying out the displacements. And ironically, the US did so on the basis of fighting so-called "narco-guerillas."

The foregoing assertions were strongly supported by a December 21, 2013, story that ran in *The Washington Post*, entitled "Covert action Colombia," about the intimate and critical role of the CIA and the NSA in helping to assassinate "at least two dozen" leaders of the Colombian FARC guerillas from "the early 2000s" to and through the date of that story. The most illuminating statement in that piece is that while the CIA and NSA—allegedly in the interest of fighting drug trafficking and

terrorism—have assisted the Colombian government in hunting down and murdering Marxist FARC guerillas with US-made smart bombs, *"for the most part, they left the violent paramilitary groups alone."*[147]

Meanwhile, as Father Giraldo explains, between 1997 and 2007— that is, roughly during the period of Plan Colombia, in which the US gave over 10 billion dollars to the Colombian military (and well after the collapse of the Soviet Union)—the most intense period of paramilitary activity occurred, in which nearly 800,000 hectares of land were captured and one million peasants displaced by the paramilitaries. In the same vein, the Colombian Victims' Unit, which recently tallied seven million total victims of the Colombian conflict, reports that "the majority of [human rights] victimization occurred after 2000 [i.e., after the initiation of Plan Colombia], peaking in 2002 at 744,799 victims."[148]

As Amnesty International explains, while there have been some efforts at the restitution of land to those displaced in this process, such efforts have been barely more than symbolic, for "[v]ery few land restitution cases have tackled land occupation by large national or international companies [many of these US companies] or others who may have been responsible for the forced displacement and dispossession of the claimant."[149]

The result is that Colombia has the largest internally displaced population on earth (even greater than Syria) at over 7 million, with a disproportionate number of the internally displaced being Afro-Colombians and indigenous tribes, many of the latter now being pushed to the point of extinction, leading some groups to raise the specter of genocide in Colombia.[150] Meanwhile, as the UN High Commission for Refugees has pointed out, the displacements are often-times accompanied by other grisly crimes such as "the forced recruitment of children and youth, sexual and gender-based violence (SGBV), threats, disappearances and murders . . . ."[151]

Again, this is all according to plan, and advances the interests of the US, which invented, and continues to support, the Colombian paramilitaries in order to make Colombia, Latin America and other

far-flung countries safe for maximum corporate penetration and resource extraction.

A recent article in the *New York Times*, entitled "The Secret History of Colombia's Paramilitaries & The US War on Drugs," contains useful clues as to the US's true views towards the Colombian death squads and their massive war crimes and human rights abuses.[152] In short, it reveals a high-level of tolerance of, and condonation by, US policy-makers for the suffering of the Colombian people at the hands of our long-time friends and allies, the right-wing paramilitaries.

The gist of the *New York Times* story is that, beginning in 2008, the US has extradited "several dozen" top paramilitary leaders, thereby helping them to evade a transitional justice process which would have held them accountable for their war crimes and crimes against humanity. They have been instead brought to the US, where they have been tried for drug-related offenses only, and given cushy sentences of 10 years in prison on average. And, even more incredibly, "for some, there is a special dividend at the end of their incarceration. Though wanted by Colombian authorities, two have won permission to stay in the United States, and their families have joined them. There are more seeking the same haven, and still others are expected to follow suit."

That these paramilitaries—forty in all that the *New York Times* investigated—are being given such preferential treatment is shocking given the magnitude of their crimes. For example, paramilitary leader Salvatore Mancuso, "who the government said 'may well be one of the most prolific cocaine traffickers ever prosecuted in a United States District Court,'" has been found by Colombian courts to be *responsible for the death or disappearance of more than 1,000 people.*" Yet, as a result of his cooperation with US authorities, Mr. Mancuso "will spend little more than 12 years behind bars in the US."

Another paramilitary, the one the article focuses on most, is Hernan Giraldo Serna, who committed "1800 serious human rights violations with over 4,000 victims . . . ." Mr. Giraldo was known as "The Drill" because of his penchant for raping young girls, some as young

as 9 years old. Indeed, he has been "labeled . . . the biggest sexual predator of paramilitarism." While being prosecuted in the US for drug-related crimes only, Mr. Giraldo too is being shielded by the US from prosecution back in Colombia for his most atrocious crimes.

The *New York Times* gives some quite illuminating details as to why the US would protect such "designated terrorists responsible for massacres, forced disappearances and the displacement of entire villages," and then give them "relatively lenient treatment."

First, it correctly explains that former President Alvaro Uribe asked the US to extradite these paramilitary leaders because, back home in Colombia, they had begun "confessing not only their war crimes but also their ties to his allies and relatives."

While the story does not mention it, the potential confession of paramilitary leaders to their links with the US government, as well as to US multinationals, was most certainly another reason for their extradition and treatment with kid gloves. As just one example, paramilitary leader Salvatore Mancuso told investigators nearly 10 years ago that it was not only Chiquita that provided financial support to the paramilitaries (this is already known because Chiquita pled guilty to such conduct and received a small $25 million fine for doing so), but also companies like Del Monte and Dole.[153] However, given that Mancuso was never put on trial (the *New York Times* notes that none of the paramilitary leaders have been) but instead was given a light sentence based upon a plea deal, such statements have never gone on the court record, were never pursued by authorities and have largely been forgotten.

The *New York Times* also quite correctly states that former President Alvaro Uribe has a "shared ideology" with these paramilitaries and their leaders. This is of course true. But what does this say about the United States, which gave billions of dollars of military assistance to Colombia when Uribe was President, all the while knowing that he had a long history of paramilitary ties and drug trafficking and that his military was working alongside the paramilitaries in carrying out

abuses on a massive scale? And, how about the fact that Uribe was also awarded the Presidential Medal of Freedom by President George W. Bush, who considered Uribe his best friend in the region?

The fact is that the US also shares an ideology with both Uribe and his paramilitary friends. The *New York Times* touches upon this issue too when it states that "the paramilitaries, while opponents in the war on drugs, were technically on the same side as the Colombian and American governments in the civil war." Indeed, the *New York Times* quotes US lawyers, a retired US prosecutor, and the US judge who gave a light sentence to vicious paramilitary leader Rodrigo Tovar-Pupo (alias, "Jorge 40") to support the proposition that these paramilitaries are viewed as "freedom fighters" whose role in the Colombian civil war is actually a "mitigating rather than aggravating factor in their cases."

Of course, with the old Cold War against the USSR over, supporting such "freedom fighters" is a bit harder to justify to the American public. And so we've had to come up with other pretexts for our war against social change in countries like Colombia. A recent article in *The Washington Post* describes this reality, as well as the pretextual nature of the so-called "anti-drug war," quite well[154]:

> With US backing, the Colombian government launched a scorched-earth counteroffensive against the FARC's rural strongholds after President Álvaro Uribe was elected in 2002. Government troops were often followed by right-wing militias that targeted suspected rebel sympathizers *and massacred civilians*. More Colombians were driven from their homes during the first stages of Plan Colombia than at any other time in the half-century conflict.
>
> In the aftermath of the Cold War, when Plan Colombia was hatched, revelations of atrocities committed by Guatemala's genocidal military and the US-backed government of El Salvador had stigmatized the idea of US military intervention in Latin America. So the plan's promoters advertised it primarily as a counternarcotics program.

Even at a superficial glance, this "counternarcotics" rationale breaks down, for, as the *New York Times* article on the paramilitary extraditions notes, in spite of the US dumping around $10 billion in military aid into Colombia since 2000, "[c]oca cultivation has been soaring in Colombia, with a significant increase over the last couple of years in acreage dedicated to drug crops."

Indeed, the pretextual nature of the war on drugs became quite evident to me when I visited the US Embassy in Bogota in March of 2017. I was in Colombia this time to give a presentation about the phenomenon of forced disappearances at the Autonomous University of Colombia, as well as to accompany an Afro-Colombian and indigenous delegation on meetings with US and Colombian officials about the need to protect their land and their physical integrity against continued paramilitary threats and incursions. While at the US Embassy, the officials there admitted that they anticipated a record coca crop in Colombia for the most recent period measured (2016). (And, as I write this book, it has just been made public that Colombia's coca crops are their biggest in two decades.[155]) Still, these officials frequently patted themselves on the back for the "success" of US policies in Colombia, showing once again, apparently, that there is no success like failure. Or, more to the point, this points to the conclusion that something else is afoot with our policies in Colombia.

In the end, the only plausible explanation for the US partnership in such crimes is its quest for a disproportionate share of the world's resources, and any countries trying to lay claim to their just portion (whether it be Colombia, or Russia, or China) need to be put in their place.

* * *

On Sept. 11, 1973, General Augusto Pinochet led a violent coup against the elected government of President (and medical doctor) Salvador Allende, bringing an end to democratic rule in that country for

the next sixteen-plus years. Many refer to this as the "First 9/11," and it would be much more devastating than the 9/11 the US suffered in 2001 in terms of its body count and historical significance for a number of countries.

At the time of the coup, Chile had been the longest-standing constitutional democracy in Latin America—something the United States would claim to support. However, because the United States did not like the left-leaning (but not Communist) Dr. Allende, it chose to help foment the coup that toppled his government, and then continued to support the Pinochet dictatorship even as its human rights crimes became apparent. Mr. Pinochet's regime ultimately was responsible for the murder of at least 3,197 individuals and the torture of over 30,000.[156]

As the *Washington Post* summarized, in September of 1973, "the Chilean military, aided by training and financing from the US Central Intelligence Agency, gained absolute control of the country in less than a week. The new regime waged raids, executions, 'disappearances' and the arrest and torture of thousands of Chilean citizens—establishing a climate of fear and intimidation that would remain for years to come."[157]

In addition to the CIA, another key actor in the coup was the International Telephone and Telegraph Company (ITT), which wanted Allende gone for fear that he might be a threat to their interests in Chile. ITT, which was also involved in the military coup in Brazil in 1964, and which owned 70% of the Chilean Telephone Company as well as The Sheraton Hotel at the time, backed Allende's opponents in the 1970 elections and provided crucial financial support to the coup plotters against Allende.[158] Shortly before the coup in which he would die, Dr. Allende gave an impassioned speech at the UN decrying the interference of ITT, as well as Kennecott Copper, in his country:

> Two firms that are part of the central nucleus of the large transnational companies that sunk their claws into my country, the

International Telegraph and Telephone Company and the Kennecott Copper Corporation, tried to run our political life.

ITT, a huge corporation whose capital is greater than the budget of several Latin American nations put together and greater than that of some industrialized countries, began, from the very moment that the people's movement was victorious in the elections of September 1970, a sinister action to keep me from taking office as President.

This speech had a huge impact on me when I listened to it, obviously well after the fact, while studying about the evils of US intervention back in College. A Sept. 19, 2000, document released by the CIA revealed that the CIA "sought to instigate a [military] coup" against Mr. Allende even before he took office in 1970.[159] As the CIA relates, it "was working with three different groups of plotters," all of which "made it clear that any coup would require the kidnapping of army Cmdr. Rene Schneider, who felt deeply that the constitution required that the army allow Allende to assume power." The CIA, not having any qualms about constitutionality or civilian rule, admits that it agreed with the assessment that the kidnapping (though it claims not killing) of Schneider was necessary, and so it provided weapons for the kidnapping operation. Not surprisingly, the kidnapping operation ended in the killing of Schneider when he tried to defend himself, and the path was cleared for the military coup.

The CIA continued to assist the coup-plotters through the time Mr. Allende was overthrown. Once the coup took place, the United States continued to support the Pinochet regime, including Manuel Contereras, who served as an agent of the CIA from 1974 to 1977, and went on to head Chile's intelligence agency, known as the DINA, which played the key role in the human rights abuses carried out in Chile. The CIA concedes that its friend Contereras "became notorious for his involvement in human rights abuse," and had a key role in the car-bombing of former Chilean Ambassador to Washington Orlando

Letelier and his young American assistant Ronnie Moffit in the middle of Washington D.C. in 1976.

In the end, the CIA claims that it aided and abetted such a historic subversion of democracy and human rights because of Cold War hysteria. As it explains:

> The historical backdrop sheds important light on the policies, practices, and perceived urgency prevalent at that time. The Cuban revolution and emergence of Communist parties in Latin America had brought the Cold War to the Western Hemisphere. Thousands of Chilean military officers came to the United States for training, which included presentations on the impact of global communism on their own country. After Allende won a plurality in the Presidential election on 4 September 1970, the consensus at the highest levels of the US Government was that an Allende Presidency would seriously hurt US national interests.
>
> These Cold War attitudes persisted into the Pinochet era. After Pinochet came to power, senior policymakers appeared reluctant to criticize human rights violations, taking to task US diplomats urging greater attention to the problem. US military assistance and sales grew significantly during the years of greatest human rights abuses. According to a previously released Memorandum of Conversation, Kissinger in June 1976 indicated to Pinochet that the US Government was sympathetic to his regime, although Kissinger advised some progress on human rights in order to improve Chile's image in the US Congress.

A few notable points here. First, notice that the CIA does not reference any direct Russian involvement in Chile at this time, and this is because the movement supporting Allende was home-grown and not dependent on any outside support, Russian included. Moreover, while the CIA talks about "global communism," Allende was not in fact a Communist. In other words, the US overthrew a constitutional

democracy citing Cold War concerns, but such concerns were not bona fide in this case. Rather, the Chilean 9/11, as so many US interventions, was about keeping Chile in a subservient economic role, and the US trusted that Pinochet was the man to ensure this. The Red Scare was just a pretext.

The Chilean coup had dire reverberations throughout the Southern Cone of South America, as the CIA itself recognizes. As it relates, "Within a year after the coup, the CIA and other US Government agencies were aware of bilateral cooperation among regional intelligence services to track the activities of and, in at least a few cases, kill political opponents. This was the precursor to Operation Condor, an intelligence-sharing arrangement among Chile, Argentina, Brazil, Paraguay and Uruguay established in 1975." More than a "few" political opponents were killed by these regimes, some of them, as in the case of Argentina, openly fascist, if not Nazi. As journalist Ben Norton explains, anywhere between 60 and 80,000 people were either killed or disappeared in Operation Condor, which grew out of the Chilean coup.[160]

I must point out that Colombia is currently the Western Hemisphere's leader in disappeared persons, with well over 92,000 persons disappeared and counting—this according to the International Committee of the Red Cross (ICRC) back in 2014.[161] That is, Colombia has more disappeared people than Chile, Argentina, Brazil, Paraguay and Uruguay *combined* during the Operation Condor years. And this is a direct consequence of the US's continued support—continuing years after the collapse of the Soviet Union and the end of the first Cold War—for a repressive military that colludes with death squad forces in that country.

9

BILL CLINTON AND "HUMANITARIAN INTERVENTION"

AFTER THE COLLAPSE OF THE SOVIET Union in 1991 and the end of the first Cold War, the US had a huge problem—how could it continue building and running its war machine without the threat of the USSR to point to? This indeed was a conundrum.

Bill Clinton, a very intelligent and savvy politician, quickly came up with a plan—we would now go to war and intervene in other countries in the name of defending human rights. And thus, "humanitarian intervention" was born, or at least re-born.

In fact, "humanitarian intervention" is nothing new. The first known instance of it, that I know of anyway, was practiced by King Leopold II of Belgium, and best described in the wonderful *King Leopold's Ghost*, by Adam Hochschild.

As Hochschild explains, during the period 1885 to 1908, King Leopold enslaved, mutilated and killed millions of poor souls in the Congo (all told, possibly 10 million were killed) in order to plunder the Congo of its riches, such as rubber. He was able to get away with this for so long, moreover, by convincing many in the West that he

was actually in the Congo for philanthropic purposes—under the auspices of an altruistic group known as the "International African Association"—and that he was helping the Congolese. An American plantation owner, General Henry Shelton Sanford, helped promote Leopold's story in Washington, thus prevailing upon the US to be the first country in the world to recognize Leopold's claim to the Congo.

As Hochschild points out, King Leopold's little game was eventually foiled by such good folks as Mark Twain, one of the co-founders of the Anti-Imperialist League, who helped to expose and petition for an end of Leopold's atrocities in Africa. Twain, who also decried the massive slaughter of civilians in the Philippines by US "liberation" forces, had this to say about King Leopold and the Congo: "In fourteen years Leopold has deliberately destroyed more lives than have suffered death on all the battlefields of this planet for the past thousand years. In this vast statement I am well within the mark, several millions of lives with the mark. It is curious that the most advanced and most enlightened century of all the centuries the sun has looked upon should have the ghastly distinction of having produced this moldy and piety-mouthing hypocrite, this bloody monster whose mate is not findable in human history anywhere, and whose personality will surely shame hell itself when he arrives there—which will be soon, let us hope and trust."

Sadly, there are few writers and journalists of Twain's integrity today. Instead, we have what a real journalist, John Pilger, refers to as "anti-journalists," who merely parrot the state's line in service of the empire. If there were such journalists, however, they might have things to say about Bill Clinton quite similar to what Twain said about King Leopold.

Clinton, borrowing a page from Leopold's playbook, and armed with the ideology of "human rights" and the Right to Protect (R2P), began to run amok in the world on the pretense that he was doing so to advance the cause of the countrymen with whom he was meddling. And, quite appropriately, one of the areas Clinton most effectively tried

out this practice was in the Congo (soon to be called the DRC)—which is still uniquely rich in valuable resources—and its neighbor Rwanda. And, just as King Leopold, his foray was absolutely cataclysmic for the people living there.

Clinton's first disastrous move was to aid and abet the genocide in Rwanda in 1994. As we know now from declassified documents,[162] as well as from Dr. Gregory Stanton[163] who worked in Clinton's State Department at the time, Bill Clinton knew about the genocide just as it was beginning to unfold in Rwanda; Clinton "lied" (in Stanton's words) that he did not know about it; and the Clinton Administration then affirmatively acted at the UN Security Council to have UN peace-keeping troops, then on the ground, removed at a critical moment.

As the National Security Archive at Georgetown University explains:

> By April 15, [just over a week into the genocide] the US dele-gation at the UN dropped a "bombshell" on the Security Council's secret deliberations, arguing for total termination of the mission and pullout of the peacekeepers, only to find they did not have the votes given opposition from the Non-Aligned Movement and others. On April 21, the Security Council voted to reduce the force in Rwanda from over 2,000 troops down to 270, which US ambassador Made-leine Albright in an earlier cable had all-too-accurately called a "skel-etal staff."
>
> Experts and former officials gathered at The Hague last year for a critical oral history conference reviewing the Rwanda tragedy agreed that the UN pullout decision was a turning point, a "green light" for genocide, a "disastrous decision [with] horrendous consequences," as the Nigerian UN envoy Ibrahim Gambari called it.

As we know, about 800,000 Rwandans lost their lives as a result of Clinton's machinations, which, according to the National Security Archives, were carried out for the pretty meager *quid pro quo* of getting

the French to agree to send peace keepers to Somalia after the "Black Hawk Down" debacle.

And, believe it or not, the worst bloodshed was yet to come. Paul Kagame's Rwandan Patriotic Front (RPF) forces, which committed their own mass slaughter during the 100-day genocide in 1994, as the US knew full well,[164] took power after the genocide and hold power still. Clinton hailed Kagame as a human rights hero, as he has often been portrayed in such popular films as "Hotel Rwanda," but he was anything but. Nonetheless, Clinton would support Kagame in his invasion of what is now the Democratic Republic of the Congo (DRC) under the "humanitarian" pretext of going after the Hutu *genocidaires* there. In the process, Kagame's forces would commit an even greater genocide in the DRC.

As an excellent report by The World Policy Institute explains,

> The Clinton administration attempted to make up for its shameful efforts to stop humanitarian intervention into Rwanda during the genocide by sending a hefty shipment of arms and military training to Paul Kagame's government after the genocide. The US sent $75 million in emergency military assistance to Rwanda in 1994, *after* Kagame drove the government that had perpetrated the Rwandan genocide from power; but when it could have supported efforts to stop the killing, the Clinton administration was instead actively lobbying to withdraw UN forces from the country.[165]

Rwanda would use that military assistance, and continued military training from the US, to invade the DRC, along with Uganda, from the East in 1996, and then again in 1998. With the U.S.'s full backing, Rwanda and Uganda helped Congo rebel Laurent Kabila overthrow the U.S.'s former client - the brutal dictator Mobutu Sese Seko who had become less compliant in his old age. Laurent Kabila, who quickly made sweetheart deals with U.S. mining interests, took power in 1997. And, when Laurent Kabila himself became less compliant,

particularly in regard to granting mining contracts to foreign firms, Clinton supported Rwanda and Uganda in moving against him in 1998, and he was successfully removed at the very end of the Clinton Administration in January of 2001.[166]

Meanwhile, other African nations invaded the DRC from the West. This became known as "Africa's First World War," though it received little press here at the time.

Incredibly, the US, under Bill Clinton, would give military training and hardware to *every country* involved in that conflict—including to the DRC itself—even as the conflict escalated and the death toll surged. Thus, in addition to the $75 million given to Rwanda after the genocide, the US gave significant military support to Angola, Burundi, Chad, DRC, Namibia, Rwanda, Sudan, Uganda, and Zimbabwe, all of which had a role in this war.[167] And the Clinton Administration continued to give military support and training to Rwanda, Uganda, Namibia and Zimbabwe even as they continued to occupy, ravage and plunder the DRC into Clinton's last year in office (2000).[168]

As the World Policy Institute put it succinctly, "[u]nder Clinton's watch approximately three million people in Rwanda and the eastern region of the DRC died, even as US corporations were participating in questionable mining deals in the region." And indeed, it appears that it was US mining interests, rather than any humanitarian concerns, that may have been the motivating factor for Clinton to support the invasion of the DRC, which is known for some of the purest untapped minerals on earth, including high-grade copper, cobalt, gold and coltan (which is critical for electronics and cell phones).[169]

One very telling piece of evidence of this is that, "in a classic case of cronyism," as the World Policy Institute puts it, the very first mining company to receive a mining contract with the new Laurent Kabila government in DRC was American Mineral Fields (AMF).[170] The notable thing about AMF, as Forbes Magazine also noted in an article entitled, "Friends In High Places," was that AMF was headquartered in Hope, Arkansas, the hometown of Bill Clinton, and had "interesting Clinton

Administration connections."[171] For its part, the UN Security Council, in a 2002 report largely ignored by the media, also concluded that the Rwandan and Ugandan occupation of the DRC was not done for humanitarian purposes, but rather to secure mineral wealth there.[172]

Thus, Kagame's troops, with the full knowledge of Bill Clinton and with a massive arms shipment sent by Clinton for this purpose, invaded the DRC, and began murdering civilians by the hundreds, including women and children, and engaging in rape on a mass scale.[173] The troops not only went after Hutus who had fled to refugee camps in the DRC, but also Congolese as well. And Kagame, along with the US-backed Ugandan military as well, has continued his rampage through the DRC with the knowledge, acquiescence and support of the United States.

All told, nearly six million people have been murdered in the DRC since 1996,[174] and Bill Clinton bears a large responsibility helping to set this slaughter in motion, with, of course, George W. Bush and Barack Obama continuing what Clinton had started and with the plunder of the DRC's resources continuing to this day. Indeed, some argue persuasively that Bill Clinton intentionally set the entire DRC war in motion in order to secure mining rights there.[175] And Clinton did so, though all the while trumpeting his human rights bona fides. In the end, though, as one commentator on Huffington Post detailed, "According to Human Rights Watch, Clinton's foreign policy generally adopted a "selective approach to human rights," turning a "blind eye in African countries considered to be strategically or economically important."[176] Indeed!

As a consequence of the Congo War, Rwanda and Uganda's economies boomed from coltan and cobalt, and Western corporations such as American Mineral Fields and Barrick Gold (whose board included George H.W. Bush and former Canadian Prime Minister Brian Mulroney), received concessions for mining and mineral resources worth over $157 billion.

As my friend, Kambale Musavuli, a Congolese activist with Friends

of the Congo, also explains, it has been US economic and geopolitical interests that have motivated its continuing support for the bloodbath in the Congo:

> Economic interests in Congo are that which we need in our daily life. The coltan which comes out the Congo can be found in your cell phone, the cobalt of the Congo can be found in the battery of the broker of Congo's minerals, and they loot Congo's mineral resources while they commit atrocities. ... Chaos allows resources to leave from the Congo at a cheap price, and of course it's not actually just leaving, it's actually being stolen from the Congolese people.
>
> The second [factor] is military interest. The militaries of Rwanda and Uganda have both been trained by the United States. Since the era when the American soldier was killed in Somalia in Mogadishu, the US did not want to have any of the troops in Africa anymore. So the US created a system in which they would train all the foreign military missions. I mean, can you imagine that ... today, we have Ugandan soldiers in Afghanistan fighting the war on terror. How many Americans know that? We have Rwandan soldiers in Haiti and in Sudan. These missions can be deployed across the world to protect US interests around the world. . . .

Kambale, speaking for himself and many other Congolese, decries the silence which has allowed the nightmare in the DRC to unfold:

> If you are aware, just as we took action to end the Holocaust in Europe, if we know in the Congo millions have died from—estimates take the number to over 6 million, and half of them are children under the age of 5—and we remain silent when we know what is happening, we are really complicit. And in a very tangible way because we are supporting the two oppressive regimes in Rwanda and Uganda, and in turn these nations are using the support that we are giving them to

create, fabricate militia groups which are committing war crimes and crimes against humanity.

Clinton, a modern day King Leopold II, would continue to wage war in support of human rights elsewhere in the world, as detailed elsewhere in this book. What is instructive about the Rwanda and DRC episodes, however, is that (1) pretexts for war and intervention (whether they be human rights or anti-Russian hatred) must be looked at quite closely and with a critical eye. On this score, I would argue quite adamantly that it is the very rare instance indeed that any state, including the US, truly acts for altruistic purposes, such as "democracy promotion," human rights, or freedom. And, (2) the US press is all too willing to push any pretext for war that the US government puts forth, and it will rarely question the claims made in support of armed conflict. Again, these lessons should be applied to the current claims about Russia and Putin.

Finally, it is worth repeating here that even if we were to accept as true the claims about Putin's lack of sanity, foreign aggressiveness, and imperialist ambitions, he is not even in the ball park of someone like Bill Clinton in these respects. But we in the United States have been collectively lulled into accepting our country's worst and most depraved crimes, and believing them to be acts of mercy and kindness. This is the greatest propaganda trick ever performed, and it undermines our society more than any alleged shenanigans by Moscow ever could.

To be clear, the Congolese friends I have, some of whom I have assisted with asylum applications in the US, are not fooled. They know who has been turning the screws on them in the DRC, and they are understandably outraged about it. Their scorn is particularly focused on Bill Clinton. And they made it clear to me that they did not want Hillary Clinton to become President, even in lieu of Trump, because of what the Clinton Administration had done to their country. However,

I quite doubt that the Congolese vote made much of a difference in the 2016 elections.

But there has been much discussion about another group who feels greatly wronged by the Clintons and who might have impacted the outcome of the 2016 vote: the Haitians.

The main issue which the press has focused on in this regard has been the Clintons' failure in managing the hundreds of millions of dollars donated for Haiti earthquake relief, most notably to the Clinton Foundation, with little actually reaching the Haitian people, and with the Foundation doing a very poor job in accounting for the monies spent.[177] This has left a bitter taste in the mouths of Haitians, and the Haitian immigrant community, whose country is still a basket case post-earthquake. With that said, I think it's only fair to point out that this does not distinguish the Clintons from all of the Western NGOs, including the Red Cross, which have largely squandered the ample generosity of the many people who have donated to Haiti relief. As an aside, I note that the two countries that actually did something positive for Haiti post-earthquake, were the also-vilified Cuba and Venezuela, whose medical teams have been on the forefront of the campaign to fight cholera in that country.[178]

Meanwhile, what is largely forgotten is that Bill Clinton, as President, was quite tough on Haiti, by his own admission. Thus, he admitted after the fact that his trade policies in Haiti, which allowed farmers, including Arkansas farmers Clinton emphasizes, to dump cheap, subsidized food products into Haiti, destroyed the livelihood of small Haitian farmers. Clinton admitted that those policies undermined the Haitian peoples' ability to feed themselves, much like Clinton's NAFTA policies did in Mexico. The *New York Times* put this succinctly, explaining that Clinton's policies in Haiti "included his destruction of domestic rice growing in the pursuit of free trade and a new market for American rice farmers."[179] As Clinton lamented later, "I have to live every day with the consequences of the lost capacity to produce a rice crop in Haiti to feed those people, because of what I did."[180]

Recall that Clinton had imposed these draconian policies upon Haiti as a condition for re-instating the democratically-elected president, former liberation priest Jean-Bertrand Aristide, to power after Aristide had been removed in a coup carried out by the Front for the Advancement and Progress of Haiti (FRAPH) in 1991.[181] Not surprisingly, the FRAPH, in turn, was backed by the US, and in particular the CIA, at the time of the coup and thereafter. And, quite strangely, Clinton was always playing both sides of the fence, continuing to back the brutal and violent FRAPH before, during and even after Aristide's return to power. Clinton did so in order to "balance out" Aristide, in the words of FRAPH leader Emmanuel Constant. Indeed, despite Constant's known brutality, which included rape and murder, Clinton allowed Constant to live freely in the US, rather than return him to Haiti to face justice for his crimes, in order to conceal the US support for the FRAPH.

Ultimately, the US grew tired of Aristide again, and, along with France and Canada, kidnapped him and forced him into exile in the Central African Republic in 2004. But that, of course, happened later, under George W. Bush.

In addition to helping starve the Haitians while also supporting the FRAPH goons who killed and raped them, Clinton was incredibly tough, if not downright cruel, in his treatment of Haitian refugees. This, despite his 1992 campaign pledge to improve their treatment. To wit, Clinton continued George H.W. Bush's policy of refusing Haitian boat people entry into the US and instead housing them, children included, indefinitely in a detention center on Guantanamo Bay.[182] But Clinton saw Bush's cruel policy and raised it by requiring the detained Haitians to be tested for HIV, and then segregating those who tested positive in filthy conditions, including tents, in what came to be known as "the world's first HIV detention camp." And he did so for two years until a US federal court, finding this treatment to be "outrageous, callous, and reprehensible," ordered him to stop.

As a *Huffington Post* article explains, in light of the Clintons' abuse

of Haiti, and after a successful Trump rally in the Little Haiti section of Miami, Florida, the Haitian Florida community—the second largest voting bloc in Florida—may have shifted significantly enough to Trump to have affected the outcome in that state.[183]

Again, in analyzing the 2016 election failure of Hillary Clinton, the Democrats might do better to focus on the failings of the Clintons which led to this defeat. The fixation on Putin at this point is simply a distraction from this analysis, but maybe that is the very point of this fixation.

10

HILLARY AND THE HONDURAN COUP

NOTWITHSTANDING THE ABOVE, WE HAVE CONVINCED ourselves of our inherent goodness and our inherent generosity towards the rest of the world. And we have done so by erasing all such miserable chapters of our country out of our memory. This phenomenon might have best been explained by writer Harold Pinter in his 2005 Nobel Prize acceptance speech, and so I quote part of it here:

> The United States supported and in many cases engendered every right wing military dictatorship in the world after the end of the Second World War. I refer to Indonesia, Greece, Uruguay, Brazil, Paraguay, Haiti, Turkey, the Philippines, Guatemala, El Salvador, and, of course, Chile. The horror the United States inflicted upon Chile in 1973 can never be purged and can never be forgiven.
>
> Hundreds of thousands of deaths took place throughout these countries. Did they take place? And are they in all cases attributable to US foreign policy? The answer is yes they did take place and they are attributable to American foreign policy. But you wouldn't know it.
>
> It never happened. Nothing ever happened. Even while it was happening it wasn't happening. It didn't matter. It was of no interest.

The crimes of the United States have been systematic, constant, vicious, remorseless, but very few people have actually talked about them. You have to hand it to America. It has exercised a quite clinical manipulation of power worldwide while masquerading as a force for universal good. It's a brilliant, even witty, highly successful act of hypnosis.[184]

Something else that never happened, or is certainly not worth mentioning, is the recent overthrow of democracy in Honduras with a little help from its giant neighbor in the North.

Thus, not to be outdone in cruelty by their predecessors, President Obama and Secretary of State Clinton played an important role in the most recent military coup in Latin America—the 2009 coup which deposed democratically-elected President, Manuel Zelaya. As the AP reported at the time, "Honduran President Manuel Zelaya was ousted in a military coup after betraying his own kind: a small clique of families that dominates the economy."[185] Zelaya's biggest sin was to have raised the minimum wage by 60%, infuriating business elites, both domestic and foreign (including, again, Chiquita Banana).

Given such audacious crimes, Zelaya had to be gotten rid of. And so, the military took the direct route, kidnapping Zelaya at gun-point in the middle of the night and flying him out of the country to Costa Rica. Not surprisingly, the two key military generals who carried out this coup were trained by the US at its infamous US Army School of the Americas (SOA), now located in Columbus, Georgia, and now known as the Western Hemisphere Institute for Security Cooperation (WHINSEC). WHINSEC trained over 500 Honduran officers from 2001 through 2009, and the General who violently kidnapped Zelaya (Romeo Orlando Vásquez Velásquez) is a two-time graduate.[186] Gen. Luis Javier Prince Suazo, the head of the Honduran Air Force, who arranged to have Zelaya flown into exile, was also trained at the School of the Americas.

Moreover, in the months leading up to the coup, the US National

Endowment for Democracy (NED), a Reagan-era organization created to use "soft power" to meddle in other country's affairs and even help foment regime change, provided $1.2 million to the International Republican Institute to organize against Zelaya and his reforms, and to support the opposition groups which ended up toppling him.[187] The NED did the very same in helping to organize the coup against Hugo Chavez in 2002. This is important to keep in mind when, as so often happens, Putin is ridiculed for complaining about NED and NGO interference in the affairs of Russia and neighboring states. It turns out there is much to complain about here. Further, as the *National Catholic Reporter* wrote at the time, while "[t]he Foreign Operations Appropriations Act requires that US military aid and training be suspended when a country undergoes a military coup, and the Obama administration has indicated those steps have been taken," those steps in fact were never taken. Indeed, as the article points out, I, along with Father Roy Bourgeois and other supporters of SOA Watch, personally would witness firsthand the falsehood of Obama's claim when we travelled to Honduras days after the coup.

Our first stop on this trip was to visit the US's Soto Cano/Palmerola Air Base northwest of Tegucigalpa, where the US Southern Command's Joint Task Force-Bravo is stationed. The base was humming with activity, seemingly unaffected by the coup which had just happened, and we asked a Sgt. Reyes at the base point blank whether it was true that the US military had halted its joint operations with the Honduran military post-coup. Reyes responded, and I took notes of this at the time, that the US relationship with the Honduran military after the coup was "stable. Nothing has changed. That's just something they're telling the press." In addition, Lee Rials, public affairs officer for WHINSEC, confirmed post-coup that Honduran officers were still being trained at the SOA.

In addition, the US stood nearly alone in the Western Hemisphere in recognizing the election of President Porfirio Lobo Sosa that followed the coup, though this election took place in the absence of

Zelaya being returned to Honduras and able to participate in the election. Dana Frank, writing in the *New York Times*, explained the significance of this:

> President Obama quickly recognized Mr. Lobo's victory, even when most of Latin America would not. Mr. Lobo's government is, in fact, a child of the coup. It retains most of the military figures who perpetrated the coup, and no one has gone to jail for starting it.
>
> This chain of events—a coup that the United States didn't stop, a fraudulent election that it accepted—has now allowed corruption to mushroom. The judicial system hardly functions. Impunity reigns. At least 34 members of the opposition have disappeared or been killed, and more than 300 people have been killed by state security forces since the coup, according to the leading human rights organization COFADEH. At least 13 journalists have been killed since Mr. Lobo took office, according to the Committee to Protect Journalists.

Frank, citing a report by the Fellowship of Reconciliation, noted that, "[s]ince the coup the United States has maintained and in some areas increased military and police financing for Honduras and has been enlarging its military bases there . . . ."[188]

As we would find out later in Hillary Clinton's vanity work, *Hard Choices*, she had proudly worked behind the scenes to ensure that elections would go forward in Honduras after the coup swiftly, without Zelaya, and in such a way as to "render the question of Zelaya moot." Quite tellingly, Clinton would later excise this passage from her book when the paperback edition came out,[189] after she was shocked to realize that people were inexplicably upset by her cynical maneuvers to undermine democracy in Honduras.

The reader might also recall that a key public relations spokesman for the new coup regime was none other than Clinton campaign team member Lanny Davis.[190]

One individual who took umbrage at Clinton's pro-coup

machinations and then shameless bragging about them, was Honduran Berta Cáceras, the acclaimed environmental and human right activist, who was murdered by four gunmen in 2016 after receiving numerous death threats. As Berta was quoted as saying shortly before her death, "We're coming out of a coup that we can't put behind us. We can't reverse it. It just kept going. And after, there was the issue of the elections. The same Hillary Clinton, in her book, *Hard Choices*, practically said what was going to happen in Honduras. This demonstrates the meddling of North Americans in our country."[191]

Meanwhile, it has been revealed that, not too surprisingly, the special forces who actually killed Berta were themselves trained by the US. As *The Guardian* recently reported:

> Leaked court documents raise concerns that the murder of the Honduran environmentalist Berta Cáceres was an extrajudicial killing planned by military intelligence specialists linked to the country's US-trained special forces, a Guardian investigation can reveal.
>
> A legal source close to the investigation told the Guardian: "The murder of Berta Cáceres has all the characteristics of a well-planned operation designed by military intelligence, where it is absolutely normal to contract civilians as assassins."[192]

To this day, the U.S remains closely allied to Honduras, continuing to use it as a giant military base from which to project its power throughout the region. Indeed, Honduras has once been described as "USS Honduras"—"a stationary, unsinkable aircraft carrier, strategically anchored" in the middle of Latin America.[193] And the terrible repression unleashed by the 2009 coup continues at the hands of a military the US continues to support.

As Latin American specialist Greg Grandin recently explained, "hundreds of peasant activists and indigenous activists have been killed. Scores of gay rights activists have been killed . . . . [I]t's just a nightmare in Honduras. . . . And Berta Cáceres, in that interview,

says what was installed after the coup was something like a permanent counterinsurgency on behalf of transnational capital. And that
wouldn't have been possible if it were not for Hillary Clinton's normal-
ization of that election, or legitimacy."[194]

In addition, Honduras is the most dangerous country in the Hemisphere to be a journalist, with scores of journalists killed since the 2009
coup.[195] Moreover, as has recently been reported, the Garifunas—Hon-
durans of African descent who have been there for centuries—are being
subjected to intense discrimination and are being forced off their land
in large numbers by real estate developers and others who covet their
land, with many being forced to leave Honduras altogether.[196]

The case of Honduras is worth considering in light of the current
concerns about Russia. While Clinton and her supporters cry foul
about alleged Russian hacking, they seem to feel no shame about Clinton's very real meddling, which has destroyed the democratic system of
Honduras and unleashed terror upon that population.

Similarly, while there seems to be mass hysteria in this country
about Putin's conduct in Ukraine and Crimea, there is barely a whisper
about the US misdeeds in countries like Honduras.

Moreover, as much concern (real and feigned) is expressed about
the fate of journalists in Russia, there is very little said about the
extraordinary killing of journalists in Honduras post-coup. The same
can be said about journalists in Mexico, who are also being killed in
huge numbers with little concern expressed by the US press.

Indeed, a great example of the selective concern of the US press
again comes from NPR, and its reporting for the day of March 23, 2017.
On that day, and the next one as well, NPR had significant reportage
of the murder of a former Russian lawmaker in Kiev[197]—by whom, we
don't know, but all trails always lead to Putin, as NPR would have us
believe. Of course, this is important for NPR's 24/7 Russia bashing.
Meanwhile, on the same day, it was reported by Venezuela's Telesur,
but of course NOT by NPR, that a third Mexican journalist was murdered this month![198] As Telesur further explains, 48 journalists were

killed in 2016 and 72 were killed in 2015. But again, because this has nothing to do with Vladimir Putin, or other ostensible enemies of the US for that matter, it is not worth reporting by the liberal NPR. However, to give NPR its due, it did cover a story about a journalist in Mexico on March 21—that is, about Tom Brady's Super Bowl jersey being found in the possession of a journalist in Mexico. And thank God for that!

In the same vein, while gay activists are being killed in Honduras by forces armed and trained by the US, they do so in the almost total absence of criticism by folks in the US, even while Russia is criticized for its comparatively softer (or at least non-lethal) anti-gay policies.

Meanwhile, I do not recall that the Russians had much to say about the US role in the Honduran coup, quite possibly because they do not view what happens in this hemisphere as any of their business. And when Trump goes ahead and builds his wall on the Mexican border, I truly doubt that Putin will be making some Reaganesque speech (recall his admonition to Gorbachev about the Berlin Wall) about the need for tearing down walls.

The selective concern about such issues says much about the hypocrisy and foggy thinking which permeates the discourse in this country. Possibly, it is worth considering this before such thinking gets us into another world war.

11

THE US EXPANDS AS RUSSIA CONTRACTS: BROKEN PROMISES AND HUMILIATION

As we all know, the USSR and the East Bloc began to disintegrate during the late 1980s. There were many reasons for this, but one major reason was that the reformer, Premier Mikhail Gorbachev, had decided to voluntarily let the Soviet empire go. While the USSR had already abandoned the Brezhnev Doctrine—pursuant to which the Soviet Union could intervene to protect its interests in the East Bloc—Gorbachev made this break even more explicit, telling the East Bloc governments that they were now on their own. Gorbachev made it clear to these governments that if they had trouble holding on to power, they should not expect the USSR to come along (as in Hungary in 1956 and Czechoslovakia in 1968) to save them.

As a result, one East Bloc communist government fell after another. This process was relatively peaceful, which, as Michael Parenti has pointed out, might say something about the nature of those communist

leaders—to wit, maybe they weren't as repressive and power hungry as they were accused of.

In any case, in 1989, the Berlin wall came down, and it was time to decide about a huge issue for Russia and the USSR—the re-unification of Germany. Russia, having had two destructive wars with Germany—WWI, which played a giant roll in the rise of the Bolsheviks to power in 1917, and WWII, in which the Soviet Union lost over 25 million lives—was predictably wary of a re-united and powerful Germany.

Joshua R. Itzkowitz Shifrinson, writing recently in the *LA Times*, explains how the West put Russia's concerns at ease:

> In early February 1990, US leaders made the Soviets an offer. According to transcripts of meetings in Moscow on Feb. 9, then-Secretary of State James Baker suggested that in exchange for cooperation on Germany, US could make 'iron-clad guarantees' that NATO would not expand "one inch eastward." Less than a week later, Soviet President Mikhail Gorbachev agreed to begin reunification talks. No formal deal was struck, but from all the evidence, the quid pro quo was clear: Gorbachev acceded to Germany's western alignment and the US would limit NATO's expansion.[199]

Through such a bargain, the final nail had been placed in the Cold War coffin, or so Russia had thought, for, as we all know, the West's promises were swiftly broken, with Poland, Hungary, the Czech Republic, the Baltic states and other formerly East Bloc countries being admitted to NATO membership in 1999, and Bulgaria, Estonia, Latvia, Lithuania, Romania, Slovakia and Slovenia admitted in 2004.[200]

This expansion has continued to the present, with NATO deciding in 2008 that the former Soviet state of Georgia would eventually be allowed to join NATO when it meets all necessary criteria,[201] and with NATO entering into closer and closer cooperative ties with the former Soviet state of Ukraine.[202] Meanwhile, the US has sold extended-range

missiles to Poland that could easily hit Russia, as well as new cruise and air-to-air missiles for Poland's F-16 fleet.[203]

Even putting aside the fact that such actions of the US and NATO constituted a grave breach of trust with post-Soviet Russia, these actions must be viewed as objectively provocative of Russia.

Indeed, the one time ever that Russia engaged in an analogous action—putting missiles and advisers in Cuba in 1962—the world was brought to the brink of nuclear war. And, in the end, Khrushchev agreed within a matter of days to take the missiles out of Cuba in return for *the secret* promise that the US would take its missiles out of Turkey months later. Of course, the part of the deal about the US removing its missiles from Turkey was secret because the US insisted that it be able to save face and not be made to look weak by having caved in to Soviet demands. Of course, the gesture of saving face was not extended to the Russians, who will always be seen as the ones who "blinked" during this crisis. Though if "blinked" means being the one to back down and lose face so as to ensure the salvation of our planet, that is not something to be too ashamed of. But, despite Russia's quick responsiveness to the US demand to leave Cuba, the US did not relent in its continued milking of the "Soviet threat" to justify its military build-up.

In any case, the idea that Russia would now put troops and missiles in Cuba and/or Mexico and/or Central America would simply be inconceivable, and would in no case be tolerated by the US. But, as usual, the US, insisting on running the world, can have its way with Russia while not risking, and certainly never tolerating, reciprocal treatment. And, when Russia dares to even assert itself on its own borders, the US cries foul and accuses Russia of imperialist ambitions. I cannot describe such an attitude as anything other than galling, but I seem to be in the minority in this country with such a view. Meanwhile, the US continues to hold on to Guantanamo Bay, Cuba—which it acquired by force in 1898 and then obtained a lease through threat of force in 1903—against the Cubans' wishes, and without apparently

seeing any irony in that or feeling any apparent shame. And Obama's promises, eight years ago, to shut down the prison there have long been forgotten. The quick and extensive expansion of NATO to the Russian frontier after the Soviet collapse was not the end of what Russia reasonably viewed as the US and West's provocations. It is worth remembering, for example, that the US and NATO bombed the former Yugoslavia in the 1990s, leading even the compliant Boris Yeltsin to respond, "'This is the first sign of what could happen when NATO comes right up to the Russian Federation's borders. . . . The flame of war could burst out across the whole of Europe.'"[204]

However one regards the US/NATO bombings in the former Yugoslavia in 1995 and then again in 1999—bombings which Clinton characterized (as was his wont) as a "humanitarian intervention" carried out to protect civilians from human rights abuses—one has to at least understand the trepidation with which the Russians viewed this event. Imagine if, for example, the Russians engaged in major bombing campaigns, lasting weeks at a time, in Honduras or Colombia to halt the horrible human rights abuses there, abuses which include ethnic cleansing on a huge scale. I suspect that there might be an outcry in Washington over this. Indeed, such a scenario seems too absurd to even seriously contemplate.

Moreover, there is cause to doubt the humanitarian intentions of the U.S and NATO in carrying out the Yugoslav intervention. Indeed, there is good reason to believe, as asserted by commentators such as George Szamuely in his *Bombs for Peace*, that this intervention was really motivated by the desire of the US to destroy the last socialist state in Europe and to prime the Western world for a post-Soviet, unipolar world order in which the US would use NATO to intervene anywhere in the world as it saw fit. The "humanitarian war" model was a perfect pretext for this goal, and has remained a powerful ideology to justify the multiple wars of the US to this day, though they invariably cause more suffering than they allay.

In the case of the Yugoslav intervention, Szamuely details how

the West worked toward the goal of partitioning Yugoslavia, by first encouraging the secession of Slovenia and Croatia and then the breaking away of Bosnia-Hercegovina—events which would inevitably lead to the brutal internecine violence that followed. Then, at every turn, the US intervened to prevent peace.

First, the US, through Ambassador Warren Zimmerman, convinced Bosnian leader Alija Izetbegovic to renounce the 1992 Lisbon Agreement, which could have prevented the civil war from breaking out in the first place, and which Izetbegovic had already signed.

In his wonderful *Humanitarian Imperialism*, Jean Bricmont explains, "of the Lisbon agreements of February 1992, the Canadian Ambassador to Yugoslavia at that time, James Bissett, has written, 'The entire diplomatic corps was very happy that the civil war had been avoided—except the Americans. The American Ambassador, Warren Zimmerman, immediately took off for Sarajevo to convince [the Bosnian Muslim leader] Izetbegovic not to sign the agreement.' As Bricmont relates, Zimmerman would later admit this, and an anonymous, high-ranking State Department would tell the *New York Times* that Zimmerman was not acting on his own; that "[t]he policy was to encourage Izetbegovic to break the partition plan." As per usual, the US was afraid that peace might break out, and did all it could to prevent this.

After the Lisbon accords were intentionally scuttled, the civil war broke out with disastrous consequences for all sides of the conflict. The major bombing campaign of NATO then occurred in 1999, and lasted for eleven weeks. As Professor Adam Roberts explains, this "was the first sustained use of armed force by the NATO alliance in its 50-year existence; [and] the first time a major use of destructive armed force had been undertaken with the stated purpose of implementing UN Security Council authorization but without Security Council authorization," as Russia and China made it clear they would not give such authorization.[205]

Given the lack of UN Security Council authorization, the NATO

intervention was arguably illegal under international law, particularly under the UN Charter, which (1) generally forbids the use or threat of force; and (2) gives the Security Council the sole authority to authorize the use of force in the interest of "maintaining international peace and security." Moreover, the Security Council is required by the UN Charter to attempt to use "pacific means" to achieve this goal before authorizing force. In the case of Yugoslavia, the US actually prevented any "pacific means" from succeeding.

Moreover, as a number of critics have noted, the NATO bombing seemed to only intensify the human rights abuses against the Kosovars that the bombing was allegedly intended to prevent, with Roberts explaining that,

> [I]t is not disputed that, in the words of a White House spokesman on 26 March, the situation in Kosovo took 'a dramatic and serious turn for the worse' in the day after the bombing commenced. Many refugees fleeing from Kosovo saw the Serb onslaught against them as a direct consequence of the NATO action. . . . Within one month of the start of the bombing campaign, over half a million people had fled from Kosovo into neighboring countries, and many thousands were displaced within Kosovo itself. During the whole period of the bombing, according to NATO figures, almost one million inhabitants left Kosovo, and a half-a-million were internally displaced. Thousands of Kosovar Albanians were killed.[206]

In addition, the 78-day NATO bombing, in which, of course, no NATO soldiers risked their lives in what amounted to shooting fish in a barrel, did much damage to the civilian population and infrastructure of Serbia. Roberts quotes then UN High Commissioner for Human Rights, Mary Robinson, who complained, "[i]n the NATO bombing of the Federal Republic of Yugoslavia, large numbers of civilians have incontestably been killed, civilian installations targeted on the basis that they are or could be of military application, and NATO remains

the sole judge of what is or is not acceptable to bomb." She then expressed the concern for whether the international humanitarian law norm requiring proportionality was being followed.

Roberts does put forward the counter-argument that, notwithstanding the above, "[i]t might have been better to bring the crisis to a head [with NATO intervention] than to let it fester on, albeit in a less intense form, from year to year . . . ." This is an interesting argument, albeit a possibly callous one, and one that also ignores the fact that in 1999, just before the bombing began, there was another chance for peace that the US prevented. Thus, it is pretty clear that Slobodan Milosevic would have accepted an agreement pursuant to which Serbian troops would be removed from Kosovo—allegedly the goal of the bombing that ultimately ensued—but the US inserted a poison pill in the agreement (the 1999 Rambouillet Accord) in the form of Appendix B, which would have required Serbia to essentially give up its sovereignty to NATO occupation.

The description of this by Lewis MacKenzie in the *Globe & Mail* certainly comports with my recollection from that time—and puts it so well: "unfortunately—but intentionally," the March 18, 1999 accord contained a requirement "that Mr. Milosevic could never accept, making war or at least the allied bombing of a sovereign state inevitable." To wit, the agreement "demanded that NATO have freedom of movement throughout the entire land, sea and airspace of the former Federal Republic of Yugoslavia." No self-respecting country, of course, would have accepted such an arrangement. The other predictably unacceptable portion of the agreement, MacKenzie explains, would have required "a referendum be held within three years to determine the will of those citizens living in Kosovo regarding independence. The fact that Kosovo's population was overwhelmingly Albanian Muslim guaranteed that the outcome of any such referendum would be a vote for independence and the loss of the Serbian nation's historic heart." As a consequence, "Mr. Milosevic refused to sign the accord, and NATO began bombing Serbia on March 24, 1999, without a Security Council

resolution, citing a 'humanitarian emergency'—a decision still widely challenged by many international legal scholars."[207]

Moreover, if we were to apply Roberts's argument in favor of NATO intervention to Syria now, it would seem to justify the Russian strategy of trying to end the seemingly intractable conflict there quickly by supporting the one unified force in Syria that seems to be able to win militarily and to bring some sense of peace and stability to Syria—that of the Assad government. But of course, that is crazy talk.

In any case, the US/NATO campaign in Yugoslavia, over the objections of Russia, and against Serbia, with whom the Russians were allied, was another humiliating event for Russia, which was simply powerless to do anything to stop it. This event reminded them of their lost glory as the USSR, whose existence had prevented such bombing raids in Europe after World War II.

In addition to the Yugoslav intervention, the US has also decided to meddle in the former Soviet Republics, most recently and notably in Ukraine, in quite dangerous ways, which have now undermined the stability of the region. Of course, the press blames all of the problems in Ukraine on Putin, but the facts are at least more complex than this one-sided account.

First of all, let's start from the premise that there was an illegal *coup d'etat* in February, 2014 that overthrew the democratically elected government of Viktor Yanukovych, a leader who was at least favorably disposed towards Russia. The ouster of Yanukovych, which came under pressure from street protests, some violent, was prompted by his "offense"—or at least the press here considered it an offense—of re-considering whether to enter an association agreement with the European Union in light of a pretty decent deal being offered from Vladimir Putin to stay economically integrated with Russia—a deal that included Russia buying $15 billion of Ukrainian government bonds and cutting gas prices.[208]

For Yanukovych to at least consider the deal offered by Putin was not irrational, especially given that "[e]conomic experts [at the time]

say Ukraine desperately needs at least $10b in the coming months to avoid bankruptcy."[209]

Moreover, it is fair to say that Ukraine was under a great deal of pressure from the West in the form of the US-dominated IMF, which had approved a $15.1 billion loan for Ukraine in 2010 and then suspended it, after only paying out $3 billion of the loan, in light of Ukraine's failure to pursue austerity measures, such as pension "reforms" (meaning cuts) and the increase of consumer gas prices.[210] And the IMF would only approve a new loan deal on condition that Ukraine "drastically increasing the gas bills of Ukrainians while freezing salaries at the current level and doing additional budget cuts."[211] Indeed, Yanukovych's Prime Minister at the time cited the onerous requirements of the IMF loan then on the table as a big reason for backing out of the EU deal.[212] An IMF deal, by the way, ended up being approved very shortly after the coup that unseated Yanukovych.

In addition, buried within the EU deal were provisos that would have required Ukraine to submit to NATO military security policy, a controversial requirement indeed.[213] And, as it has turned out, Kiev's relationship with NATO deepened after the toppling of Yanukovych and after the new government entered the Association Agreement with the EU. As NATO gloated thereafter, "[w]e will continue to promote the development of greater interoperability between Ukrainian and NATO forces. NATO's enhanced advisory presence in Kyiv is already in place and will continue to grow. As requested by Ukraine, Allies will continue to provide expertise as Ukraine completes its comprehensive defense and security sector review. The comprehensive reform agenda undertaken by Ukraine in the context of its ANP [Annual National Program] with NATO, as well as in the context of its Association Agreement with the EU, will further strengthen Ukraine."[214]

As the *New York Times* acknowledged when the new President, Poreshenko, signed the EU Agreement, "[o]ne of Mr. Putin's major objections to closer political and economic relations between Ukraine and the West was widely understood to be a concern about NATO

expansion, and the risk that would pose to Russia's military interests in the Crimean peninsula."[215] But, of course, why should we care what Putin or Russia fears, or believe is in their self-interest?

Meanwhile, there can be no doubt that many in Ukraine, particularly in the West, which has strong anti-Russian sentiment, were angered by Yanukovych's vacillation on the EU deal, and that this anger led to Yanukovych's undoing. What was bizarre, however, was how the US press reacted to Putin's offer, portraying it as somehow illegitimate for Putin to try to keep Ukraine within Russia's orbit by offering favorable terms.

Again, while it is obviously understandable that the EU was upset by this turn of events, why this was a major concern for the US simply does not stand to reason. It would be akin to Russia being upset about NAFTA—the three-way trade agreement between the US, Canada and Mexico, which, by the way, has been devastating for Mexico in terms of destroying the livelihood of about 2 million Mexican small farmers, and which helped make Mexico a failed state[216]—because it preferred that Mexico be more closely integrated with Brazil.

No one would care what Russia thought about such goings-on in this hemisphere anyway. Meanwhile, we seem to begrudge Russia for any assertion of self-interest even at its borders. It is as if Russia is to have no self-interest anywhere in the world, while the US should be able to assert its self-interest everywhere.

In any case, as we know, Yanukovych's backing away from the EU deal proved to be his undoing, with people taking to the streets and his being forced from office. Many of those protesting were regular folks who had legitimate concerns about the policies of Yanukovych—many of which were quite undemocratic and corrupt, no doubt—while some of those involved in the events of 2013-2014 were quite sinister.

Indeed, there were, and there are, those very closely aligned to the post-Yanukovych government of President Petro Poreshenko— who himself has asked the Ukraine Supreme Court to declare that the unseating of Yanukovych constituted an unconstitutional coup (most

likely because he is afraid the same will happen to him)[217]—who are themselves violent, anti-democratic, and indeed neo-Nazi, and who are carrying out acts in accord with such a heinous philosophy.

And there are certainly sectors of the US government who support these forces in Ukraine. These are undeniable facts, and yet it is rarely reported in the US press, and few seem concerned about it. From all appearances, the mainstream US media would prefer neo-Nazis running amok in Ukraine, and even taking charge, than having a Ukraine integrated with Russia.

Max Blumenthal, writing at the time of the EuroMaiden protests in February of 2014, which unseated Yanukovych, explained the facts on the ground:

> As the Euromaidan protests in the Ukrainian capital of Kiev culminated this week, displays of open fascism and neo-Nazi extremism became too glaring to ignore. Since demonstrators filled the downtown square to battle Ukrainian riot police and demand the ouster of the corruption-stained, pro-Russian President Viktor Yanukovych, it has been filled with far-right streetfighting men pledging to defend their country's ethnic purity.
>
> White supremacist banners and Confederate flags were draped inside Kiev's occupied City Hall, and demonstrators have hoisted Nazi SS and white power symbols over a toppled memorial to V.I. Lenin. After Yanukovych fled his palatial estate by helicopter, Euro-Maidan protesters destroyed a memorial to Ukrainians who died battling German occupation during World War II. *Sieg heil* salutes and the Nazi Wolfsangel symbol have become an increasingly common site in Maidan Square, and neo-Nazi forces have established "autonomous zones" in and around Kiev.[218]

As Blumenthal explains, "[o]ne of the "Big Three" political parties behind the protests is the ultra-nationalist Svoboda, whose leader, Oleh Tyahnybok, has called for the liberation of his country from the

"Muscovite-Jewish mafia."[219] Despite Tyahnybok's openly neo-Nazi and anti-Semitic philosophy, Senator John McCain has proudly rallied alongside him in Kiev.[220]

More disturbingly, as the recording of a call between Geoffrey Pyatt, the US ambassador to Ukraine, and Obama's Assistant Secretary of State, Victoria Nuland, reveal, Nuland maneuvered behind the scenes to make sure that the neo-Nazi Tyahnybok, while remaining officially "on the outside" of the new government, consults with the US's choice for Prime Minister, Arseniy Yatsenyuk "four times a week."[221]

As Nuland states in the same conversation, "I think Yats [Yatsenyuk] is the guy . . . ," as if it were for the US to hand-pick the new government.[222] And indeed, Nuland has admitted that, since 2004, the US has spent over $5 billion on promoting groups in Ukraine which would help align that country with the interests of the United States.[223] For his part, Barack Obama would later admit in an interview with CNN that he "had brokered a deal to transition power in Ukraine."[224] Again, the US may meddle wherever and whenever it wants, even half way around the world, while Russia must not assert its own interests even at its frontiers.

Even if it can be said that Putin overplayed his hand in trying to coax Yanukovych into rejecting the EU deal and accepting a deal with Russia, it is not at all surprising that Putin was nonetheless spooked by the events in Ukraine wherein neo-Nazis seemed to have a role in both the coup which deposed Yanukovych, and in the new government in Kiev. The fact that the US seemed to have a hand in these events, and to acquiesce in, if not outright encourage, the participation of ultra-nationalists in the Ukraine government, was predictably disturbing to Putin as well.

It is also not lost on the Russians that the US has had a hand in supporting Nazis in the Ukraine and elsewhere for a very long time. As an expert on this issue, Russ Bellant, told *The Nation* magazine back in 2014,[225] "the key organization" in the 2014 Ukrainian coup was the Organization of Ukrainian Nationalists (OUN), which was founded

in the 1920's, was actively in alliance with Nazi Germany as the "14th Waffen SS Division," and continues to defend its war-time role today. This group, which continues to wear the "SS" insignia on its uniforms, openly calls for the purging of Jews, Poles—and, yes, of Russians as well—from Ukrainian society. Thousands of Ukrainian emigres associated with the OUN were re-settled in the US after the war, and they have had great influence in the US, particularly within the Republican Party.

Bellant points out the inconvenient fact that the US has aggressively supported the OUN since WWII "through the intelligence agencies, initially military intelligence, later the CIA."

The OUN was also a key factor in the 2004 Orange Revolution—which the US was also behind—and Viktor Yuschenko, who was the Prime Minister of the Ukraine from 2005-2010, was closely aligned with them as they proceeded, among other things, to erect monuments to Nazi leaders throughout Ukraine. As Bellant explains, "[t]he United States was very aggressive in trying to keep the nationalists in power, but they lost the election" in 2010.

And so the US pumped millions of dollars into the Ukraine in the intervening period to help these nationalists return to power in the 2014 coup that precipitated the current crisis in Ukraine. The US has continued to provide military training to the ultra-nationalist forces post-coup—at first directly, and now, after Congress passed a law forbidding such training, as a consequence of their being so embedded in Kiev's regular forces.[226]

I share the view of a number of commentators that, given the foregoing, Putin's response to the coup in the Ukraine was predictable, and even understandable.

As John J. Mearsheimer, writing for *Foreign Affairs*, I think quite correctly states:

> [T]he United States and its European allies share most of the responsibility for the crisis. The taproot of the trouble is NATO enlargement, the central element of a larger strategy to move

Ukraine out of Russia's orbit and integrate it into the West. At the same time, the EU's expansion eastward and the West's backing of the pro-democracy movement in Ukraine—beginning with the Orange Revolution in 2004—were critical elements, too. Since the mid-1990s, Russian leaders have adamantly opposed NATO enlargement, and in recent years, they have made it clear that they would not stand by while their strategically important neighbor turned into a Western bastion. For Putin, the illegal overthrow of Ukraine's democratically elected and pro-Russian president—which he rightly labeled a "coup"—was the final straw.[227]

Even if one does not go as far as putting the lion's share of the blame on the West for the Ukraine crisis, one at least has to understand why Putin and Russia would feel very threatened by these events. And frankly, the downplaying of the role of neo-Nazis in the current Ukrainian conflict is just baffling. For example, in the NPR piece I mentioned earlier, in which Steve Inskeep interviewed the CEO of Voice of America, Inskeep mocked what he characterized as the "false flag" conspiracies of some who, apparently, deserve no voice in the Ukraine debate. The truth is, these alternative viewpoints have little to do with alarm over "false flags," but over Nazi flags. One would think this to be a worthy news item, but instead, it is dismissed out of hand.

Moreover, it would be unfair to say that it was only Putin and Russia that were disturbed by these events. The fact is that Ukrainians of Russian descent in the east of the country, particularly in the Donbass region, were also frightened by the nature of the new government, as were the residents of Crimea. And again, with good reason. It was not long before violent tensions began, and the blame for the violence that unfolded cannot be laid solely, or even primarily, at Putin's feet.

Again, former Reagan official, Paul Craig Roberts:

What has happened in Ukraine is the United States organized and financed a coup. And the coup occurred in Kiev, the capital.

Either from intention or carelessness, the coup elements include
ultra-right-wing nationalists whose roots go back to organizations
that fought for Hitler in the Second World War against the Soviet
Union. These elements destroyed Russian war memorials celebrating
the liberation of the Ukraine from the Nazis by the Red Army and
also celebrating Gen. Kutuzov's defeat of Napoleon's Grande Armée.
So this spread a great deal of alarm in southern and eastern Ukraine,
which are traditionally Russian provinces.

The other act which alarmed the "traditionally Russian provinces"
was the vote in the Kiev parliament, almost immediately after the coup,
to ban Russian as the second official language.

The result was that pro-Russian separatists in Ukraine, without
any prompting or support from Vladimir Putin—though that support
would certainly come later—seized parts of the eastern Donetsk and
Luhansk regions in March of 2014—very shortly after the coup—and
declared their own "People's Republics," of course harkening back to
the old Soviet Union.

In response, the new government in Kiev attacked the separatists
in these regions in what they dubbed as "anti-terrorist" operations,
and a brutal civil war has broken out. While the separatists have been
vilified in the US media as pawns of Putin, this is just not the case.
They are homegrown militants who want independence from the Kiev
government, which they view as illegitimate and fascist.

Of course, the US has been happy to support such separatists
when it has served its own ends, as it did when it helped to break
up the former Yugoslavia—even supporting, and indeed keeping on
life support at a critical moment, the Kosovo Liberation Army (KLA),
which was a designated terrorist organization[228]—and as it has done in
Sudan when it helped South Sudan break away into its own independent state (that's going swimmingly, by the way, with South Sudan
now facing a potential genocide within its borders[229]).

Moreover, and quite ironically, while the US insisted on elections

in Kosovo in regards to independence from Serbia as a condition to avoid the 1999 bombing—an insistence that helped derail a possible peace—the US and E.U. were dead set against elections which the two Donbass regions called in November of 2014 to elect their own governments.[230] And both the US and E.U. were critical of Russia's willingness to honor these elections. Of course, this goes to show again that it is the US which decides whether and when people can decide to declare their independence.

But even assuming that the people of the Donbass are not entitled to their own country, and even assuming that one is troubled that Putin's government in Moscow ended up following the lead of independent Russian militias in joining the fray in the Donbass, it is still fair to consider the forces on the other side that the Western governments and media are supporting against these peoples. While it is rare to hear this in the US mainstream press,

> Kiev's use of volunteer paramilitaries to stamp out the Russian-backed Donetsk and Luhansk "people's republics," proclaimed in eastern Ukraine in March, should send a shiver down Europe's spine. Recently formed battalions such as Donbas, Dnipro and Azov, with several thousand men under their command, are officially under the control of the interior ministry but their financing is murky, their training inadequate and their ideology often alarming.
>
> The Azov men use the neo-Nazi Wolfsangel (Wolf's Hook) symbol on their banner and members of the battalion are openly white supremacists, or anti-Semites.[231]

This same article from *The Telegraph* of London cites Mark Galeotti, an expert on Russian and Ukrainian security affairs at New York University, for the proposition that battalions like Azov are becoming "'magnets to attract violent fringe elements from across Ukraine and beyond,'" and "[t]he danger is that this is part of the building up of a toxic legacy for when the war ends."

How the proliferation of Nazis is not, by all appearances, of concern to the US press, while the concern about Putin has risen to pathological levels, is simply beyond me.

And, the fact is that the neo-Nazis are winning, with the civilian population of the Donbass taking a very bad beating as a result of the fighting, as well as from the siege being laid to that area by the government in Kiev.

Thus, as UNICEF has recently reported, *one million children in East Ukraine* are now in grave need of aid to survive.[232] UNICEF explains, not surprisingly given the horrible coverage of this situation, that *"[t]his is an invisible emergency—a crisis most of the world has forgotten."* (emphasis added). UNICEF further explains, "Children in eastern Ukraine have been living under the constant threat of unpredictable fighting and shelling for the past three years. Their schools have been destroyed, they have been forced from their homes and their access to basic commodities like heat and water has been cut off." And, it is not the Russians, but the pro-West government in Kiev which is carrying out this destruction, again to the collective yawn of the US media.

I find it quite ironic that NPR has recently been promoting the film called *Bitter Harvest*, about the famine in the Ukraine in 1932-1933 which is generally explained as an intentional man-made famine imposed by Joseph Stalin, and yet it has had nothing to say about the current starvation of children in Ukraine. Similarly, the press has very little to say about the US-Saudi imposed famine upon Yemen, which may kill up to seven million people through starvation.[233]—about the same as the highest estimates of those who died in the Ukraine famine of the early 1930s. But, of course, it is always easier to dwell upon the crimes of Joseph Stalin over eighty years ago rather than focus on our own crimes, which are causing people to starve now and which we could actually do something to stop.

Meanwhile, in its same announcement, UNICEF recommends that, in the interest of peace and the end of such suffering, all parties abide by what is known as the Minsk Agreements—the most recent version

of which was put together by Germany's Angela Merkel and France's François Hollande. As *The Economist* explains, the Minsk Agreements offer "a detailed roadmap for resolving the conflict. The 13 point-plan begins with a ceasefire and the withdrawal of heavy weapons from the front lines, to be monitored by the Organization for Security and Co-operation in Europe (OSCE)."[234] One might recall that Putin has committed Russia to the Minsk Agreements, and that then US Secretary of State John Kerry flew to Sochi with the express purpose to tell Putin that the US would back these Agreements as well.[235] However, before he even left Sochi, Kerry was intentionally undermined by the Biden wing of the Obama Administration. As an article in *Foreign Policy* by James Cardin explains:

> Meanwhile, in the US, the hawks took aim at Kerry. Julianne Smith, a former top national security adviser to Vice President Joe Biden, complained to the *New York Times* that Kerry's trip to Sochi was "counterproductive" and that "it created this kind of cloud of controversy around what is the US strategy, why did he go?"[236]

It is also Stephen F. Cohen's take, as he explained to me in our interview, that it was the Biden team which interfered with Kerry's attempt to show the US's buy-in for Minsk. And indeed, The *New York Times* acknowledges Joe Biden's sizeable role in the Ukrainian issue, explaining that the "Vice President Biden has played a leading role in American policy toward Ukraine as Washington seeks to counter Russian intervention in Eastern Ukraine."[237]

While we may never know for sure, and while neither Cardin nor Cohen mention it, the explanation may lie with Joe Biden's son, Hunter, who has strong business interests in Ukraine.[238] Indeed, Hunter Biden was suspiciously named to the board of a Ukrainian natural gas company in April, 2014—just after the 2014 coup in Ukraine.[239] But again, few have bothered to look into this curious lead, and few seem to care.

In addition to the Donbass conflict, of course, is the question of

the Crimea, which I often hear folks talk about as cause to fear Vladimir Putin and Russia. The facts are largely undisputed that on March 1, 2014, shortly after the coup, Putin, with Russian Parliamentary approval and in the context of much unrest in Crimea provoked by the change of government in Kiev, decided to send troops to secure Crimea, which included a long-standing Russian navy base in the port city of Sevastopol on the Black Sea. Crimea had been a part of Russia, and then the Soviet Union, from 1783 until 1954 when Nikita Khrushchev voluntarily "gifted" it to Ukraine. Meanwhile, Russia had maintained its naval base in Sevastopol, pursuant to a lease with Ukraine, even after 1954.[240]

As the *Washington Post* explains, "Crimea has a modern history intrinsically linked with Russia, contains the largest population of ethnic Russians within Ukraine, and harbors a significant portion of Russia's navy in Sevastopol . . . ."[241] Given this, it is not all too surprising that, in the time of crisis precipitated by the overthrow of Yanukovych, Russia would want to protect its interests, naval base and the Russian speakers in Crimea.

I have little doubt that the US, confronted with a similar situation—and currently occupying foreign territories with at best a dubious right to do so (for example, its base and torture chamber on Guantanamo, Cuba)—would do the same thing.

In any case, a couple of weeks after the Russian military intervention, on March 16, 2014, the Crimeans voted overwhelmingly in a referendum to secede from Ukraine and join Russia. This is not too surprising given that sixty percent of Crimeans are Russian speakers. And, while both the EU and US called this referendum a sham and refused to honor it, polls show (1) that the Crimeans themselves believe this referendum to be valid; and (2) that the Crimeans, including the Tartar minority which is reasonably wary of Russia, are happier under Russian governance than Ukrainian.

As the radical, pro-Putin *Forbes* magazine relates, "[t]he US and European Union may want to save Crimeans from themselves. But the

Crimeans are happy right where they are. One year after the annexation of the Ukrainian peninsula in the Black Sea, poll after poll shows that the locals there—be they Ukrainians, ethnic Russians or Tatars are mostly all in agreement: life with Russia is better than life with Ukraine."[242]

Again, I fully understand that the US takes the position that what country Crimea is a part of is none of the Crimeans' business, and while I also get the point that Russia should never stray beyond its borders for any reason, it is hard for me to feel too excited by any of this, and equally hard for me to believe that others in this country feel as strongly about this as they apparently do. At a minimum, it is not clear to me how Russia's actions regarding Crimea, especially as they ended up being welcomed by the Crimeans, is any cause for Americans to believe that Russia is somehow a threat to humanity.

* * *

Meanwhile, the US used the collapse of the USSR, which had once put some brakes on US Empire, to expand throughout the entire globe. As of 2015, the US had at least 800 military bases in over 70 nations, while Britain, France and Russia had only 30 military bases *combined*.[243] And Russia has no bases outside the former Soviet Union with the sole exception of Syria.[244]

As David Vine, in his new book, *Base Nation*, explains, the US has bases in many undemocratic, and indeed "despotic," nations, such as Qatar, Bahrain, Saudi Arabia and Honduras. Vine reminds us that Osama bin Laden cited the US's presence in the Muslim holy land of Saudi Arabia as a motivation for the 911 attacks.

In addition, these bases cause untold environmental degradation, have a huge carbon footprint, and encourage the proliferation of commercial sex zones around the US's worldwide bases. These are the modern day comfort women that few will talk about. To add to the humiliation of post-Soviet Russia, women from Russia and the

former Soviet Republics have replaced Korean women as sex workers in South Korea.[245]

The position of the US, which seems beyond question in this country, is that we have the right to project our power and our presence anywhere and everywhere throughout the world, while countries like Russia, and China too, are deemed to be acting aggressively and unreasonably if they claim any right to be free from the military presence of the US and other Western countries, even on their borders.

As just one example, I'll never stop feeling shocked, and even quite irate really, when I hear a US government spokesman and/or news pundit accuse China of military aggression because it is seeking some control over the South China Sea and because it takes some umbrage at the US's attempt instead to assert control there. "It's called the 'South *China* Sea,' after all," I think, as I throw my remote at the radio. In any case, the US even has China, and Russia as well, outgunned in the South China Sea, with three aircraft carrier strike groups deployed there at the end of Obama's term, to just one aircraft carrier each for China and Russia.[246] But again, I seem to be nearly alone in such thoughts.

That we clearly do not understand how arrogant and insulting such a position is only reveals the depths of our own psychosis. Meanwhile, it is Russia and Vladimir Putin who are accused of being the crazy ones.

12

UNLEASHING TERROR TO WIN THE COLD WAR

ONE OF THE MOST FATEFUL INTERVENTIONS by the US motivated, at least in part, by Cold War hysteria, was the US overthrow of the democratically elected government of Prime Minister Mohammad Mosaddeq in Iran in 1953.

As *The Guardian* explains, "Mosaddeq epitomised a unique 'anti-colonial' figure who was also committed to democratic values and human rights . . . ."[247] The US moved against him because of his decision to nationalize Iran's oil concerns, including some owned by British Petroleum, and because they distrusted this left-leaning leader as a possible communist who could not be relied upon to keep Iran's vast oil wealth out of the hands of Russia. And so, the US, with help from Britain, acted to put in place a government—the old monarchy of the Shah—that it could count on to "safeguard the west's oil interests in the country."[248]

And, to ensure the Shah's hold over Iran for the next 26 years, the US helped set up the repressive secret police services known as the SAVAK. As one CIA agent revealed, "the CIA sent an operative to teach interrogation methods to SAVAK, the Shah's secret police, that the training included instructions in torture, and the techniques were copied from the Nazis."[249]

Not surprisingly, the Iranians still resent the US for its role in overthrowing a democratic government and setting up what can only be described as a torture state. This explains the antipathy the current Iranian government—which came to power in 1979 after overthrowing this torture state and then immediately proceeded to kidnap 52 Americans at the US Embassy in retaliation—has toward the United States, and why Iran has instead cozied up to the US's old Cold War rival, Russia. Lest one forget, there is very solid evidence that our beloved Ronald Reagan, in order to win the 1980 election, undermined then President Jimmy Carter's negotiations with Iran to free the hostages, and indeed prevailed upon Iran (with whom Reagan would later sell arms to fund his Contra terrorists) to hold the hostages months longer, until after he was inaugurated in January of 1981. As Robert Parry, the journalist most responsible for breaking this "October Surprise" story, relates, even if we accept the current allegations against Trump regarding collusion with Russia prove true, they would pale in comparison to Reagan's treacherous collusion with Iran to win the 1980 elections.[250]

* * *

Another momentous, and arguably more disastrous, Cold War maneuver of the US was its support for the Mujahideen in Afghanistan, which at that time shared a 1000-mile-long border with the Soviet Union.

The Mujahideen was a motley group of foreign fighters, including Osama Bin Laden, trained and armed by the CIA,[251] we were told at the time, to confront and beat back the Soviet invasion of Afghanistan. All told, over 15,000 such fighters (whom we of course deemed "freedom fighters" at the time), many of whom were Islamist extremists such as Osama Bin Laden, were trained by the CIA "in bomb-making, sabotage and urban guerrilla warfare in Afghan camps the CIA helped to

set up." It goes without saying that there has been some terrible blow-back from this operation, blowback which we continue to experience to this day.

What makes this all the more troubling, as we would find out years later, was that the US began to train, arm and support these fighters—or, if you would allow me, terrorists—BEFORE the Soviet invasion of Afghanistan. Thus, as Zbigniew Brzezinski, Jimmy Carter's National Security Adviser, explained in an interview to a French publication in 1998:

> According to the official version of history, CIA aid to the Muja-hiddin began during 1980, that is to say, after the Soviet army invaded Afghanistan on December 24, 1979. But the reality, closely guarded until now, is completely otherwise: Indeed, it was July 3, 1979 that President Carter signed the first directive for secret aid to the opponents of the pro-Soviet regime in Kabul. And that very day, I wrote a note to the president in which I explained to him that *in my opinion this aid was going to induce a Soviet military intervention.*[252]
> (emphasis in original).

When asked whether he regretted this course of action given the explosion of terrorism which was unleashed as a consequence, Brzezinski responded:

> Regret what? That secret operation was an excellent idea. It had the effect of *drawing the Russians into the Afghan trap* and you want me to regret it? The day that the Soviets officially crossed the border, *I wrote to President Carter, essentially: "We now have the opportunity of giving to the USSR its Vietnam War."* Indeed, for almost 10 years, Moscow had to carry on a war that was unsustainable for the regime, a conflict that bought about the demoralization and finally the breakup of the Soviet empire. . . .

What is more important in world history? The Taliban or the collapse of the Soviet empire? Some agitated Moslems or the liberation
of Central Europe and the end of the cold war?[253]

Of course, in our post-9/11 world, I would hope that even someone
like Brzezinski would have to concede that the calculus as to whether
the Afghan escapade was worth it in terms of US blood and treasure
is now much different. And, for Russia, as Brzezinski himself bragged,
the results were devastating, as they were for the poor Afghanis whom
the US willingly sacrificed for their Cold War chess game. In the
end, 15,000 Russian soldiers were killed in the war, while one million
Afghanis lost their lives.[254]

If the US did not support jihadists in Afghanistan to halt a Soviet
invasion, as we had been led to believe, then what was it fighting in
Afghanistan? As one of my favorite philosophers and writers, Michael
Parenti, explains, the US was in reality fighting modernization efforts
of a socialist government, albeit supported by the Soviet Union but
not controlled by it. As Parenti has explained, the Afghan government
so reviled by the US at the time

> proceeded to legalize labor unions, and set up a minimum wage,
> a progressive income tax, a literacy campaign, and programs that
> gave ordinary people greater access to health care, housing, and pub-
> lic sanitation. . . .
>
> The government also continued a campaign begun by the king
> to emancipate women from their age-old tribal bondage. It provided
> public education for girls and for the children of various tribes.[255]

Parenti goes on to also explain that the government also engaged
in a program to eradicate the cultivation of opium poppy in Afghanistan, which, up to that point, was providing 70% of the world's supply.
Oh, the horror!

As we know, with the help of the US, and despite the invasion of

the Soviet Union, which did come, the jihadists were able to overthrow this progressive government, though the government did hold out for six months after the Soviets left. The jihadist victory ushered in the Taliban, whose retrograde, medieval reign was marked by a return to the repression of women's rights, religious intolerance and the destruction of ancient historical ruins.

Of course, the US would intervene against the Taliban government right after the 9/11 attacks, having come to understand that, quite possibly, Brzezinski's cost/benefit analysis in supporting extremists to throw Afghanistan into chaos was wrong.

In any case, the US's operations against the Taliban were greatly aided by Russia under Vladimir Putin. Russia had much to add to the efforts given the substantial assets it continued to have in Afghanistan. As CNN explained at the time, Putin was very eager to help: "[w]ithin hours of the attacks on New York and Washington, Russian President Vladimir Putin was on the phone to George W. Bush—the first international leader to call the US president on September 11."[256] CNN related that "Putin offered more than words of support" when the US decided to invade Afghanistan, providing intelligence information it had collected on the terrorist training camps, and even allowing the US to utilize military bases of the former Soviet Union.

Recall that, just a few months before the 9/11 attacks, Bush had met with Putin and claimed to have become fast friends with him. Indeed, Bush would famously state of Putin, "I looked the man in the eye. I found him to be very straight forward and trustworthy and we had a very good dialogue. I was able to get a sense of his soul."[257] One would have thought that Putin's eager help with the Afghan mission would have further solidified this friendship. However, Bush did not show much appreciation to Putin, quickly taking actions which were predictably provocative to Russia. Thus, Bush backed out of the anti-ballistic treaty which he knew Russia had greatly valued, and posted military trainers in the former Soviet country of Georgia.[258]

While Putin tolerated such hostile actions in return for promises of

greater integration with the West, [259] this integration never came. And, the US-Putin relationship seems to have gone sideways when Putin did not go along with second Gulf War in 2003. As long-time Russian analyst Mark Ames recently told Telesur reporter Abby Martin, this was Putin's unforgivable sin, and it was after this point that the US started feigning concern about democracy in Russia. [260]

Of course, history has shown that Putin was right not to go along with the 2003 invasion of Iraq on the basis that this had nothing to do with fighting terror in response to 9/11, Bush's claims notwithstanding. And, this gets into another topical issue—that of the newly-discovered phenomenon of "fake news."

The news leading up to and stoking the invasion of Iraq in 2003 was as fake as a three-dollar bill, with false intelligence being drummed up by the CIA about weapons of mass destruction that didn't exist. This fake news was also being peddled by all of the mainstream press, and most scandalously by the paper of record, The *New York Times*, which had a veritable war propagandist on its staff named Judith Miller.

As *New York* magazine would later report in an expose of the Judith Miller story, "[d]uring the winter of 2001 and throughout 2002, Miller produced a series of stunning stories about Saddam Hussein's ambition and capacity to produce weapons of mass destruction, based largely on information provided by [Ahmad] Chalabi and his allies— almost all of which have turned out to be stunningly inaccurate." [261] And, this inaccurate reporting, apparently fueled by both Miller's and the *Times*'s hubris and quest for glory, led to disaster, especially for the Iraqi people, "for the [Bush] administration specifically cited [this reporting] to buttress its case for war."

At least half a million Iraqis were killed as a result of the 2003 invasion of Iraq, [262] which many Iraqis view as leaving their country in the worst condition it has been since the Mongol invasion of 1258. Moreover, Iraq continues to be a breeding ground for jihadists, this time in the form of ISIS, which had no foothold in Iraq prior to the invasion. Indeed, say what you will about Saddam Hussein, he was a secularist

and a mortal enemy of such extremist forces. The toppling of Hussein and wiping out of his entire Republican Guard only unleashed more terror on the world, when it was claimed it was aimed at doing the opposite. As Iraqis continue to suffer from ISIS terrorism, and as the US is fighting ISIS in Mosul, it is important to remember that it was the invasion of Iraq—a war of choice if there ever was one—that caused this. One must forgive Putin, then, for having refused to go along with this insanity.

Meanwhile, it must be noted that the invasion of Afghanistan after 9/11, at least to the extent that it morphed into the toppling of the Taliban as opposed to merely attacking the al-Qaeda bases in Afghanistan, was also a disastrous decision. Over 15 years and counting, the US is still bogged down in Afghanistan, as should also have been predictable given the Russians' experience there, and countless Afghanis have lost their lives in the apparently endless war that the 2001 invasion precipitated.

In addition, it must also be pointed out that, for all of their many real faults, the Taliban had, by the time of the invasion, come close to wiping out the heroin poppy fields there. Indeed, The *New York Times* reported on this very fact in May of 2001, just several months before the 9/11 attacks and the invasion that followed.[263] Then, after the US invasion dislodged the Taliban, cultivation skyrocketed. Indeed, as Dr. Meryl Nass, M.D., explained in the *Washington's Blog* in 2015, "[t]he real surge in Afghanistan is in heroin production." Complete with a chart, Dr. Nass shows that by 2001, before the invasion, poppy production in Afghanistan was approaching zero, while post-invasion, Afghanistan now supplies 85% of the world's heroin, a "virtual monopoly."[264]

Dr. Nass, noting that there is nearly no public debate about the impact of the US invasion on heroin supply, raises some thorny questions, such as whether "heroin shipments from Afghanistan are at lower risk of being seized than heroin coming from Latin America. Might some be entering through government channels, when so much materiel and so many personnel (soldiers, aid workers, diplomats and

contractors) fly directly between the US and Afghanistan?" This is an obvious question, of course, given that the US has military and intelligence services, like the CIA, swarm all over Afghanistan, and yet the heroin flows out the doors.

Indeed, Dr. Nass makes an appropriate quip about the CIA-Contra-Cocaine connection in her piece. But few dare to ask such questions. One of the few willing to do so, like veteran journalist Douglas Valentine, is certain that the CIA, which also helped to run drugs to support the US war efforts in Vietnam and to support the Kuomintang's fight against Mao's forces in China, is indeed helping smuggle heroin out of Afghanistan. [265] The CIA does so, he explains, by partnering with Afghani drug kingpins, for example, with the late Ahmed Karzai—the half-brother of Hamid Karzai, who was the first President installed by the US after the 2001 invasion—who was coincidentally killed after it became public that he was running drugs.

In any case, when a loved one of yours dies of a heroin overdose, and it's a good chance one will, given the thousands (over 13,000 in 2016) dying of such overdoses every year—that's the equivalent of over three World Trade Center attacks per year—know that the US foray into Afghanistan bears a significant responsibility.

In short, the over $5 trillion and counting the US has spent on its post-9/11 interventions[266] has not appeared to do the world or the US very much good, as judged by the countless lives lost, the unleashing of only more terror, and the increased proliferation of drugs.

And, just when it appeared that US foreign policy couldn't get any crazier, it did. Thus, as we learned from Seymour Hersh back in 2007, the US began at that time to try to weaken Iran and Syria by supporting Sunni extremist groups to subvert those countries. As Hersh explained in the *New Yorker*,[267] "[t]o undermine Iran, which is predominantly Shiite, the Bush Administration has decided, in effect, to reconfigure its priorities in the Middle East," partnering with Saudi Arabia's government, which is Sunni [and from where nearly all of the 9/11 attackers came], in clandestine operations" against Iran, against

Hezbollah in Lebanon and against Assad's government in Syria. As Hersh explained, "[a] by-product of these activities has been the bolstering of Sunni extremist groups that espouse a militant vision of Islam and are hostile to America and sympathetic to Al Qaeda."

For his part, Bobby Kennedy, Jr., wrote a very provocative piece in 2016, entitled "Why the Arabs Don't Want Us in Syria."[268] This article opens with the line about his father being "murdered by an Arab," and about Bobby Jr.'s consequent attempt to understand US policy in the Middle East. It goes on to detail the decades-long interference of the US in Syrian affairs. And, it further postulates that the US actually decided to go so far as overthrowing the regime in Syria in 2009 after Assad refused to allow an oil pipeline which would have allowed Qatar to connect through Syria to Turkey, in lieu of a pipeline allowing Russia to connect a pipeline from Syria through Iran and onward to Russia. While Kennedy has been greatly maligned for this piece, his argument seems at least plausible, especially given the US's general propensity to intervene internationally to protect Western interests in such valuable assets as oil. For me, though, the piece is equally important for Bobby, Jr.'s attempt at soul-searching in light of his father's assassination. The piece is a classic case of trying to "love thine enemy," which I have always believed we are called on to do, but which few dare to put into practice.

In any case, the US continues to intervene in Syria, as we know, in the most incoherent ways. For starters, it is now generally accepted that the CIA and the Pentagon have been at times backing opposing militant groups that are fighting each other![269] Moreover, as Hersh was reporting a decade ago, we have been arming, and assisting Saudi Arabia in arming, brutal and retrograde forces in their own right that fight alongside with and provide supplies of arms to groups even the US recognizes as terrorist, such as al-Qaeda.

Veteran Middle East reporter, Robert Fisk, explained this truth, which is largely *verboten* to speak of, in a great article in *Counterpunch* entitled, "There Is More Than One Terrible Truth To Tell In The Story

of Aleppo."[270] As he writes, "many of the 'rebels' whom we in the West have been supporting . . . are among the cruellest and most ruthless of fighters in the Middle East. And while we have been tut-tutting at the frightfulness of Isis during the siege of Mosul (an event all too similar to Aleppo, although you wouldn't think so from reading our narrative of the story), we have been willfully ignoring the behaviour of the rebels of Aleppo." As to the US's fight in Mosul, it was just reported as I write this that the US killed over 100 innocents in a bombing raid on that town. But again, I'm sure that this won't stop the US media's "tut-tutting" about Aleppo.

Fisk also relates what many of us already know—that, as Syrian soldiers predicted, the US has willfully allowed ISIS forces it has pushed out of Mosul, Iraq to cross the border into Syria to fight against the Syrian government. As Fisk notes, these forces quickly moved in to "seize the beautiful city of Palmyra all over again," and to continue its destruction of the ancient Roman architecture in that city.

Similarly, while the media fixates on Russia's alleged crimes in Syria, there is nearly no discussion about the unfolding destruction of Yemen, one of the poorest countries on earth, by Saudi forces armed with US weapons, including cluster bombs, and assisted by the US with mid-flight refueling of their bomber planes. According to Human Rights Watch, "[t]he Saudi coalition continues to use cluster bombs, and other US-supplied weapons, to bomb civilian sites, including homes, factories, markets, hospitals, children's schools, and a funeral."[271] And St. Obama continued to supply such lethal weaponry even as the slaughter in Yemen accelerated, and Trump continues this supply even still. In addition, the UN has been saying for some time, and it has just reiterated, that Yemen is now on the verge of a massive famine which could kill millions, and this would not be happening but for the US-Saudi war on that country. And yet this news is being greeted with the sound of crickets chirping.

Again, when you can obsess about the crimes of others, like Putin, you don't have to worry about your own country's horrible atrocities.

While the media has a field day worrying about Trump's allegedly being some type of Russian pawn, why is there so little concern about the real hold that the retrograde monarchy of Saudi Arabia has over the United States? President after President, Trump included, inexplicably continue to partner with the Saudi monarchy despite its suppression of women's rights, and its authoritarian nature, despite the fact that Saudi Arabia does more than any other country to spread Islamist terrorism, including in the form of al-Qaeda, and despite the fact that fifteen of the nineteen 9/11 attackers were Saudi. One might think this deserves some looking into. This is not even to mention the biggest elephant in the room, which is never to be spoken of, and that is Israel and its outsized influence over US foreign policy.

Meanwhile, Putin's Russia came much later to the game in Syria, not intervening militarily in that country until late September, 2015.[272] As *The Guardian* of London noted, "*[i]t was the first time that Russia had launched major military action outside the borders of the former Soviet Union since the end of the cold war.*" (emphasis added).

Let's just pause on this fact. While the dreaded Putin has been President on and off since 1999, he did not stray beyond the old Soviet borders, and really not all that far, until nearly the end of 2015. During that same time, the US has itself militarily intervened in Syria, both covertly and overtly through major bombing raids; engaged in its major bombing campaign of Serbia (very close to Russia); overthrew the democratically elected government of Jean Bertrand Aristide; invaded Afghanistan, which it has yet to leave; invaded Iraq, which it has yet to leave; engaged in what it termed "anti-terrorist" operations in Georgia (on the border of Russia), Djibouti, Kenya, Ethiopia, Yemen, and Eritrea; engaged in military actions in Somalia which ended up destabilizing that country for years to come; supported the coup against the democratic government of Manuel Zelaya in Honduras; and participated in the NATO invasion and dismantling of Libya.

It was the invasion of Libya, moreover, that would ultimately lead to Putin's decision to intervene in Syria. This was another case

of the West, the US included, removing a secular leader in Muammar Gaddafi, quite possibly the greatest enemy of al-Qaeda, and allowing the country to be overridden by religious extremists. Indeed, post-invasion, ISIS itself controls huge swaths of the country, including the once-prosperous town of Sirte, which lies on the Mediterranean close to Europe.[273] It is well-accepted that the Libyan invasion was the major precipitating event leading to the massive influx of refugees into Europe, with over 50,000 refugees entering Europe through Libya.[274]

In addition, the security of Tunisia, Mali and the Lake Chad Region (Nigeria, Niger, Chad, and Cameroon) has been profoundly undermined by the spill-over from the Libya conflict.[275] And, though the NATO intervention in Libya was allegedly undertaken on humanitarian grounds, the human rights situation in Libya is a disaster, as "thousands of detainees [including children] languish in prisons without proper judicial review," and "kidnappings and targeted killings are rampant."[276]

As the LA Times explained in an article entitled, "US Intervention In Libya Seen As a Cautionary Tale," "in three years [post-invasion] Libya has turned into the kind of place US officials most fear: a lawless land that attracts terrorists, pumps out illegal arms and drugs and destabilizes its neighbors." [277] It may be time to ask, how many cautionary tales do we need, for goodness' sake?

In any case, Vladimir Putin, who had been watching the US rampage through the Middle East like a bull in a china shop, finally decided that he had had enough, not just because of the ultimately disastrous results of the intervention, but because he rightly felt that Russia was bamboozled by NATO's act of regime change in Libya. Thus, Russia, along with China, ultimately abstained from the Security Council resolution (1973) which authorized military action in Libya because of its explicitly limited goal of only authorizing a no-fly zone to protect civilians. Neither Russia nor China wanted regime change in Libya and never authorized it.

And yet NATO wasted no time after setting up the no-fly zone

before moving quickly to regime change. When this became apparent, Putin, then Prime Minister, publicly stated that NATO had no right to engage in regime change,[278] and certainly had no right to kill Gaddafi as NATO was trying to do and ultimately helped to do. Indeed, Putin ultimately watched the video of Gaddafi being killed, and sodomized in the process, with horror, and this played a big part in his deciding that the same thing would not be allowed to play out in Syria with the similar disruptive results. Putin publicly described the killing as "repulsive," and publicly expressed his fear that the West was actively and intentionally moving to destabilize various societies, including Russia.[279]

For her part, Secretary of State Hillary Clinton famously responded to the violent murder of Gaddafi, not with horror, but with uncontrollable joy, saying, as she laughed maniacally, "we came, we saw, he died."[280] Of course, in making this statement, Clinton was channeling another great imperialist, Roman general and consul Julius Caesar, who is purported to have coined the similar phrase "*veni, vidi, vici*" (we came, we saw, we conquered). This is most appropriate, given that Clinton was the real architect behind NATO's imperial assault against Libya. And, as usual with such interventions, the Clinton team (Hillary, along with Samantha Power and Susan Rice), with the always-willing support of the media, peddled the most absurd lies to justify the NATO action.

The general lie which led the US and NATO into Libya, and promoted even by such left-wing sources as DemocracyNow!, was that we needed to intervene to protect the human rights of the Libyan people from Gaddafi. That is, the US, and Clinton's team in particular, put forth the now-commonly used pretext of humanitarian intervention. However, as Clinton's own emails show—the ones released by the US State Department, not the ones allegedly hacked—the Clinton team itself did not believe, by the time the intervention started on March 17, that there was an impending human rights disaster that the Libyans needed protection from.

As I wrote in a *Huffington Post* article in which I analyzed Clinton's

Libyan emails,[281] Huma Abedin emailed on February 21, 2011, nearly a
month before the intervention, that:

> Based on numerous eyewitness reports, it is the [US] Embassy's
> assessment that the [Gaddafi] government no longer controls Beng-
> hazi. This is likely the case for Ajdabiyah as well. Numerous sources in
> Benghazi report that Libyan Interior Minister Abdul Fattah Younes
> has "changed sides" and is "now with the protesters in Benghazi." The
> mood in Benghazi and Ajdabiyah is allegedly "celebratory" and all
> posters of Qadhafi have been knocked down. . . .

Then, on March 2, a couple of weeks before Resolution 1973 was
passed, Harriet Spanos of USAID sent an email describing the relative
calm in Benghazi. Thus, she explains that "Security Reports . . . confirm that Benghazi has been calm over the past couple of days." She
explains that "economic activity is going on in Benghazi," that shops
and banks are open and that "[m]obile and landline phones are working and Internet has returned."

Probably the most revealing email is dated March 30, 2011, just
eleven days into the NATO bombing campaign which would go on
until October, 20, when Qaddafi was finally murdered (after being
sodomized). In this email (C05782459), entitled "Win this War,"
Clinton's closest adviser, Sidney Blumenthal, makes it clear that, in
terms of the continuing reasons for the war, any *humanitarian motive
offered is limited, conditional and refers to a specific past situation.*" (emphasis added). In other words, while NATO would go on bombing for
another 7 months, Blumenthal is already admitting that there is really
no humanitarian basis for continuing the conflict.

Still, Blumenthal insists on the importance for pressing on until
final victory (i.e., the overthrow of Qaddafi, whom he calls "Q"). And,
he explains that the reasons for doing so include, first and foremost,
boosting Obama's then-anemic approval ratings. The other reasons he
outlines are "establishing security in North Africa, securing democracy

in Egypt and Tunisia, economic development, effect throughout Arab world and Africa, extending US influence, counter-balancing Iran, etc." Again, the pretext of saving Libyan lives is notably absent from this list.

Moreover, in terms of the alleged goal of promoting regional security, a number of emails reflect the awareness that the bombing campaign, and the toppling of the aggressively anti-al-Qaeda Gaddafi, might very well open a space for al-Qaeda and allied forces to take over many parts of Libya, as they actually have. For example, one email, again from Blumenthal to Clinton, explains that "[t]raditionally, the eastern part of Libya has been a stronghold for radical Islamist groups, including the al-Qaeda-linked Libyan Islamic Fighting Group. While Qaddafi's regime has been successful in suppressing the jihadist threat in Libya, the current situation opens the door for jihadist resurgence." Given this knowledge, how Blumenthal could then argue that "winning the war" against Qaddafi was somehow necessary for regional security is bizarre in the extreme.

Meanwhile, the emails actually demonstrate a complete lack of concern for humanitarian violations by the pro-NATO rebels. Thus, in but another email to Hillary, dated March 27, 2011, Blumenthal explains, "[s]peaking in strict confidence, one rebel commander stated that his troops continue to summarily execute all foreign mercenaries in the fighting." Now, summarily executing even armed combatants is a clear violation of the Geneva Conventions, but neither Blumenthal nor Hillary demonstrate much concern about such trifles.

Even more concerning, it became known during the course of the NATO invasion that the claims of foreign mercenaries fighting for Qaddafi were false;[282] that, in fact, the alleged foreign mercenaries were really African guest workers. What was really happening was that the rebels were summarily arresting and murdering people who happened to be black, and doing so in very large numbers.[283] In other words, it was the US's rebel friends who were actually carrying out genocide in Libya, and NATO, which had a UN mandate to protect civilians in Libya, was aiding and abetting them in doing it.

The most outrageous lie which primed the world for the Libya intervention was that Gaddafi was allegedly handing out Viagra to his troops so that they could carry out mass rape. I recall thinking when that claim was made with a straight face at that time by then-US Ambassador to the UN, Susan Rice—and of course repeated with equally straight face by Hillary Clinton and the US press—that this claim was patently absurd and not worthy of belief. Of course, human rights groups investigating this claim ultimately found no evidence of it.[284] But, the damage was done, paving the way for the NATO invasion and the takeover of Libya by forces who actually have, and continue to, carry out rape on a large scale.

The Clinton emails reveal one other important fact—that before and during the NATO conflict, Clinton and her team knew very well, and actually feared, that the conflict in Libya might very well have been resolved through negotiations; that indeed, Muammar Qaddafi's son Saif was actually trying to find ways to do just that.

Remember that, well before the invasion, the Gaddafi government had already been making great efforts in achieving rapprochement with Washington, giving up its nuclear arms, compensating victims of the Lockerby bombing and allowing for more (though not unrestricted) Western investment in Libya. As a number of commentators have argued persuasively, this was not enough for Washington, which was concerned that Gaddafi was still shutting the US and other Western countries out of a number of key infrastructure investment opportunities in favor of Russia and China.[285] This just would not do.

Consequently, Clinton shunned all efforts by the Gaddafis to avert an invasion, instead preferring a war—as Bill Clinton had preferred a war in Yugoslavia, and as both Bushes had preferred wars in Iraq—despite its quite predictably horrible consequences, which would give the US and its allies the hand they wanted in the future of Libyan and African affairs. In the end, the welfare of the Libyan people, and of the people of Northern Africa, were sacrificed, not protected, by such a choice.

Indeed, as with all of our supposed "humanitarian interventions," the cost to those enduring the intervention is always ignored. In the case of Libya, for example, no one seemed to care that, while NATO allegedly (though not plausibly) intervened to protect Benghazi, it proceeded to level the important port city of Sirte, which also happened to be the city in which the African Union was founded and which Gaddafi hoped would be the capital for a new United States of Africa, with its own currency in lieu of both the US dollar and the Euro. Quoting David Randall, a reporter from the *Independent* of London on this subject, author Maximillian Forte explains that Sirte after the NATO intervention "was found 'without an intact building,' with 'nearly every house . . . pulverized by a rocket or mortar, burned out or riddled with bullets'—'the infrastructure of a city upon which the Libyan leader lavished millions has simply ceased to exist.'" As Forte continues, eyewitnesses in Sirte described "endless rows of buildings on fire, corpses of the executed lying on hospital lawns, mass graves, homes looted and burned by insurgents, apartment blocks flattened by NATO bombs."

Meanwhile, Libya, with its advanced social system destroyed, went from being the most prosperous African nation pre-invasion to being the least prosperous. But, of course, this was all to the good, according to NPR, which reported that the Libyan workers would be coddled no more, and would be forced instead to enter the dog-eat-dog world of the free market that we all love. Thus, without tongue in cheek, or any note of irony, NPR, in its report, entitled, "Libya's Economy Faces New Tests After Gadhafi Era,"[286] explained that the biggest impediment to the new economic era is the Libyan worker who was simply spoiled by Gaddafi. NPR thus cited a 2007 book on the Libyan economy by authors Otman and Karlberg who called "the Libyan worker under Gadhafi 'one of the most protected in the world,'" receiving job tenure, government subsidies of around $800 a month for the average Libyan household, and gasoline at a mere 60 cents a gallon. NPR, citing the same book, explained that workers now freed from such a

tyrannical world by NATO bombs, have been left with a "subsidy men-tality" and a "job-for-life outlook which has ill-prepared Libyans for the more aggressive and cutthroat world of competition." But NPR assured the concerned listener that the new regime would see to it that the Libyans would adapt to this new world order and get to work as they damn well should.

Mission accomplished!

Not shockingly, however, other world leaders, such as Vladimir Putin, looked upon these events with grave concern, and even as directed against his country in particular, given that the US and NATO had demonstrated their willingness to ravage an entire country to keep countries like Russia out of the economic game there.

Moreover, the US blocked a UN statement, introduced by Rus-sia in the aftermath of the NATO invasion, to try to save the city of Bani Walid[287] (just as the original Security Council resolution which Russia permitted to be passed was at least ostensibly intended to save the town of Benghazi). The US blocked this resolution because it was now its jihadist friends who were threatening the city, and the US's "humanitarian concerns," if there were any, extended only to would-be victims of Gaddafi.

And the jihadists did a very thorough job of laying Bani Walid, and other areas of the country, to waste. As Amnesty International reported at the time:

> Bani Walid was among the last cities to fall under the control of anti-Gaddafi forces during Libya's internal [sic.] conflict last year. Hundreds of residents from Bani Walid have been arrested by armed militias. Many continue to be detained without charge or trial across Libyan prisons and detention centres, including Misratah. Many have been tortured or otherwise ill-treated. The entrance of anti-Gaddafi forces into Bani Walid in October 2011 was accompanied by wide-spread looting and other abuses.
>
> Thousands of individuals suspected of having fought for or

supported the government of Mu'ammar al-Gaddafi continue to be detained across Libya. The vast majority have yet to be officially charged or brought to trial. Since the fall of Tripoli and the vast majority of the country under the control of anti-Gaddafi forces in August 2011, human rights abuses by armed militias such as arbitrary arrest and detention; torture or other ill-treatment—including death; extrajudicial executions and forced displacement continued to take place in a climate of impunity. To date, armed militia seize people outside the framework of the law and hold them incommunicado in secret detention facilities, where they are vulnerable to torture of other ill-treatment.[288]

And, the mistreatment of the Bani Walid continues, with residents being subjected to "killings, sexual violence, torture and religious persecution."[289] The reaction of the US government and media has been, of course, a collective yawn.

Similarly, the heroic "freedom fighters" supported by the US (you may be starting to see a pattern here with U.S-backed "freedom fighters"), and spurred on by the Clinton and media lies about "black mercenaries" fighting for Qaddafi, laid waste to the all-black town of Tawergha, again with little attention given in the US to the carnage. Human Rights Watch continued to sound the alarm about this town a full two years after the intervention, stating: "[t]he Libyan government should take urgent steps to stop serious and ongoing human rights violations against inhabitants of the town of Tawergha, who are widely viewed as having supported Muammar Gaddafi. The forced displacement of roughly 40,000 people, arbitrary detentions, torture, and killings are widespread, systematic, and sufficiently organized to be crimes against humanity and should be condemned by the United Nations Security Council."[290] But, of course, given that these were the wrong victims, no one did condemn those who made them suffer.

As it turned out, Libya was just the first of numerous new military interventions the US would make in Africa. Indeed, "'barely a

month after the fall of Tripoli—and in the same month Gaddafi was murdered (October 2011)—the US announced it was sending troops to no less than four more African countries: the Central African Republic, Uganda, South Sudan and the Democratic Republic of Congo.'"[291] Still it is argued that it is Russia which is trying to take over the world.

In any case, the US/NATO destruction of Libya had two impacts *vis a vis* Russia. First, it undermined then-Russian President Dmitry Medvedev (Putin was Prime Minister at the time) in the eyes of Russians, who believed that he had been tricked by the West in assenting to the NATO intervention. As Stephen F. Cohen explained to me in an interview in 2015, if the West wanted Medvedev, viewed as the more moderate one between himself and Putin, to continue in the more powerful Presidential position, they made a huge error in setting him up as the fool by suckering him into believing that the intervention would merely take the form of a no-fly zone.

And indeed, in a 2015 interview on CNN, Obama claimed that he had wanted a "re-set" with Russia under Medvedev.[292] And, while Obama then goes on to, of course, blame Putin for subsequently preventing the "re-set" when he became President again, Obama takes no responsibility for his own conduct in undermining Medvedev and paving the way for the return of Putin, nor for his causing Putin to have a different view of the trustworthiness of the US after the Libya debacle.

Second, as indicated above, the intervention would play a role in leading Vladimir Putin, who would become President again in 2012, to decide to intervene militarily in Syria.

Of course, let us not forget that, before militarily intervening, Putin, notwithstanding his anger at Obama's Libya foray, pulled Obama's chestnuts out of the fire in Syria. Thus, in 2013, Putin brokered a deal over Syria's chemical weapons which saved Obama from having to greatly up the US's military intervention in Syria.[293] The reader may recall that, at that time, Obama believed that the "red line" he drew over the use of chemical weapons by the Assad government

may have been crossed (though it is not at all clear to this day that the chemical weapons use at issue was Assad's).

Quite masterfully, Putin stepped in and prevailed upon Assad to agree to have all of his chemical weapons destroyed under UN supervision to prevent an imminent attack by the US. As the *LA Times* noted at the time, "[b]y offering to broker a deal that would put Syria's chemical arsenal under control of international inspectors, the Russian president has forestalled a looming conflict and created a rare opportunity for international cooperation."[294]

It is also worth noting, in the same vein, that in 2015, Putin was instrumental in using his influence with Iran to help Obama broker the nuclear deal with that country, pursuant to which Iran agreed to limit its nuclear capability and not to pursue nuclear weapons. While Obama thanked Putin for his help at this time,[295] the US's gratitude would be short-lived, as per usual, with Putin becoming the US punching bag again in short order. But of course, as Putin knows all too well, no good deed goes unpunished.

Finally, it might also be recalled that Putin helped broker a peace deal in Syria that the United States, or at least its political leaders, agreed to, only for that deal to be scuttled within days when the US Central Command accidentally/on purpose[296] bombed a Syrian troop convoy, killing 62 soldiers and wounding 100.[297] As the *Washington Post* explained, this "marked the first time the United States has engaged the Syrian military since it began targeting the Islamic State in Syria and Iraq two years ago. The strike also came at a particularly sensitive time in US and Russian efforts to forge a cease-fire in Syria's civil war . . . ."[298]

This coincidence was simply too much for the Russians, who called an emergency meeting of the Security Council in response. Incredibly, US Ambassador to the UN Samantha Power feigned outrage, not in response to this ill-timed mass killing, which ensured there would be no peace soon in Syria, but in response to Russia's audacity in bringing

her into the UN on a weekend to hear Russia complain about who killed whom in Syria.

Thoughts of the foregoing event certainly come to my mind when friends on an almost daily basis talk about how allegedly crazy Vladimir Putin is. Honestly, it is not fathomable that he is crazier or more reckless than our leaders, who seem to make the most disastrous choices about whom our enemies and friends are, and I might suggest that it is their mental health that Americans should be worrying about.

13

THE REAL ATTACK ON US DEMOCRACY

THE US HAS A SEVERE DEMOCRACY deficit. Indeed, former President Jimmy Carter opined in July of 2015—well before anyone was concerned about alleged Russian interference—that America is no longer a democracy, but rather, "an oligarchy with unlimited political bribery being the essence of getting the nominations for president or being elected president. And the same thing applies to governors, and US Senators and congress members. So, now we've just seen a subversion of our political system as a payoff to major contributors, who want and expect, and sometimes get, favors for themselves after the election is over."[299]

As the *Washington Post* reported in March of 2016, US elections ranked dead last among Western democracies.[300] And, this is not because of Russia or Vladimir Putin. Rather, as the piece explained, it is because of the faulty, non-standardized election processes across the country, with long wait times for voting in some states, inaccurate voter registers in some locales and states, poorly trained poll workers and the breakdown of machines in states like New York. The US's poor ranking is also due, as the piece relates, to the disenfranchisement of voters, particularly people of color, through voter ID laws, as well as

to the unprecedented power that money has in the election process, a problem only exacerbated by the Supreme Court's *Citizens United* decision, which removed monetary caps on donations and opened the flood gates for secret PAC funding not subject to reporting requirements. And, of course, as the US becomes more economically unequal and disparate, this problem will only grow and magnify.

Other problems include partisan gerrymandering, particularly by the Republicans, and the removal of ex-felons who have served their time—or as we saw in Florida in 2000, thousands of individuals who were mistakenly listed as ex-felons—from the voter rolls. On this score, it is important to note that the US has over two million people in prisons—the largest absolute number as well as percentage of the population of any country on the planet—and a total of six million individuals under some type of "correctional supervision."[301] This is more people than were in Stalin's Gulag system at its height![302] And about half of the people in the US prison system are there as a result of non-violent drug offenses, which disproportionately capture African Americans in the system. This is not even to mention the outdated, anti-democratic Electoral College system, which allows someone (like Hillary Clinton, for example) to win the popular vote but lose the election anyway.

In short, the "land of the free" is not so free, and it is not so democratic. And, in the 2016 Presidential election, both major Parties ran the two most unpopular Presidential candidates in recorded memory, thereby leading many, particularly on the Democratic side, to either stay home on Election Day or vote Third Party.

I will show my cards at this point. I was one of those people who voted third party (Green) because I truly could not decide who was the lesser of the two evils in this election. For reasons I believe well-illustrated above, I could not vote for Hillary Clinton, who had a well-established record of maneuvering the US into destructive wars such as the one in Libya, and who was instrumental in making permanent the destruction of democracy in Honduras. I also could not

vote for Donald Trump, who ran on a racist and xenophobic platform that is simply unconscionable. The one redeeming attribute I did see in Trump, however, was the one at the heart of this book—that he wanted, for whatever reason, to make peace with Russia, which I sincerely believe is a worthy friend and ally.

In any case, I ended up going to the polls with the belief that both major candidates being offered to us were deeply flawed, but in different ways. And certainly, at least on the Democratic side, such an awful offering was not necessary, inevitable or desirable.

Thus, as we know specifically from the DNC emails that were either leaked or hacked, (more on that in a moment), the DNC was dead set against who could have been a more popular, change candidate in Bernie Sanders, from winning the nomination. We also know that the Clintons ran against the candidate they hoped to run against—Donald Trump—in a terrible miscalculation of his chances of winning.

Even after these historic errors which have now become quite apparent, the DNC just elected the establishment candidate, Tom Perez, as its new leader over the insurgent candidate, Keith Ellison, who was backed by Bernie Sanders, possibly sealing the Democrats' fate in the next round of elections.

Instead of doing some much needed soul-searching about how they contributed to their own loss in an election they should have been able to win easily, the Democrats have now seized upon a plan which is as dangerous as it is unprincipled, which, in my view unfortunately, appears to be working for them. To wit, they have decided to blame Russia for their own failings. This is not only misguided from the point of view of those, including myself, who would like to see a *revamped* Democratic Party poised to win the next election under the leadership of a Bernie Sanders or Elizabeth Warren, but it is also quite dangerous from the point of view of those concerned for world peace and security from nuclear war.

As an initial matter, the publication of the emails in question (that is, the Podesta and DNC emails, and not Clinton's emails, which were

voluntarily given to the State Department and are now up on the State Department's website) do not appear to have swung the election in favor of Donald Trump, and few consequently even claim this.

If any event seemed to undo Clinton's campaign in the eleventh hour, it is the infamous letter by FBI Director Comey, who announced, inexplicably to many observers, that the FBI's investigation into Hillary Clinton's private email server was still ongoing in light of emails found on the server of one Anthony Weiner—also a Democrat, and the husband at that time of Clinton's trusted adviser, Huma Abedin—in a separate investigation into Weiner's sexting with underage girls. Indeed, at the time, there was an outcry that Comey should be investigated for possible violations of the Hatch Act, which forbids government officials from engaging in conduct which could impact the outcome of an election.

It was in fact comical to hear Comey, in testifying about his investigation of the Russia-Trump collusion allegations on March 20, 2017, say that it was unusual for the F.B.I. to confirm or deny the existence of any investigations,[303] when that's exactly what he was doing at that moment, and exactly what he did just weeks before the 2016 election, thereby helping to derail Clinton's candidacy. This appears to be the case of the exception swallowing the rule.

In addition, it also seems quite convenient for Comey to now be pushing the Russian collusion story because it takes all the attention away from his own, greater misdeed (if not crime), which most certainly influenced the outcome of the 2016 elections. Indeed, it is just bizarre that he claims his bureau has been investigating the Trump-Russia connection since July 2016, but is only speaking up now. And, of course, he still isn't really saying anything, only confirming that the FBI is still investigating the matter.

For their part, the Democrats have largely stopped complaining about Comey's pre-election publication of the continuing FBI investigation into Clinton's emails, and for obvious reasons. While the Comey letter may have doomed Clinton's election bid, and may have been an

error in judgment if not much worse, the letter certainly grew out of wounds self-inflicted by the Democrats themselves.

First of all, Hillary Clinton herself, as she has admitted on several occasions, committed a huge error in judgment by maintaining a private, unsecured email server as Secretary of State. If she had not committed such a lapse in judgment, the Comey letter obviously never would have come about. And, of course, you have the ticking time bomb of Anthony Weiner, whose obsessive and bizarre sexting also played a role in this letter being issued. While it may not be polite to do so, one might also wonder what Huma was thinking by not having thrown Weiner to the curb a long time before, again possibly averting the Comey disaster. In any case, the Comey letter, as damaging as it was, is an inconvenient fact for the Democrats to focus on for these reasons.

And so the Democrats, having nothing to offer the American people in terms of policies, have now seized upon the allegation that Putin personally ordered the hacking of the DNC, with the knowledge and complicity of the Trump campaign, in order to help Trump get elected, and that the Wikileaks regular release of the product of this hacking was part of this plan. And the Democrats are pushing this alibi with reckless abandon. One example of this is the following press statement by former Speaker Nancy Pelosi: "[t]he possibility of Trump officials conspiring with a foreign adversary to influence a US election represents a grave threat to our national security and our democracy, and the American people deserve answers."

My first response to such hysterics would be: even assuming, for the sake of argument, that the Russian hacking claims were true, why should we truly care? First, no one really believes the emails did much, if anything, to affect the outcome of the election, and so the "no harm, no foul rule" may properly be invoked here.

Moreover, as I believe I have illustrated in great detail above, such an act on the part of the Kremlin would be mere child's play compared to the election interventions and even violent coups and regime changes the US has instigated and/or supported throughout the globe

over many decades, including by Hillary Clinton herself in the case of Libya and Honduras.

On this score, I cite a recent *New Yorker* article on the Russian hacking story that is accompanied by a graphic of a hovering, upside-down St. Basil's Cathedral (which most people mistakenly believe is the nearby Kremlin) ominously firing a laser down at The White House. Even this article, whose graphic tells you where they are coming from on this matter, begrudging acknowledges that "[t]he C.I.A., for its part, worked to overthrow regimes in Iran, Cuba, Haiti, Brazil, Chile, and Panama. It used cash payments, propaganda, and sometimes violent measures to sway elections away from leftist parties in Italy, Guatemala, Indonesia, South Vietnam, and Nicaragua."[304] While the *New Yorker*, as most other media sources, warns nonetheless of making "false moral equivalences" between the conduct of the US and Russia in such respects, let me say that I would never do that: the US conduct is so much worse that equating the two would not at all be fair to Russia.

In short, the outrage some Americans, mostly aligned with the Democratic Party, are expressing about the alleged Russian hacking just seems silly in light of our own track record of interfering with, and indeed destroying, democratic institutions around the globe. But again, the ferocity of the Democrats' expressions of concern on this issue is inversely proportional to what they have to offer the American people in terms of real policies.

If Putin had truly instigated a bit of computer hacking to undermine the credibility of someone who views him as another Hitler (Clinton has openly said just this), and to provide some (very minimal) support for the other candidate, who might lift sanctions against his country—sanctions which are costing Russia's already struggling economy up to 1.5% GDP per annum[305]—forgive me if my conscience is not shocked by this. And, notice how carefully I have worded this. As the *New Yorker* explains, it is very likely that Putin did not try, and did not even believe he could, affect the outcome of the election; he simply

wanted to be a conspicuous thorn in Clinton's side.[306] Again, this does not seem like anything to be too alarmed about.

And indeed, as the same *New Yorker* piece notes, the Obama Administration, which was well aware of the hacking issue during the summer, was so alarmed that it did virtually nothing in response. As the piece explains, as November, 2016 approached:

> The White House watched for signs that Russian intelligence was crossing what a senior national-security official called "the line between covert influence and adversely affecting the vote count"— and found no evidence that it had done so. At the time, Clinton was leading in the race, which, the official said, reinforced Obama's decision not to respond more aggressively. "If we have a very forceful response, it actually helps delegitimize the election."[307]

Finally, there is good reason to be skeptical of the claims surrounding this alleged plot. Let us recall, first of all, how other similar claims have been made in the past about our ostensible foes, only to be seriously questioned, if not debunked, later and then forgotten. One such alleged plot that comes to mind is the "North Korea hacked Sony" scandal a couple years back. Remember that one? Probably not so well because it has been long forgotten. And, it was quickly forgotten because it appears to have been untrue. Thus, in the end, after the FBI quickly pointed the finger at North Korea—impossibly quickly in the minds of many computer experts—and after the media gleefully went along, the press had to sheepishly admit later that the hacking was most likely an "inside job" by a disgruntled Sony employee.[308] Well, I guess it's good we didn't end up nuking North Korea over this anyway.

For what it is worth, legendary computer expert John McAfee, who correctly stated at the time that North Korea was not behind the Sony hack, guarantees that Russia was not behind the DNC hack. As he explains:

I can promise you it was not the Russians who hacked the Democratic National Committee (DNC). The software used was way too
old. The state hackers would not use an old version of software which
was less functional than the updated versions . . . . One of the things
that the CIA said and I've been saying for years is that it is virtually
impossible to find attribution for any hack because a good hacker
can hide their tracks plus make it look like someone else did it. This
happens all the time.[309]

McAfee believes, as I do, that the Russian hack story is a political-
ly-motivated ploy being pushed mainly by the Democrats who revile
Vladimir Putin, and, in my view, are desperately in need of a scapegoat
for their recent election loss.

In addition, let us consider the source of "Russia-gate,"the Russia-Trump conspiracy theory. One of the biggest players pushing
the hack theory—amongst the seventeen intelligence agencies that
allegedly have signed off on this (talk about bureaucratic redundan-
cies!)[310]—is the CIA. And there is indeed some reasonable suspicion
that the CIA is, at a minimum, lying about the Russians having hacked
the DNC, or even that the CIA was the one who procured and leaked
the DNC emails themselves in order to set up the Russians.

Let us then examine the CIA in this matter as any investigator
would a suspect in a criminal case: analyzing its propensity for carrying out such an act, its motive for doing so, and whether it had the
means and opportunity for the alleged wrongdoing.

As the reader might garner from the discussion above, the CIA is
not a reliable source, and in fact, truth be told, poses a much greater
threat to US democracy than Russia ever could, which makes it all the
more baffling that rank 'n file liberals are now cozying up to the CIA in
the midst of this "hacking scandal." To put a finer point on it, the CIA
is a nefarious, criminal organization which often misleads the American public and government into wars and misadventures which they
would have been much better off to avoid, and it should have been

done away with long ago.[311] (For more on this, see my friend Douglas Valentine's book *The CIA As a Criminal Organization*).

Legend has it that, after the Bay of Pigs fiasco, Jack and Bobby Kennedy, who were told wrongly (as per usual) by the CIA that the Cubans would rise up against Fidel Castro during this counter-revolutionary uprising, decided to disperse the CIA to the four corners of the earth. I do not know if that is truth or apostasy, but what is known is that the Kennedys never trusted the CIA after the Bay of Pigs, feeling that they had been misled about the chances of success of the operation.[312] Indeed, while the CIA had concluded that only direct US intervention against Cuba would succeed (rather than simply relying upon Cuban exiles to do the job for the US, as was done in the Bay of Pigs) it never bothered sharing this assessment with President Kennedy beforehand.[313] For a president like Trump to be wary of the CIA would not make him much of an outlier, at least when compared to Kennedy.

In any case, someone should have long ago, and certainly should now, destroy the dreaded institution of the CIA, which, among many other famous crimes, provided much of the bogus "evidence" of WMDs which justified the US invasion of Iraq in 2003.[314]

Not only is the CIA an unreliable and suspect source, it also has the motive for at least claiming the Russians hacked the DNC emails, if it did not go the further step of actually stealing the emails themselves and then pinning it on the Russians.

As the Veterans of US Intelligence Services eloquently point out, the CIA, as evidenced by their own quite unprecedented public warnings to Trump, is against a détente with Russia.[315] Of course this makes perfect sense, for as George Kennan explained years ago, such a détente is simply bad for business, in particular the business of war which so profoundly undergirds the US economy, and which also ensures that the capital that is generated is siphoned off to the few rich on top instead of being wasted on social programs for the unwashed masses.

And, the CIA has, quite uncharacteristically, shown its cards with regard to its desire that Trump not get any strange notions about

ending the new Cold War, and has even publically made not-so-veiled threats against him in the event he does. As award-winning journalist Gareth Porter said so well, then-CIA Director John Brennan, "[i]n an interview with Fox News, . . . said, 'I think Mr. Trump has to understand that absolving Russia of various actions that it's taken in the past number of years is a road that he, I think, needs to be very, very careful about moving down.'"[316] Porter goes on to quote Graham Fuller, who was a CIA operations officer for 20 years and National Intelligence Officer for the Middle East for four years under President Reagan, that, clearly, Brennan and others in the intelligence community are "dismayed at any prospect that the official narrative against Russia could start falling apart under Trump, and want to maintain the image of constant and dangerous Russian intervention into affairs of state."

As with the CIA's claims about WMDs, the US media has been all too willing to accept and regurgitate the CIA's claims about Russian hacking and Trump's alleged conspiracy with Russia to steal the election. A journalist I trust, Pulitzer Prize winner Seymour Hersh, has properly condemned the media for accepting these claims at face value.[317] I join Hersh, if he would allow me to, in asking, where is the evidence for this?

Indeed, we may have to continue asking this pointed question, as even a number of Democratic leaders are now warning their base. Thus, as Glenn Greenwald wrote in *The Intercept* on March 16, 2017, in the face of the Russia conspiracy frenzy, which has now become a "fixation" of the Democratic rank 'n file, "former acting CIA chief Michael Morell. . . . one of Clinton's most vocal CIA surrogates . . . appeared at an intelligence community forum to 'cast doubt' on 'allegations that members of the Trump campaign colluded with Russia.'"

As Greenwald continues, "'[o]n the question of the Trump campaign conspiring with the Russians here, there is smoke, but there is no fire at all,'" he [Morell] said, adding, "There's no little campfire, there's no little candle, there's no spark. And there's a lot of people looking for

it.'" Not only are they looking for it, I would emphasize, but they have been looking for it since July of 2016, and still haven't found anything. This is quite revealing.

Greenwald relates that Morell's comments echo the categorical remarks by Obama's top national security official, James Clapper, who told *Meet the Press* last week that during the time he was Obama's DNI, he saw no evidence to support claims of a Trump/Russia conspiracy." Similarly, the Senate Intelligence Committee, according to Greenwald, is starting to panic about the real possibility that no evidence of collusion between Trump and Putin will be found.

In addition, the Veterans of US Intelligence Services ("Veterans") find the claims quite dubious. They believe, in fact, that the DNC emails at issue were leaked (by someone within the DNC), and not hacked by Russia or anyone else.[318] As they explain, the NSA, which has not fully embraced the hacking theory, is "vacuuming up intelligence like crazy." And, with the technology they have—technology we know about from the leaks (not hacks) of Snowden—these Veterans explain, the NSA should be able to say with certainty who hacked the information, if it were hacked, and to whom that hacked information was sent. The fact that the NSA cannot do this, as it admits, demonstrates to the Veterans that the information was not in fact hacked at all, but leaked, for example by someone in the DNC copying the emails on a thumb drive and then sharing it from there. Such a leak—as opposed to a hack—would not have been detected by the NSA, the Veterans claim.

Of course, the other theory is that there was a hack, the NSA knows who did it, but won't say because the source of the hack is not a convenient culprit. This brings us to the new revelations of Wikileaks, which have been made as I write this book. To wit, Wikileaks has released a veritable treasure trove of CIA documents, which (1) justify fearing that organization much more than Putin; and (2) prove that the CIA had the means to hack the DNC itself and make it look like the Russians did it.

As for the first issue, The *New York Times* explains[319] that the Wikileaks documents reveal

> that the C.I.A. and allied intelligence services have managed to compromise both Apple and Android smartphones, allowing their officers to bypass the encryption on popular services such as Signal, WhatsApp and Telegram.

If this doesn't make you feel less secure about your privacy and the safety of your information and communications, I don't know what will.

But more to the point, the Wikileaks documents show that the CIA has possession of foreign hacking-software tools, including Russian, which they could have used to hack the DNC themselves and make it look like someone else did it. Again, The *New York Times*:

> Another program described in the documents, named Umbrage, is a voluminous library of cyberattack techniques that the C.I.A. has collected from malware produced by other countries, *including Russia*. According to the WikiLeaks release, the large number of techniques allows the C.I.A. to mask the origin of some of its attacks and confuse forensic investigators.[320]

(emphasis added). As a number of commentators have pointed out, what this reveal "means is that current efforts by Democratic Party leaders and . . . leakers in the government intelligence sector to pin the blame on Russia for hacking the election or for trying to help elect Trump as president, now must confront the counter-argument that . . . the CIA, may have been behind the hacks, but is making it look like the Russians did it."[321]

It is also important here to discuss the other Russia-related concern with Trump—that Russia is somehow blackmailing Trump with compromising evidence (of possibly a sexual nature). I would first

suggest that Trump appears to be blackmail proof, as he weathered so many scandals, sexual and otherwise, with ease, and is most likely correct that he could kill someone and still not lose the support of his sizable base.

Moreover, as Greenwald explains in the March 16, 2017 edition of *The Intercept*, "Obama's former CIA chief [Michael Morrell] also cast serious doubt on the credibility of the infamous, explosive 'dossier' originally published by BuzzFeed, saying that its author, Christopher Steele, paid intermediaries to talk to the sources for it. The dossier, he said, 'doesn't take you anywhere, I don't think.'"

More disturbingly, there is in fact good reason to believe that it is not the Russians at all who are blackmailing Trump, but rather, the CIA itself. Thus, from what we have been given to know, it was not the Russians who came to Trump to tell him that they had incriminating evidence on him, as any blackmailer would do. No, it was the CIA—who we know wants to pressure Trump into staying on the path toward confrontation with Russia—that not only went to Trump to tell him about the allegedly incriminating evidence on him, but also went to a number of other government officials and the public to let them know about this "evidence."

Indeed, even The *New York Times*, which describes the dossier shown to Trump and various officials as a *"summary of unsubstantiated reports* that Russia had collected compromising and salacious personal information" on him, explains that

> [t]he decision of top intelligence officials to give the president, the president-elect and the so-called Gang of Eight—Republican and Democratic leaders of Congress and the intelligence commit-tees—*what they know to be unverified, defamatory material* was extremely unusual.

(emphasis added). This conduct of US intelligence officials is not only "unusual," I would contend, but totally improper. This certainly

sounds like the conduct of a blackmailer, and it is incredible that so few in the mainstream press are concerned about the plausible black-mailing operation, by our own government, of a now-sitting US President.

The same, of course, can be said of the intelligence community's successful attempt to remove Mike Flynn, another open friend of Russia—friendship with Russia apparently being a high crime these days —as National Security Adviser. First of all, if it is true that Flynn (whom I otherwise have a lot of concerns about aside from Russia) might have spoken to the Russian Ambassador—after Trump was elected, and when it was clear that Flynn would have an official role in his administration—about the possibility of easing sanctions against Russia in the future, I don't see how that it is some crime. Of course, Flynn denies this.

It seems that, in reality, it was not the fact of the communication with the Russian Ambassador (and not a spy after all), but the sub-stance of it—which somehow threatened that peace might break out between the two countries—that was the problem.

On this point, I am in agreement with Dennis Kucinich, who broke ranks with fellow liberals over this issue, that the real crime here was the US intelligence community's spying on Flynn, and then leaking what they found to the press, in a successful attempt to remove Flynn for trying to do something constructive with Russia.[322] Indeed, such conduct by an intelligence agency is itself a great breach of the public trust. As Gareth Porter explains:

> The implications of the coy revelation of the Flynn conversation with [Ambassador] Kislyak were far-reaching. Any interception of a communication by the NSA or the FBI has always been considered one of the most highly classified secrets in the US intelligence uni-verse of secrets. And officers have long been under orders to protect the name of any American involved in any such intercepted commu-nication at all costs.

But the senior official who leaked the story of Flynn-Kislyak conversation to Ignatius—obviously for a domestic political purpose—did not feel bound by any such rule. That leak was the first move in a concerted campaign of using such leaks to suggest that Flynn had discussed the Obama administration's sanctions with Kislyak in an effort to undermine Obama administration policy.[323]

In addition to the allegations about Flynn's communications with the Russian Ambassador, the Democrats have tried to portray Flynn as being on the Russian payroll. As journalist Robert Parry explains in debunking such claims, while the Democrats try to point to Flynn's receiving payments from "several Russia-related entities, totaling nearly $68,000," the largest share of the payments came from a speech he made at an anniversary dinner for RT News, for which he received a net of $45,386.[324] As Parry explains, this sum is dwarfed by the sums others have received from similar affairs, for example, by former President Bill Clinton, who "received $500,000 for a Moscow speech from a Russian investment bank with ties to the Kremlin . . . ."

This sum is also dwarfed by the millions of dollars the Clinton Foundation has received over the years from Saudi Arabia[325]—a country that is supporting jihadists throughout the Middle East and Northern Africa, that supplied most of the 9/11 attackers, and that bizarrely seems to have much more influence over US foreign policy than it should given this fact, its repressive nature, and its relatively slight stature internationally. It is such a relationship that should be much more troubling to the American people than the quite paltry one Flynn seems to have had with Russia.

Still, the McCarthyite witch hunt against those who would dare even speak with or to the Russians continues, with Jeff Sessions now under investigation for his possible conversations with the Russian Ambassador before Trump took office.

Again, I am no fan of Jeff Sessions, Mike Flynn or Donald Trump, but at the same time, I take great umbrage at the use of the new Russian

Scare to attack them, and again, to attack the one policy of Trump's that actually makes sense. That Trump is right on Russia only proves the old adage that a broken clock is right twice a day.

Moreover, even if Trump's friendliness with Russia may be motivated by his business interests—Obama's Ukraine policy may have been motivated at least in part by the Ukrainian business interests of Vice-President Biden's son Hunter, as I explain above[326]—this does not in itself make it wrong.

14

GIVE PEACE A CHANCE

WE NOW FACE SOME OF THE greatest crises that humanity and the earth have ever seen—global warming, terrorism, nuclear proliferation, mass poverty and constant wars. To ally with a country like Russia to confront such challenges makes all the sense in the world.

Obama himself once talked about "our Sputnik" moment—a reference, of course, to the US's great strides with our space program, motivated largely by Russia's own strides before us. Not only did a once-strong Russia propel us to great advances in space travel, and consequently in science, but it is well-known that it also helped shame us into advances in civil rights as well as the creation of the very first human rights institution, the International Labor Organization (ILO) in 1918. And, of course, it was a brave and reliable ally in both WWI and WWII.

To shun the Russians now simply makes no sense, and the fact that it is Trump who is pushing a sensible policy towards Russia does not make this policy any less sane. Indeed, I agree wholeheartedly with Russian expert Robert David English, who recently wrote in *Foreign Affairs*[327]:

> Trump has enunciated a clear three-part position on Russia, which contrasts strongly with that of most of the US political elite.

First, Trump seeks Moscow's cooperation on global issues; second, he believes that Washington shares the blame for soured relations; and third, he acknowledges "the right of all nations to put their own interests first," adding that the United States does "not seek to impose our way of life on anyone."

The last of these is an essentially realist position, and if coherently implemented could prove a tonic. For 25 years, Republicans and Democrats have acted in ways that look much the same to Moscow. Washington has pursued policies that have ignored Russian interests (and sometimes international law as well) in order to encircle Moscow with military alliances and trade blocs conducive to US interests. It is no wonder that Russia pushes back. The wonder is that the US policy elite doesn't get this, even as foreign-affairs neophyte Trump apparently does.

In short, Trump's at-least-stated goal of finding ways to cooperate with Russia (though it is never clear exactly what Trump may truly be thinking or intending) is reasonable on its face and should be welcomed.

Conversely, courting a confrontation with Russia, as I believe large segments of the US government are willing if not eager to do, and as Trump may himself decide to do if he is goaded enough by the media and liberal establishment, who accuse him of being "too soft" on Russia—just as Johnson was goaded into invading Vietnam because he feared being accused of being "too soft" on Communism—is the height of folly. This not only risks a nuclear conflagration, but it will certainly serve as justification for the US's continued military expenditures and expansion, both of which are undermining the real security of the United States as well as the lives of thousands of innocents abroad.

As I tried to detail above, though not exhaustively, we have been lied and misled into nearly every war we have been involved in—by both the government and by the press which seems to be captured by

it—and the results of these wars, if not the aims, have been the opposite of what we were told they were.

The war in Vietnam, for example, was not about defending democracy, but about destroying it. The War on Terror quickly morphed into something else which actually spread the very terror, and from the very sources (e.g., Saudi Arabia), which we claimed to be fighting. The War on Drugs has done as much to spread drugs as to combat them. And our "humanitarian interventions" have only undermined the human rights and well-being of the peoples for whom we claimed to be fighting.

Meanwhile, the US, in the name of freedom and democracy, has fought against nearly every war of liberation waged by the peoples of the Third World, and has many times partnered with right-wing fascist forces, including in Ukraine at the present. And up until 1991, the US has justified such reactionary wars based on claims (usually exaggerated if not absolutely false) that the USSR was somehow behind these indigenous struggles for self-determination.

The current demonization of Russia will be used, and is indeed currently being used in such theaters as Ukraine and Syria, for similar purposes—to justify unjust wars that destroy the lives of poor people abroad; to sacrifice the lives of our poor, who are largely recruited into the armed forces for economic reasons; to deplete this country's rich resources on the continued build-up of our over-bloated military to the detriment of much-needed infrastructure and social spending; and to greatly increase our carbon footprint.

While the Democrats see the Russia-baiting as a way to get rid of Trump, either through impeachment, or in the next election, they must realize that this is a short-sighted gamble that is both unlikely to succeed, and that will do much harm to international relations even if it does. They would be better to focus on principled fights over health care, infrastructure improvement, jobs, a living wage, and ratcheting down our reliance on the military, rather than pursuing this short-end game.

Even as I write this, President Trump is proposing a massive increase in the military budget, while also proposing to slash federal jobs and social benefits. He is also doubling down on the US's involvement in the slaughter in Yemen and upping the US's aggressive posture towards Iran and North Korea. This is the exact opposite of what we should be doing, and this must be resisted.

Sadly, those who used to resist such things (liberals, for lack of a better term), have become so inured to ridiculous military spending and adventures when "their guy" is in power that they won't even resist such things when a Republican is in power. There is nearly no debate in this society about war and peace—one of the most profound and pressing issues a society must grapple with—and that is one of the greatest tragedies that I can see. The liberal Russia bashing only further precludes such discussion.

In the end, it is important for American citizens, both liberal and conservative, to stand against such madness, and to stand for a foreign policy based upon reason and facts. Confrontation with Russia is justified by neither of these.

AFTERWORD

A LOT HAS HAPPENED SINCE I wrote this book in the spring of 2017. While President Donald Trump and Vladimir Putin met at the G20 Summit and agreed to work together on a host of issues, including a cease fire in Syria and a resolution of the crisis in Ukraine, few in the United States applauded this progress. There was also much grinding and gnashing of teeth as Trump announced that he would end the CIA's covert operation to arm anti-Assad rebels in Syria,[328] a move which seems quite reasonable given the reality that the myth of the "moderate rebel" in Syria has been just that—a myth—perpetuated by the mainstream media long after any such rebels continued to exist.[329]

Trump and Putin's apparently successful meeting notwithstanding, the United States is now putting Patriot missiles in the Baltics along the Russian border, for the first time ever, and NATO just admitted another Eastern European nation, Macedonia, into its ranks.

And so, it sadly does not appear that peace between the United States and Russia is breaking out anytime soon, and there are those on both sides of the aisle who do not welcome such peace.

Thus, for example, former DNC Chair Donna Brazile disparagingly referred to Russia on Twitter as "[t]he Communists," and when told that Russia is no longer Communist, replied, "[t]hey no longer call themselves KGB either." More ominously, Democratic campaign

operative and close associate of the Clintons, Paul Begala, recently opined that the United States should bomb Russia's intelligence services in response to the alleged Russian interference in the US elections.

Of course, as we know now from the book *Shattered*, the whole blame-the-Russians excuse for Hillary Clinton's loss was consciously hatched within twenty-four hours of her concession speech by campaign manager Robby Mook and campaign chair John Podesta, and the Democrats have continued to push this excuse ever since.[330] And they continue to push this issue, moreover, despite the fact that polls show that rank 'n file Democrats have tired of the issue and are more interested in bread-and-butter issues such as health care and jobs,[331] and despite the fact that at least one study concluded that Clinton may in fact have lost the 2016 election because voters in war-weary areas of Pennsylvania, Michigan and Wisconsin saw her as a warmonger.[332] Meanwhile, despite—or possibly because of—the ceaseless playing of the blame-the-Russians card, Hillary Clinton's popularity has plummeted, with polls showing that she is even less popular than the quite unpopular Donald Trump.[333]

In addition, the Russia-gate scandal has drawn attention away from the home-grown threats to American democracy, such as the scandal uncovered by intrepid journalist Greg Palast who has written about the fact that the Republicans may have indeed stolen the 2016 elections by removing over one million voters of color from the voting rolls in key states.[334] That the Democrats have not seized upon this report seems the height of folly, though I suppose that their argument that "the Russians stole our democracy" starts to ring hollow when one acknowledges the fact that there was in fact little democracy to steal in the first place.

For its part, the influential think-tank Rand Corporation has suggested that NATO consider how it could "neutralize" Russia's military installations in Kaliningrad. Even more concerning, the Bulletin of Atomic Sciences has concluded that the United States' current modernization of its nuclear weapons systems, begun under Obama,

is intended to afford the United States first strike capability against Russia. The world is indeed on the precipice of disaster.

Meanwhile, the US House of Representatives voted in favor of a military budget *even bigger than Trump had asked for*. And, as Erik Sherman at *Forbes* magazine eloquently pointed out, 60 percent of the Democrats voted for this outsized military budget which totals $695.5 billion.[335] As Sherman explains, "[i]n other words, of the party that supposedly opposes rampant military spending and the Trump administration, 60% voted for this bill," at a time "[w]hen income inequality combines with systemic and systematic redistribution of virtually all income growth to the wealthiest while their taxes are reduced."[336]

Sherman of course hints at a truth which must be accepted—that the Democrats are not, and really never have been, a party which "opposes rampant military spending." There is bi-partisan consensus on such spending, and there is very little debate on lowering it. And this is for a number of reasons, one of which being that military spending is very lucrative for the arms manufacturers who bilk the quite willing Pentagon, and by extension the taxpayers; indeed, these are the biggest welfare cheats who few will acknowledge. Again, Sherman explains, "the Pentagon has been incapable of fiscal responsibility. This is the body that, according to news reports last fall, tried to hide $125 billion in wasted spending over a five year program. It's the only agency in the entire federal government *still* unable to pass a financial audit. And *it›s handed the largest check even as the Cold War is long over*, no other country has our military power, and major new weapons systems have been outright disasters and money sinks."[337]

Of course, as we know, while the first Cold War may be over, we are smack dab in the midst of a new one, and it is the Russia-gate canard which is helping to keep it going and grow in intensity, and thus justify both continued military spending and belligerence. Glenn Greenwald recently explained in *The Intercept* how Russia-gate is being used to justify the deepening alliance between the Democratic Party and the once-disgraced neocons:

One of the most under-discussed yet consequential changes in the
American political landscape is the reunion between the Democratic
Party and the country's most extreme and discredited neocons. . . . A
newly formed and, by all appearances, well-funded national security
advocacy group, devoted to more hawkish U.S. policies toward Russia
and other adversaries [such as Iran], provides the most vivid evidence
yet of this alliance. Calling itself the Alliance for Securing Democracy,
the group describes itself as 'a bipartisan, transatlantic initiative,' that
"will develop comprehensive strategies to defend against, deter, and
raise the costs on Russian and other state actors' efforts to undermine democracy and democratic institutions," and also "will work to
publicly document and expose Vladimir Putin's ongoing efforts to
subvert democracy in the United States and Europe.[338]

As for Putin's alleged "ongoing efforts to subvert democracy" in
Europe and elsewhere, it must be emphasized that all the claims in
this regard have been successfully debunked in recent months. Thus,
as nicely catalogued by the online muckraking journal *Moon of Alabama*, the mainstream media has ultimately had to admit, though quite
sheepishly, that their original claims that Russia hacked Ukraine artil-
lery units, the German Parliament, the recent French Presidential elections, the Qatar news agency and the UK Parliament were all false.[339]
The same journal also notes that the hysterical claims shortly after the
2016 election that Russia hacked the Vermont electrical grid were ultimately found, as admitted by *The Washington Post*, to be false.

Other fake, or at least highly suspect, news has continued to pro-
liferate, with those who question this news vilified. A notable example
is the alleged chemical attack in Syria on April 6, 2017, which was said
to claim the lives of around seventy civilians.

This ostensible attack, meanwhile, occurred less than two weeks
after the US bombing raid in Mosul, Iraq, which killed nearly three
hundred and which the *LA Times* described as "one of the largest attacks on civilians in recent memory."[340] What's more, by some

reports, Trump had killed around one thousand people in both Iraq and Syria in just the month of March alone,[341] and this body count has continued to mount. Of even more concern, Trump has also continued Obama's policy of aiding and abetting Saudi Arabia in its one-sided war upon Yemen, the poorest nation on earth, putting at least seven million people at risk of imminent starvation. Due to this war, Yemen is now suffering the greatest cholera outbreak in modern history, with 128 children under five dying every day. However, there were few, even amongst the anti-Trump "resistance," who have raised a voice against Trump's massacres of civilians in foreign lands, just as they didn't care about Obama's.

But then, seventy civilians are killed in Syria by an alleged chemical attack—an attack which the media concluded with great certainty and with great rapidity was the doing of the Russian-backed Assad government—and now everyone was calling for action. And action they got. Thus, to much applause, Trump launched fifty-nine Tomahawk missiles at Syria in an action which, by all accounts, accomplished nothing but inflaming tensions in an already tense region of the world. However, Trump did see his only spike in his ratings as a direct result of this attack.

That we have so often been tricked into war, and that the chemical attack suspiciously happened just one day after Trump said that we had to accept the idea of Assad as president of Syria, were simply not fair game for comment. Those who noted such pesky truths, and who have consequently asked for proof—for example, military veteran and Democratic Congressperson Tulsi Gabbard—have been pilloried for daring to merely ask questions. When veteran journalist and Pulitzer-prize winner Seymour Hersh published a story saying that the US military knew all along, and communicated to Trump immediately, that the Russians and Syrians did not carry out a chemical attack as claimed,[342] this elicited a collective shrug from the media which continued to be wedded to their original narrative. Indeed, for his offense of continuing to question the prevailing, pro-war narrative of the mainstream

media, Hersh has been relegated to publications further and further from US shores, with the aforementioned piece being published in the German outlet, *Welt*.

As for the greater Russia-gate story, much of that has begun to fall apart as well, though again you would not know it from the mainstream press which seems absolutely obsessed with the issue. It turns out that the long-time claim that seventeen intelligence agencies concluded that Russia was responsible for the hacking of the DNC e-mails was never true, and that hand-picked analysts from only three agencies were responsible for this report, as the *Associated Press* and *New York Times* had to later admit.[343] And, of course, none of these agencies ever analyzed the allegedly-hacked computer themselves because the DNC refused to turn over the computer for government analysis. Instead, it turned the computer over to a private security firm, Crowd Strike, to do the analysis.[344] And, as the Veteran Intelligence Professionals for Sanity stated in a July 24, 2017 article, they are now convinced that the information on the DNC computer was leaked by insiders, and not hacked by the Russians. As this group explains:

> After examining metadata from the "Guccifer 2.0" July 5, 2016 intrusion into the DNC server, independent cyber investigators have concluded that an insider copied DNC data onto an external storage device, and that "telltale signs" implicating Russia were then inserted.
>
> Key among the findings of the independent forensic investigations is the conclusion that the DNC data was copied onto a storage device at a speed that far exceeds an Internet capability for a remote hack. Of equal importance, the forensics show that the copying and doctoring were performed on the East coast of the U.S. Thus far, mainstream media have ignored the findings of these independent studies.[345]

It appeared that the Russia-gate narrative might finally implode after a CNN producer was caught on tape saying that CNN's coverage

of this issue was largely "bullshit" and being done simply to boost ratings. This admission coincided with CNN's retraction of a story purporting to link Trump associate and hedge-fund manager, Anthony Scaramucci, to a Russian investment firm—a story which turned out to be untrue—and the subsequent resignation of three CNN journalists responsible for the story.

However, as we all know, the Russia saga was quickly revived with the revelation of a meeting which Donald Trump, Jr. had with a Russian lawyer named Natalia Veselnitskaya and several others. What we know about the meeting is that Trump, Jr. eagerly went to it upon the promise that he would receive damaging information on Hillary Clinton from a Russian government source. As far as we know, though, no such information was given and instead the conversation turned to the issue of the 2012 Magnitsky Act, a US sanctions bill meant to punish human rights abusers in Russia, and to Putin's retaliatory measures forbidding US adoption of Russian children.[346] Moreover, it turns out that Natalia Veselnitskaya is most likely not a Russian government operative, but instead the lawyer for a private company which was implicated in the Magnitsky affair which led to the sanctions act being passed in the first place.

As an initial matter, if it does turn out that no dirt on Hillary Clinton was given to Trump, Jr. at this or a subsequent meeting of the parties involved, this can provide no proof whatsoever of Russia's intentions to "collude" with the Trump campaign, even if it shows some ill intent (or at least poor judgment) on the part of Trump, Jr. Indeed, there is no proof that the Russian government itself was behind this meeting at all as Trump, Jr. was originally led to believe.

I note that this lack of Russian intent to "collude" was demonstrated at an analogous meeting in which Trump's son-in-law, Jared Kushner, met with then Russian Ambassador Sergey Kislyak. In this meeting, held during the transition period, Kushner apparently proposed to set up a back-channel communication system with Russia which could not be monitored by US intelligence agencies. First of

all, I agree with those who suggest that there would be nothing wrong with having such a backchannel with a major nuclear power, as other Administrations have had before, and that such a backchannel may even be helpful to avert disaster between our two countries. But even if one has another view of this, what we know from *The Washington Post* is that "Kislyak reportedly was taken aback by the suggestion," reported back to Moscow about it, and the idea ended up going nowhere.[347] Again, the Russians in this instance showed no desire to "collude" with the Trump team even if "collusion" was what was being offered.

Going back to the Trump, Jr. meeting with the Russian lawyer, there are a few other notable facts. First of all, as Robert Parry explains, the whole Magnitsky affair itself—a significant pillar of the new anti-Russia hysteria—may very well be a myth propagated by an American businessman named William Browder.[348] As Parry relates, an anti-Putin documentary filmmaker who began a film along the lines of Browder's version of events—that of a Sergei Magnitsky who was a crusading lawyer jailed in Russia for exposing massive corporate fraud in Russia and who died in prison in 2009—ended up making a film which debunked Browder's story. As it turns out, Magnitsky may in fact have been an accountant involved in covering up corporate corruption himself and was jailed accordingly. Apparently, one of the chief reasons Natalia Veselnitskaya was in the United States at the time of the Trump, Jr. meeting was to lobby against the Magnitsky Act and to help debut this documentary film.

In other words, we again see reasons to question the entire anti-Russian narrative which we have been fed for years. This narrative, in fact, appears to be myths built upon myths.

Another fascinating fact turned up as a result of the Trump, Jr. meeting revelation is that Hillary Clinton, while serving as secretary of state, ended up publicly opposing the 2012 Magnitsky Act shortly after Bill Clinton received five hundred thousand dollars from a Russian investment bank for a speech he gave in Moscow.[349] In terms of Bill Clinton's own deep Russia involvement, I must also note that,

subsequent to writing my book, I discovered that Dick Morris, Bill Clinton's closest adviser, admitted that Bill Clinton was personally involved in Boris Yeltsin's re-election campaign in 1996, stating, "We, Clinton and I, would go through it and Bill would pick up the hotline and talk to Yeltsin and tell him what commercials to run, where to campaign, what positions to take. He basically became Yeltsin's political consultant."[350]

This evidence of the Clintons' own ethically-challenged behavior and Russian meddling is quite inconvenient for the Democrats who are trying so hard to keep the public's attention fixated on Trump's alleged collusion with the Russians.

In short, the passage of time has yet to disprove my book's thesis that Russia is being unfairly scapegoated for our own country's shortcomings—both foreign and domestic—and that this scapegoating is continuing to help fuel the United States' unjustifiable military spending and permanent war-footing, while also leading us closer and closer to a potentially disastrous confrontation with Russia.

But you don't have to take my word for it that Russia and Putin are indeed being unfairly scapegoated. Even Nadezhda Tolokonnikova—the founder of the Russian punk group Pussy Riot, whose members were imprisoned in Russia in response to their anti-government protest at an Orthodox Church—recently expressed such an opinion. As Tolokonnikova explained in an interview with David Sirota in the *International Business Times*, "I'm not terrified of him [Putin] at all. I don't think you have to be terrified of him. He's just a guy who claims that he has power, but I claim to have power too and you have power. . . . If you talk here about mainstream liberal media in America, which speak a lot about Putin, I think it's just a trick. . . . They don't really want to talk about internal American problems. . . . They're just looking for a scapegoat and, you know, for Trump its Muslims and Mexican workers. And for liberal media in America it is Putin."

I could not agree more!

ENDNOTES

1   "Five Takeaways From The Senate Hearing On Russian Hacks," Erin Kelly, *USA Today* (Jan. 5, 2017). Retrieved at: http://www.usatoday.com/story/news/politics/onpolitics/2017/01/05/5-takeaways-senate-hearing-russian-hacks/96209760/

2   "The House I Live In, by Frank Sinatra," Song Facts. Retrieved at: http://www.songfacts.com/detail.php?id=2306

3   "Ethel Rosenberg's Sons Still Seek Justice for Their Mother," Miriam Schneir, *The Nation* (Jan. 19, 2017). Retrieved at: https://www.thenation.com/article/ethel-rosenbergs-sons-still-seek-justice-for-their-mother/

4   "Downplaying US Contribution to Potential Yemen Famine,"Adam Johnson, Fairness & Accuracy in Reporting (Feb. 27, 2017). Retrieved at: http://fair.org/home/downplaying-us-contribution-to-potential-yemen-famine/

5   "Famine 'Largest Humanitarian Crisis in UN History,'" Associated Press (March 2017). Retrieved at: http://www.aljazeera.com/news/2017/03/famine-united-nations-170310234132946.html

6   "Hillary Clinton Oversaw Arms Deals to Clinton Foundation Donors," Brian Schatz, *Mother Jones* (May 28, 2015). Retrieved at: http://www.motherjones.com/politics/2015/05/hillary-clinton-foundation-state-arms-deals

7   "Philip Agee, 72, Is Dead; Exposed Other CIA Officers," Scott Shane, *New York Times* (Jan. 10, 2008). Retrieved at: https://mobile.nytimes.com/2008/01/10/obituaries/10agee.html

8   Ibid.

9   "Frozen Conflicts And Disputed Borders Create Uncertainty In Russia's

Shadow," Stephanie Joyce and David Greene, NPR (March 13, 2017). Retrieved at: http://www.npr.org/2017/03/13/519954275/the-complications-of-living-in-russia-occupied-south-ossetia

10   "Medvedev: Russia's top priority in S.Ossetia war was to defend our citizens, interests," *RT News* (August 4, 2013). Retrieved at: https://www.rt.com/news/georgia-south-ossetia-medvedev-interview-012/

11   "Scott Simon Essay: People Under Those Bombs," Scott Simon, NPR (March 22, 2003). Retrieved at: http://www.npr.org/templates/story/story.php?storyId=1199967

12   "The Secret Wars of the CIA," Excerpts from a Talk with John Stockwell, Retrieved at: http://www.serendipity.li/cia/stock1.html

13   "Bolivia expels US aid agency after Kerry 'backyard' comment," Reuters (May 1, 2013). Retrieved at: http://www.reuters.com/article/us-bolivia-usaid-idUSBRE94013V20130501 As Reuters explained, "the term evokes strong emotions in the region, which experienced several US-backed coups during the Cold War." See also, "Is Trump Resurrecting The Monroe Doctrine," Max Paul Friedman, *Christian Science Monitor* (Feb. 5, 2017). Retrieved at: http://www.csmonitor.com/World/Americas/Latin-America-Monitor/2017/0205/Is-Trump-resurrecting-the-Monroe-Doctrine

14   "Why Nicaraguan Kids Aren't Fleeing to the US" Retrieved at: http://www.kpbs.org/news/2014/jul/29/why-nicaraguan-kids-arent-fleeing-to-the-us/

15   Nicaragua v. United States, International Court of Justice (June 27, 1986). Retrieved at: http://www.icj-cij.org/docket/?sum=367&p1=3&p2=3&case=70&p3=5

16   "Only Africans Have Been Tried At The Court For The Worst Crimes On Earth," Alexandra Zavis and Robyn Dixon, *LA Times* (Oct. 23, 2016). http://www.latimes.com/world/africa/la-fg-icc-africa-snap-story.html

17   "'The New York Times' Wants Gary Webb to Stay Dead," Greg Grandin, *The Nation* (Oct. 10, 2014). Retrieved at: https://www.thenation.com/article/new-york-times-wants-gary-webb-stay-dead/

18   "Kill The Messenger, How The Media Destroyed Garry Webb," Ryan Grim, *Huffington Post* (Oct. 10, 2014). Retrieved at: http://www.huffingtonpost.com/2014/10/10/kill-the-messenger_n_5962708.html

19   "Reagan's Great Lie In The Sky," David Usborne, *The Independent* (Aug. 28, 1993). Retrieved at: http://www.independent.co.uk/news/world/

reagans-great-lie-in-the-sky-star-wars-scientists-may-have-deceived-mos-
cow-and-congress-about-the-1463972.html

20   "Top Air Force Official Told JCS in 1971: 'We Could Lose Two Hundred
      Million People [in a Nuclear War] and Still Have More Than We Had at
      the Time of the Civil War,'" William Burr, The National Security Archive
      (Feb. 15, 2017). Retrieved at: http://nsarchive.gwu.edu/nukevault/
      ebb580-JCS-chairmans-diary-from-1971-reveals-high-level-deliberations/

21   "The Doomsday Clock is Now at Two and a Half Minutes to Midnight,"
      James Carden, The Nation (January 31, 2017). Retrieved at: https://www.then-
      ation.com/article/the-doomsday-clock-is-now-at-two-and-a-half-minutes
      -to-midnight/

22   Ibid.

23   "The Politics Behind 'Russia Gate,'" Robert Parry, Consortium News
      (March 4, 2017). Retrieved at: https://consortiumnews.com/2017/03/04/
      the-politics-behind-russia-gate/

24   "Eat your Spinach," Tony Wood, London Review of Books (Feb. 23, 2016).
      Accessed at: https://www.lrb.co.uk/v39/n05/tony-wood/eat-your-spinach

25   "Trump's Proposed Increase In US Defense Spending Would be 80
      Percent of Russia's Entire Military Budget," Alex Emmons, The Inter-
      cept (Feb. 27, 2017). Retrieved at: https://theintercept.com/2017/02/27/
      trumps-proposed-increase-in-u-s-defense-spending-would-be-80-percent-
      of-russias-entire-military-budget/

26   "US Is The Greatest Threat to World Peace: Poll," Post Editorial Board,
      New York Post (Jan. 5, 2014). Retrieved at: http://nypost.com/2014/01/05/
      us-is-the-greatest-threat-to-world-peace-poll/

27   Hobsbawn, Eric, On Empire: America, War, and Global Supremacy (Pan-
      theon Books 2008).

28   "Broadcasting Board of Governors' Chief On The Future Of VOA,"
      Morning Edition, NPR (Feb. 10, 2017). Retrieved at: http://www.npr.
      org/2017/02/10/514458676/broadcasting-board-of-governors-chief-on-the-future
      -of-voa

29   "Most Russians regret USSR collapse, dream of its return, poll
      shows," RT News (April 19, 2016). Retrieved at: https://www.rt.com/
      politics/340158-most-russians-regret-ussr-has/

30   Ibid.

31   Keeran, Roger, and Kenny, Thomas, Socialism Betrayed, p. 212 (iUniverse,
      Inc. 2010).

32 "SPECIAL REPORT: In eastern Europe, people pine for socialism," Anna Mudeva, Reuters (Nov. 8, 2009). Retrieved at: http://www.reuters.com/article/us-communism-nostalgia-idUSTRE5A701320091108; "Homesick for a Dictatorship, Majority of Eastern Germans Feel Life Better under Communism," Julia Bonstein, Der Spiegel (July 3, 2009). Retrieved at: http://www.spiegel.de/international/germany/homesick-for-a-dictatorship-majority-of-eastern-germans-feel-life-better-under-commnism-a-634122.html

33 Mudeva, ibid.

34 "We Lived Better Then," Stephen Gowans, *what's left* Retrieved at: https://gowans.wordpress.com/2011/12/20/we-lived-better-then/

35 "US ON ROAD TO THIRD WORLD," Paul Craig Roberts, *InfoWars* (Oct. 30, 2015). Retrieved at: https://www.infowars.com/us-on-road-to-third-world/

36 Keeran and Kenny, ibid.

37 "The End of Welfare as We Know It," Alana Semuels, *The Atlantic* (April 1, 2016). Retrieved at: https://www.theatlantic.com/business/archive/2016/04/the-end-of-welfare-as-we-know-it/476322/

38 Hobsbawn, Eric, *On Empire: America, War, and Global Supremacy* (Pantheon Books 2008).

39 "NAFTA at 20: One Million US Jobs Lost, Higher Income Inequality," Lori Wallach , Huffington Post (2014). Retrieved at: http://www.huffingtonpost.com/lori-wallach/nafta-at-20-one-million-u_b_4550207.html

40 See generally, Bowden, Charles, Murder City: Ciudad Juarez and The Global Economy's New Killing Fields (Nation Books, 2010).

41 Hobsbawm, ibid.

42 "Former CIA spy says he helped South Africa arrest 'communist toy' Nelson Mandela," Aislinn Laing, *The Telegraph* (May 14, 2016). Retrieved at: http://www.telegraph.co.uk/news/2016/05/15/former-cia-spy-says-he-helped-south-africa-arrest-communist-toy/

43 "Nelson Mandela on How Cuba "Destroyed the Myth of the Invincibility of the White Oppressor," *Democracy Now!* (Dec. 11, 2013). Retrieved at: https://www.democracynow.org/2013/12/11/nelson_mandela_on_how_cuba_destroyed

44 "Obama Has Deported More People Than Any Other President," Serena Marshall, ABC News (Aug. 29, 2016). Retrieved at: http://abcnews.go.com/Politics/obamas-deportation-policy-numbers/story?id=41715661

45 "President Orders Drone Air Strikes On Villages In Tribal Areas," Ewan MacAskill, *The Guardian* (Jan. 23, 2009). Retrieved at: https://www.theguardian.com/world/2009/jan/24/pakistan-barack-obama-air-strike

46 "American Dropped 26,171 Bombs in 2016. What a Bloody End to Obama's Reign," Medea Benjamin, *The Guardian* (Jan. 9, 2017). Retrieved at: https://www.theguardian.com/commentisfree/2017/jan/09/america-dropped-26171-bombs-2016-obama-legacy

47 "Secret 'Kill List' Proves a Test of Obama's Principles and Will," Jo Becker and Scott Shane, *New York Times* (May 29, 2012). Retrieved at: http://www.nytimes.com/2012/05/29/world/obamas-leadership-in-war-on-al-qaeda.html

48 "Last Year President Obama Reportedly Told His Aides That He's 'Really Good at Killing People,'" Michael B. Kelley, *Business Insider* (Nov. 2, 2013). Retrieved at: http://www.businessinsider.com/obama-said-hes-really-good-at-killing-people-2013-11

49 Ibid.

50 Herman, Edward, and David Peterson, *The Politics of Genocide* (Monthly Review Press 2010).

51 See, e.g., "Yemen says US drone struck a wedding convoy, killing 14," Hakim Almasmari, CNN (Dec. 13, 2013). Retrieved at: http://www.cnn.com/2013/12/12/world/meast/yemen-u-s-drone-wedding/?utm_source=huffingtonpost.com&utm_medium=referral&utm_campaign=pubexchange_article

52 "Nearly 90 Percent of People Killed In Drone Strike Were Not The Target," Marina Fang, *Huffington Post* (Jan. 3, 2017). Retrieved at: http://www.huffingtonpost.com/entry/civilian-deaths-drone-strikes_us_561fafe2e4b028dd7ea6c4ff

53 Ibid.

54 "How Team Obama Justifies the Killing of a 16-Year-Old American," Conor Friedersdor, *The Atlantic* (Oct. 24, 2012). Retrieved at: https://www.theatlantic.com/politics/archive/2012/10/how-team-obama-justifies-the-killing-of-a-16-year-old-american/264028/

55 "Obama Said he's 'Really good at killing people," Michael B. Kelley, *Business Insider*, http://www.businessinsider.com/obama-said-hes-really-good-at-killing-people-2013-11

56 Friedersdor, ibid.

57 Kelley, Michael, ibid.

58 "US Military acknowledges it launched strike against ISIS that allegedly killed more than 100 people in Iraq," Missy Ryan, *Washington Post* (March

25, 2017). Retrieved at: https://www.washingtonpost.com/news/check-point/wp/2017/03/25/u-s-military-acknowledges-strike-on-mosul-site-where-over-100-were-allegedly-killed/

59   "Congress Is Missing In Action as Trump Escalates War in Syria Amid Russia Probe," Mike Ludwig, *Truthout* (March 25, 2017). Retrieved at: http://www.truth-out.org/news/item/39987-congress-is-missing-in-action-as-trump-escalates-war-in-syria-amid-russia-probe

60   Ibid.

61   "Killer, Kleptocrat, Genius, Spy: The Many Myths of Vladimir Putin," Keith Gessen, *The Guardian* (Feb. 22, 2017). Retrieved at: https://www.theguardian.com/world/2017/feb/22/vladimir-putin-killer-genius-kleptocrat-spy-myths

62   "Is it fair to call Putin a killer," Leonid Bershidsky, *Chicago Tribune* (Feb. 2, 2017). Retrieved at: http://www.chicagotribune.com/news/opinion/commentary/ct-putin-kills-enemies-journalists-poison-20170207-story.html

63   Gessen, ibid.

64   "Who Really Did Kill Russian Journalist Anna Politkosvskaya," Mary Dejevsky, *The Independent* (June 13, 2014). Retrieved at: http://www.independent.co.uk/news/world/europe/who-really-did-kill-russian-journalist-anna-politkovskaya-9535772.html

65   Ibid.

66   "Russia: Five Men Stand Trial For The Boris Nestov Murder," *Al Jazeera* (Oct. 3, 2016). Retrieved at: http://www.aljazeera.com/news/2016/10/russia-men-stand-trial-boris-nemtsov-murder-161003084451436.html

67   Bershidsky, ibid.

68   "Obama's War on Whistle Blowers: The Trial of Bradley Manning," Dylan Murphy, Global Research (June 1, 2013). Retrieved at: http://www.globalresearch.ca/obamas-war-on-whistle-blowers-the-trial-of-bradley-manning/5337212

69   "American Special Forces Are Deployed to 70 Percent of the World's Countries," Nick Turse, *The Nation* (Jan. 5, 2017). Retrieved at: https://www.thenation.com/article/american-special-forces-are-deployed-to-70-percent-of-the-worlds-countries/

70   "Blaming America First," Editorial Board, *New York Times* (Feb. 7, 2017). Retrieved at: https://mobile.nytimes.com/2017/02/07/opinion/blaming-america-first.html For an excellent critique of this article, see FAIR's piece

by Adam Johnson, entitled, "NYT: Unlike Russian Wars, US Wars 'Promote Freedom and Democracy'" (Feb. 9, 2017) at: http://fair.org/home/nyt-unlike-russian-wars-us-wars-promote-freedom-and-democracy/

71   Ibid.

72   "Don't Forget How The Soviet Union Saved The World From Hitler," Ishaan Tharoor, *Washington Post* (May 8, 2015). Retrieved at: https://www.washingtonpost.com/news/worldviews/wp/2015/05/08/dont-forget-how-the-soviet-union-saved-the-world-from-hitler/?utm_term=.5810fd34cf42

73   "Liberation of Nazi Camps," United States Holocaust Memorial Museum. Retrieved at: https://www.ushmm.org/wlc/mobile/en/article.php?ModuleId=10005131

74   "The Responsibility of Intellectuals Redux," Noam Chomsky, *Boston Review* (Sept. 1, 2011). Retrieved at: http://bostonreview.net/noam-chomsky-responsibility-of-intellectuals-redux

75   "Memo PP23," George Kennan. Retrieved at: https://en.wikisource.org/wiki/Memo_PPS23_by_George_Kennan This work is in the public domain in the US because it is a work of the US federal government (see 17 USC. 105).

76   "The State of Consumption Today," World Watch Institute. Retrieved at: http://www.worldwatch.org/node/810; "Use It and Lose It: The Outsize Effect of US Consumption on the Environment," Roddy Scheer and Doug Mos, *Scientific American*. Retrieved at: https://www.scientificamerican.com/article/american-consumption-habits/

77   "The Exaggeration of The Threat: Then & Now." Melvin A. Goodman, *The Public Record* (Sep. 14, 2009). Retrieved at: http://pubrecord.org/commentary/5161/exaggeration-threat-then/

78   "US Military Spending v. The World," National Priorities Project, Retrieved at: https://www.nationalpriorities.org/campaigns/us-military-spending-vs-world/

79   "Russia announces deepest defence budget cuts since 1990s," Craig Caffery, *Jane's Defense Weekly* (March 16, 2017). Retrieved at: http://www.janes.com/article/68766/russia-announces-deepest-defence-budget-cuts-since-1990s

80   "Military Spending In The United States," National Priorities Project, Retrieved at: https://www.nationalpriorities.org/campaigns/military-spending-united-states/

81 "War Profiteering and the Concentration of Income and Wealth in America," Prof. Ismael Hossein-Zadeh, Global Research (April 13, 2007). Retrieved at: http://www.globalresearch.ca/war-profiteering-and-the-concentration-of-income-and-wealth-in-america/5368

82 "Hiroshima: Last Military Act of World War II or First Act of the Cold War?" William Blum (Jan. 1994). Retrieved at: https://williamblum.org/essays/read/hiroshima-last-military-act-of-world-war-ii-or-first-act-of-the-cold-war

83 "Veterans of Atomic Test Blast: No Warning and Late Amends," Clyde Haberman, New York Times (May 29, 2016). Retrieved at: https://www.nytimes.com/2016/05/30/us/veterans-of-atomic-test-blasts-no-warning-and-late-amends.html?_r=0

84 "In the Nation, Serving His Country," Tom Wicker, New York Times (Aug. 29, 1983). Retrieved at: http://www.nytimes.com/1983/08/29/obituaries/in-the-nation-serving-his-country.html

85 "In the Nation, Serving His Country," Tom Wicker, New York Times (Aug. 29, 1983). Retrieved at: http://www.nytimes.com/1983/08/29/obituaries/in-the-nation-serving-his-country.html

86 Valentine, Douglas. The CIA as Organized Crime: How Illegal Operations Corrupt America and the World (Clarity Press, 2017).

87 "Did the U.S. Cause Fallujah Birth Defects?" Al Jazeera (Aug. 3, 2012). Retrieved at: http://www.aljazeera.com/programmes/insidestoryamericas/2012/08/2012815458859755.html

88 "The United States Used Depleted Uranium in Syria," Samuel Oakford, Foreign Policy (Feb. 14, 2017) Retrieved at: http://foreignpolicy.com/2017/02/14/the-united-states-used-depleted-uranium-in-syria/

89 Ibid.

90 "Iraq War Anniversary: Birth Defects and Cancer Rates At Devastating High in Basra and Fallujah," Eline Gordts, Huffington Post (March 20, 2013). Retrieved at: http://m.huffpost.com/us/entry/2917701

91 "Who Supported The Khmer Rouge," Gregory Elich, Counterpunch (Oct. 16, 2014). Retrieved at: http://www.counterpunch.org/2014/10/16/who-supported-the-khmer-rouge/

92 Hobsbawm, ibid at p. xv.

93 Ibid.

94 Turse, ibid

95 Blum, ibid.

96   Hobsbawm, ibid.

97   Chomsky, "Responsibility of Intellectuals, Redux," Ibid.

98   "People on War," Country Report El Salvador International Committee of the Red Cross Worldwide Consultation on the Rules of War (Nov. 1999). Retrieved at: https://www.icrc.org/eng/assets/files/other/salvador.pdf

99   See, e.g., Cornwell, John, *Hitler's Pope: The Secret History of Pius XII* (Penguin Books, 2008).

100 "The Gulf War: Moscow's Role," Jill Dougherty, CNN (Jan. 17, 2001). Retrieved at: http://www.edition.cnn.com/2001/WORLD/europe/01/16/russia.iraq/index.html

101 "The First Iraq War Was Sold to the Public Based on a Packs of Lies," Joshua Holland, BillMoyers.com (June 27, 2014). Retrieved at: http://billmoyers.com/2014/06/27/the-first-iraq-war-was-also-sold-to-the-public-based-on-a-pack-of-lies/

102 Ibid.

103 "How the Iraq War Began in Panama, 1989 Invasion Set Path for Future US Attacks," Greg Grandin and Amy Goodman, *Democracy Now!* (Dec. 23, 2014). Retrieved at: http://m.democracynow.org/web_exclusives/2366

104 Ibid.

105 "Deception on Capitol Hill," Editorial Board, *New York Times* (Jan. 15, 1992). Retrieved at: http://www.nytimes.com/1992/01/15/opinion/deception-on-capitol-hill.html

106 Clark, Ramsey, *The Fire This Time: US War Crimes In The Gulf* (Thunder's Mouth Press, 1992).

107 "In the Gulf War, every last nail was accounted for, but the Iraqi dead went untallied. At last, their story is being told," John Pilger (June 26, 2000). Retrieved at: http://johnpilger.com/articles/in-the-gulf-war-every-last-nail-was-accounted-for-but-the-iraqi-dead-went-untallied-at-last-their-story-is-being-told

108 "Twenty Years Later, First Iraq War Still Resonates," Alan Greenblatt, NPR (Feb. 24, 2011). Retrieved at: http://www.npr.org/2011/02/24/133991181/twenty-years-later-first-iraq-war-still-resonates

109 "College protests revive accusations against 'war criminal' Madeleine Albright, who defended deaths of 500,000 Iraqi kids," Ben Norton, *Salon* (May 11, 2016). Retrieved at: http://www.salon.com/2016/05/11/college_protests_revive_accusations_against_war_criminal_madeleine_albright_who_defended_deaths_of_500000_iraqi_kids/

110 Ibid.

111 "Albright: 'special place in hell' for women who don't support Clinton," Tom McCarthy, *The Guardian* (Feb. 6, 2016). https://www.theguardian.com/us-news/2016/feb/06/madeleine-albright-campaigns-for-hillary-clinton

112 Cohen, Stephen F., *Soviet Fates and Lost Alternatives*, (Columbia University Press, 1993) at 154–155.

113 https://www.ncbi.nlm.nih.gov/pmc/articles/PMC259165/ National Center for Biotechnology Information, US National Library of Medicine, Tamara Men, scientist, Paul Brennan, scientist, Paolo Boffetta, unit chief, and David Zaridze, director (Oct. 25, 2003).

114 "Meddling in Presidential Elections: Two Cases," Markar Melkonian at http://hetq.am/eng/news/74607/meddling-in-presidential-elections-two-cases.html, citing, "Boris Yeltsin," David Satter, *Wall Street Journal*, April 4, 2007 at https://hudson.org/research/4893-boris-yeltsin

115 Congressional Research Service, Report 98-725, Stuart D. Goldman, Foreign Affairs and National Defense Division https://file.wikileaks.org/file/crs/98-725.pdf

116 Rescuing Boris, Michael Kramer/Moscow, *Time*, July 15, 1996. http://content.time.com/time/subscriber/article/0,33009,984833,00.html

117 Ibid.; and "Americans Claim Role in Yeltsin Win," Eleanor Randolph, *LA Times*, July 9, 1996 http://articles.latimes.com/1996-07-09/news/mn-22423_1_boris-yeltsin

118 Melkonian, ibid

119 "Americans Claim Role in Yeltsin Win," Eleanor Randolph, *LA Times*, July 9, 1996 http://articles.latimes.com/1996-07-09/news/mn-22423_1_boris-yeltsin

120 Melkonian, ibid.

121 "How October 1993 led to President Putin," Alexander Kolesnichenko, *Russia Beyond The Headlines*, October 3, 2013 at http://rbth.com/amp/500009

122 Ibid.

123 Ibid.

124 "White House: China Should Account for Tiananmen Square Victims," Julie Makinen, *LA Times* (June 4, 2014). Retrieved at http://www.latimes.com/world/asia/la-fg-tiananmen-white-house-china-victims-20140604-story.html Of course, the White House never asked Yeltsin to account for the Duma massacre victims.

125 It is worth noting that the US also had no problem with a similar event which took place in the very same year as the Tiananmen Square massacre. This event, which the US media has entirely ignored, involved the state murder of hundreds (at least 300), if not thousands (possibly 3,000) of protestors in Venezuela.. See, "Victims of Venezuela's Caracazo Clashes Reburied," Sarah Grainger, BBC News (Feb. 28, 2011). Retrieved at http://www.bbc.com/news/world-latin-america-12593085. In other words, the estimates of those protestors killed in Venezuela are identical to the estimates of those killed in Beijing, China. Of course, given that Venezuela has a tiny population (around 30 million) compared to that of China (over 1 billion), these numbers are proportionately much greater. But of course, the Caracazo massacre deserves no commemoration by the US government or media because these killings were carried out by a government—that of President Carlos Andres Perez—that was aligned with the United States at the time, and because the Caracazo was an important factor in the rise of our perceived nemesis, Hugo Chavez, who stood up against this repression.

126 "Victims of Venezuela's Caracazo clashes Reburied," Sarah Grainger, BBC News (Feb. 28, 2011). Retrieved at http://www.bbc.com/news/world-latin-america-12593085

127 Cohen, ibid.

128 Helsinki Watch 1996 Human Rights Report on Russian Federation. Retrieved at: https://www.hrw.org/reports/1996/WR96/Helsinki-16.htm (Creative Commons License)

129 Ibid.

130 Ibid.

131 Cohen, ibid.

132 "Paul Craig Roberts on Crimea, US Foreign Policy and the Transformation of Mainstream Media," Harrison Samphir, *Truthout* (March 18, 2014). Retrieved at: http://www.truth-out.org/news/item/22542-paul-craig-roberts-on-crimea-us-foreign-policy-and-the-transformation-of-mainstream-media

133 "'Silent Genocide': The Mayan Genocide," Center for Justice & Accountability. Retrieved at: http://cja.org/where-we-work/guatemala/

134 Ibid.

135 "Noam Chomsky on Colombia," *Znet* (Retrieved at: http://colombiasupport.net/archive/200004/znet-chomsky-0424.html

136 Ibid.

137 "Lawyer for Chiquita in Colombia Death Squad Case May be Next US Attorney General," Dan Kovalik, *Huffington Post* (Dec. 7, 2008). Retrieved at: http://www.huffingtonpost.com/dan-kovalik/lawyer-for-chiquita-in-co_b_141919.html

138 "The Dark Side of Plan Colombia," Teo Ballve, *The Nation* (May 27, 2009). Retrieved at: https://www.thenation.com/article/dark-side-plan-colombia/

139 "The History of the Military-Paramilitary Partnership," Human Rights Watch (1996). Retrieved at: http://www.hrw.org/reports/1996/killer2.htm (Creative Commons License).

140 "Aportes sobre el Origen del Conflicto Armado en Colombia, Su Persistencia y Sus Impactos," Javier Giraldo Moreno, S. J. Retrieved at: http://www.javiergiraldo.org/IMG/pdf/CHCV_Aporte_de_Javier_Giraldo_SJ.pdf

141 "Colombian Priest Killed in Continuing Trend of Violence," Catholic News Agency (Feb. 5 2013). http://www.catholicnewsagency.com/news/colombian-priest-killed-in-continuing-trend-of-violence/

142 Chomsky, "Responsbility of Intellectuals, Redux," Ibid.

143 "Report: The Rise and Fall of 'False Positive' Killings in Colombia: The Role of US Military Assistance, 2000–2010," Fellowship of Reconciliation (2014), Retrieved at: http://forusa.org/content/report-rise-fall-false-positive-killings-colombia-role-us-military-assistance-2000-2010

144 Giraldo, Javier, ibid.

145 "Did Pablo Escobar Work for the CIA? US Media Quiet As Son's Memoir Says 'Yes,'" Zachary Volkert, *Inquisiter* (Feb. 19, 2017). Retrieved at: http://www.inquisitr.com/3995210/did-pablo-escobar-work-for-the-cia-us-media-quiet-as-sons-memoir-says-yes/

146 "US Intelligence Listed Colombian President Uribe Among 'Important Colombian Narco-Traffickers' in 1991," Michael Evans, National Security Archive (Aug. 2, 2004). Retrieved at: http://nsarchive.gwu.edu/NSAEBB/NSAEBB131/

147 "Covert Action In Colombia," Dana Priest, *Washington Post* (Dec. 21, 2013). Retrieved at: http://www.washingtonpost.com/sf/investigative/2013/12/21/covert-action-in-colombia/

148 "7 Million Victims of Colombian Conflict," Telesur (Nov. 18, 2014) http://www.telesurtv.net/english/news/7-Million-Victims-of-Colombias-Conflict-20141118-0008.html

149 "15 Facts About Colombia's Land Restitution Process," Amnesty International (Nov. 16, 2014). Retrieved at: http://www.amnestyusa.org/news/news-item/15-facts-about-colombia-s-land-restitution-process

150 "The Risk of Genocide In Colombia," The Sentinel Project for Genocide Prevention (August, 2013). Retrieved at: https://thesentinelproject.org/wp-content/uploads/2013/09/Risk-Assessment-Colombia-2013.pdf

151 UN High Commission on Refugees, Colombia Report. Retrieved at: http://www.unhcr.org/pages/49e492ad6.html (link is now dead)

152 "The Secret History of the Paramilitaries & The US War on Drugs," Deborah Sontag, *New York Times* (Sep. 10, 2016). Retrieved at: http://www.nytimes.com/2016/09/11/world/americas/colombia-cocaine-human-rights.html?_r=0

153 "Chiquita, Dole & Del Monte Funded Murderous Militias," *Daily Kos* (May 19, 2007). Retrieved at: http://www.dailykos.com/story/2007/5/19/336518/-

154 "Plan Colombia: How Washington Learned to Love Latin America Again," Nick Miroff, *Washington Post* (Sept. 18, 2016). Retrieved at: http://wapo.st/2ciSuPV

155 "Colombia's coca production soars to highest level in two decades, US says," Associated Press, *The Guardian* (March 14, 2017); Retrieved at: https://www.theguardian.com/world/2017/mar/14/colombia-coca-cocaine-us-drugs

156 "A Chilean Dictator's Dark Legacy," Monte Reel and J.Y. Smith, *Washington Post* (Dec. 11, 2006). Retrieved at: http://www.washingtonpost.com/wp-dyn/content/article/2006/12/10/AR2006121000302.html

157 "Pinochet's Chile," *Washington Post* (Dec. 10, 2006). Retrieved at: http://www.washingtonpost.com/wp-srv/inatl/longterm/pinochet/overview.htm

158 "The Pinochet File: How US Politicians, Bankers and Corporations Aided Chilean Coup, Dictatorship," Juan Garces and Peter Kornbluh, *Democracy Now!* (Sept. 10, 2013). Retrieved at: http://m.democracynow.org/web_exclusives/1883

159 "CIA Activities in Chile," Sept. 18, 2000. Retrieved at: https://www.cia.gov/library/reports/general-reports-1/chile/

160 "Victims of Operation Condor By Country,' Ben Norton (May 28, 2015). Retrieved at: http://bennorton.com/victims-of-operation-condor-by-country/

161 "Silence Surrounds Colombia's 92,000 Disappeared: ICRC," Anastasia

Maloney, Reuters (Aug. 29, 2014). Retrieved at: http://www.reuters.com/article/us-foundation-colombia-missing-idUSKBN0GT22520140829

162 "1994 Rwanda Pull-Out Driven by Clinton White House," The National Security Archive (April 16, 2015). Retrieved at: http://nsarchive.gwu.edu/NSAEBB/NSAEBB511/

163 Excerpt from "Crisis in The Congo." Retrieved at: https://www.youtube.com/watch?v=G1gYQseoCpU

164 See, e.g., "What Really Happened in Rwanda," BBC (2014). Retrieved at: https://vimeo.com/107867605

165 "The Clinton Legacy: Uplifting Rhetoric, Grim Realities" William D. Hartung and Dena Montague, World Policy Institute (March 22, 2001). Retrieved at: http://www.worldpolicy.org/projects/arms/reports/update032201.htm

166 See, *Crisis in the Congo*, and Gregory Stanton's remarks therein about Clinton's military support for the invasion of the Congo: https://www.youtube.com/watch?v=vLV9szEu9Ag; see also, Herman and Peterson, *The Politics of Genocide* (Monthly Review Press, 2010).

167 The World Policy Institute, ibid.

168 Ibid.

169 "American Companies Exploit The Congo," Project Censored (Aug. 29, 2010). Retrieved at: http://projectcensored.org/19-american-companies-exploit-the-congo/

170 The World Policy Institute, ibid.

171 "Friends in High Places," Richard C. Morais, *Forbes* (Aug. 10, 1998). Retrieved at: https://www.forbes.com/global/1998/0810/0109038a.html

172 UN Security Council Report (Oct. 16, 2002). Retrieved at: https://documents-dds-ny.un.org/doc/UNDOC/GEN/N02/621/79/PDF/N0262179.pdf?OpenElement

173 See, *Crisis in the Congo*, and Gregory Stanton's remarks therein about Clinton's military support for the invasion of the Congo: https://www.youtube.com/watch?v=vLV9szEu9Ag; see also, Herman and Peterson, *The Politics of Genocide* (Monthly Review Press, 2010).

174 "The World Capital of Killing," Nicholas Kristof, *New York Times* (Feb. 6, 2010). Retrieved at: http://www.nytimes.com/2010/02/07/opinion/07kristof.html; see also, UN Mapping Report of the Conflict in the DRC, 1993–2003 (August, 2010). Retrieved at: http://friendsofthecongo.org/pdf/mapping_report_en.pdf

175   "Trump and the Contradictions," *The African Communist*, Issue 194, Feb.
       2017.

176   "Black Lives Matter, But Not for Clinton," Jerry Kuzmarov, *Huffington Post*
       (April 22, 2016). Retrieved at: http://www.huffingtonpost.com/jeremy-
       kuzmarov/black-african-lives-matte_b_9763346.html

177   See, e.g., "The Clinton Foundation's Legacy in Haiti—'Haitians are more
       than upset...,'" H.A. Goodman, *Huffington Post* (Oct. 6, 2016). Retrieved
       at: http://www.huffingtonpost.com/entry/the-clinton-foundations-legacy
       -in-haiti-haitians_us_57f604f9e4b087a29a5486fd

178   "Cuba Takes Lead Role in Haiti's Cholera Fight," Randal C. Archibold,
       New York Times (Nov. 7, 2011). Retrieved at: https://mobile.nytimes.
       com/2011/11/08/world/americas/in-haitis-cholera-fight-cuba-takes-lead-
       role.html

179   "With All Eyes On Haiti, Its Diaspora In Florida Could Swing A Close
       Election," Ryan Grim, *New York Times* (Oct. 4, 2016). Retrieved at: http://
       www.huffingtonpost.com/entry/with-eyes-on-haiti-its-diaspora-in-florida-
       could-swing-a-close-election_us_57f313bce4b0703f7590a99d

180   "Bill Clinton's Trade Policies Destroyed Haitian Rice Forming, Now Haiti
       Faces Post-Hurricane Famine," Amy Goodman and Ninaj Raoul, *Democracy
       Now!* (Oct. 11, 2016). Retrieved at: http://m.democracynow.org/stories/16696

181   "Haiti's Clinton Problem," Nathan J. Robinson, *Jacobin*. Retrieved at:
       https://www.jacobinmag.com/2016/10/haiti-clinton-guantanamo-hiv-
       aristide-constant/

182   Ibid.

183   "Did Trump's Visit to Little Haiti Help Him Win Florida?" Georgianne
       Nienaber, *Huffington Post* (Nov. 12, 2016). Retrieved at: http://m.huffpost.
       com/us/entry/12930834

184   Nobel Lecture: "Art, Truth & Politics," Harold Pinter, The Nobel Founda-
       tion 2005. Reprinted with Permission by the Nobel Committee. Retrieved
       at: http://www.nobelprize.org/nobel_prizes/literature/laureates/2005/
       pinter-lecture-e.html

185   "Honduran coup shows business elite still in charge," Alexandra Olson.
       Associated Press (Aug. 2009). Retrieved at: http://www.newsday.com/
       honduran-coup-shows-business-elite-still-in-charge-1.1353372

186   "US Continues To Train Honduras Troops," James Hodge and
       Linda Cooper, *National Catholic Reporter* (July 14, 2009). Retrieved at:

https://www.ncronline.org/news/global/us-continues-train-honduran-soldiers

187 "What Happens When Empire Intervenes in the Affairs of Other Countries," Mark Taliano, *Huffington Post* (Dec. 19, 2014). Retrieved at: http://www.huffingtonpost.ca/mark-taliano/canada-foreign-affairs_b_6011844.html

188 "In Honduras, A Mess Made in America," Dana Frank, *New York Times* (Jan. 27, 2012). http://www.nytimes.com/2012/01/27/opinion/in-honduras-a-mess-helped-by-the-us.html

189 "Hillary Clinton's Response To Honduran Coup Was Scrubbed From Her Paperback Memoirs," Roque Planas, *Huffington Post* (March 12, 2016). Retrieved at: http://www.huffingtonpost.com/entry/hillary-clinton-honduras-coup-memoirs_us_56e34161e4b0b25c91820a08

190 "During Honduras Crisis, Clinton Suggested Back Channel With Lobbyist Lanny Davis," Lee Fang, *The Intercept* (July 6, 2015). Retrieved at: https://theintercept.com/2015/07/06/clinton-honduras-coup/

191 "Before Her Assassination, Berta Cáceres Singled Out Hillary Clinton for Backing Honduran Coup", *Democracy Now!* (March 11, 2016). Retrieved at: https://www.democracynow.org/2016/3/11/before_her_assassination_berta_caceres_singled

192 "Berta Cáceres court papers show murder suspects' links to US-trained elite troops", Nina Lakhani, *The Guardian* (Feb. 28, 2017). Retrieved at: https://www.theguardian.com/world/2017/feb/28/berta-caceres-honduras-military-intelligence-us-trained-special-forces

193 Vine, David, *Base Nation: How US Military Bases Abroad Harm America and The World* (Metropolitan Books Henry Holt and Company, LLC, 2015).

194 *Democracy Now!*, ibid.

195 "Honduras: the most deadly place for journalists in the Americas," Corey Kane, *Latin Correspondent* (Nov. 5, 2015). Retrieved at: http://latincorrespondent.com/2015/11/honduras-the-most-deadly-place-for-journalists-in-the-americas/#R5AuAP8me7A6WdAG.97

196 "Garifunas Flee Discrimination and Land Grabs In Record Numbers," Anna Catherine Brigida, Telesur (Feb. 23, 2017). Retrieved at: http://www.telesurtv.net/english/news/Garifuna-Flee-Discrimination-and-Land-Grabs-in-Record-Numbers-20170223-0002.html. See also the piece that I wrote on the same subject shortly after the coup: "Honduran Coup Government Continues Attack on the Poor with Plan to Seize

Indigenous Hospital," *Huffington Post*. Retrieved at: http://www.huffing-tonpost.com/dan-kovalik/honduran-coup-government_b_254033.html

197 "Former Russian Lawmaker Is Shot to Death Outside Hotel in Kiev," Bill Chappell, NPR (March 23, 2017). Retrieved at: http://www.npr. org/sections/thetwo-way/2017/03/23/521215078/former-russian-law-maker-is-shot-to-death-outside-hotel-in-kiev; "Former Russian Law-maker And Putin Critic Killed In Ukraine," Lucian Kim, NPR (March 24, 2017). Retrieved at: http://www.npr.org/2017/03/24/521337546/former-russian-lawmaker-and-putin-critic-killed-in-ukraine

198 "Third Mexican Journalist Slain This Month," Telesur (March 23, 2017). Retrieved at: http://www.telesurtv.net/english/news/Third-Mexican-Journalist-Slain-This-Month—20170323-0019.html

199 "Russia's Got a Point: The US Broke a NATO Promise," Joshua R. Itzkow-itz Shifrinson, *LA Times* (May 30, 2016) Retrieved at: http://www.latimes. com/opinion/op-ed/la-oe-shifrinson-russia-us-nato-deal—20160530-snap-story.html

200 Ibid.; see also, "Why the Ukraine Crisis Is the West's Fault, The Liberal Delusions That Provoked Putin," John J. Mearsheimer, *Foreign Affairs* (Aug. 18, 2014). Retrieved at: https://www.foreignaffairs.com/articles/russia-fsu/2014-08-18/why-ukraine-crisis-west-s-fault

201 NATO Relations with Georgia. Retrieved at: http://www.nato.int/cps/en/natohq/topics_38988.htm

202 NATO Relations with Ukraine. Retrieved at: http://www.nato.int/cps/en/natolive/topics_37750.htm

203 "Poland to equip F-16s with new US cruise missiles—military," *RT News* (Dec. 24, 2016). Retrieved at: https://www.rt.com/news/371605-us-poland-missiles-deal/

204 Mearsheimer, ibid.

205 "NATO's 'Humanitarian War' Over Kosovo," Adam Roberts, *Survival*, vol. 41, no. 3, Autumn 1999, The International Institute of Strategic Stud-ies. Retrieved at: http://www.columbia.edu/itc/sipa/S6800/courseworks/NATOhumanitarian.pdf

206 Ibid.

207 "NATO's Libya 'hope' strategy is bombing," Lewis Mackenzie, *The Globe and Mail* (Jun. 10, 2011). Retrieved at: http://www.theglobeandmail. com/opinion/natos-libya-hope-strategy-is-bombing/article598629/

208 "Vladimir Putin offers Ukraine financial incentives to stick with Russia," Shaun Walker, *The Guardian* (Dec. 18, 2013). Retrieved at: https://www.theguardian.com/world/2013/dec/17/ukraine-russia-leaders -talks-kremlin-loan-deal

209 Ibid.

210 "Putin victorious as Ukraine postpones 'trade suicide', halts talks with EU," *RT News* (Nov. 24, 2013). Retrieved at: https://www.rt.com/business/ ukraine-eu-deal-suspended-088/

211 Ibid.

212 "Ukraine Blames I.M.F. for Halt to Agreements With Europe," David M. Herszenhorn, *New York Times* (Nov. 22, 2013). Retrieved at: http://www. nytimes.com/2013/11/23/world/europe/ukraine-blames-imf-for-collapse-of-accord-with-european-union.html

213 Stephen F. Cohen interview with author, June 2015.

214 "Joint statement of the NATO-Ukraine Commission," (Dec. 2014). Retrieved at: http://www.nato.int/cps/en/natohq/official_texts_115474.htm

215 "Defying Russia, Ukraine Signs E.U. Trade Pact," Andrew Higgins and David M. Herszenhorn, *New York Times* (June 27, 2014). Retrieved at: https://www.nytimes.com/2014/06/28/world/europe/ukraine-signs-trade-agreement-with-european-union.html?_r=0

216 "Under Nafta, Mexico Suffered, and the United States Felt Its Pain," Laura Carlsen, *New York Times* (Nov. 14, 2013). Retrieved at: http://www.nytimes.com/roomfordebate/2013/11/24/what-weve-learned-from-nafta/under-nafta-mexico-suffered-and-the-united-states-felt-its-pain

217 "Ukraine's Pres. Poroshenko Says Overthrow of Yanukovych Was a Coup," Eric Zuesse, *Washington's Blog* (June 22, 2015). Retrieved at: http://www.washingtonsblog.com/2015/06/ukraines-pres-poroshenko-says-overthrow-of-yanukovych-was-a-coup.html

218 "Is the US Backing Neo-Nazis in the Ukraine?" Max Blumenthal, *Salon* (Feb. 25, 2014). Retrieved at: http://www.salon.com/2014/02/25/ is_the_us_backing_neo_nazis_in_ukraine_partner/

219 Ibid.

220 Ibid.

221 Ibid.

222 "Ukraine crisis: Transcript of leaked Nuland-Pyatt call," Transcript w/

analysis by Jonathan Marcus, BBC (Feb. 7, 2014). Retrieved at: http://
www.bbc.com/news/world-europe-26079957

223   Paul Craig Roberts, ibid.

224   "Pres Obama on Fareed Zakaria GPS," CNN (Feb. 1, 2015). Retrieved at:
http://cnnpressroom.blogs.cnn.com/2015/02/01/pres-obama-on-fareed
-zakaria-gps-cnn-exclusive/

225   "Seven Decades of Nazi Collaboration: America's Dirty Little Ukraine
Secret," Paul H. Rosenberg and Russ Bellant, *The Nation* (March 28,
2014). Retrieved at: https://www.thenation.com/article/seven-decades
-nazi-collaboration-americas-dirty-little-ukraine-secret/

226   "Is America Training Neo-Nazis in the Ukraine?" Will Cathcart and
Joseph Epstein, *Daily Beast* (July 4, 2015). Retrieved at: http://www.thedai-
lybeast.com/articles/2015/07/04/is-the-u-s-training-neo-nazis-in-ukraine.html

227   Mearsheimer, ibid.

228   "NATO Gives Air Support to KLA Forces," Dana Priest and Peter Finn,
Washington Post (June 2, 1999), Retrieved at: http://www.washingtonpost
.com/wp-srv/inatl/longterm/balkans/stories/military060299.htm

229   "We're ignoring a possible genocide in South Sudan," Princeton Lyman
and Nancy Lindborg, CNN (Dec. 15, 2016). Retrieved at: http://www.
cnn.com/2016/12/15/opinions/south-sudan-genocide-looming/

230   "Why are Ukraine separatist elections controversial?" BBC News (Nov. 1,
2014). Retrieved at: http://www.bbc.com/news/world-europe-29831028

231   "Ukraine crisis: the neo-Nazi brigade fighting pro-Russian separatists,"
Tom Parfitt, *The Telegraph* (Aug. 11, 2014). Retrieved at: http://www.tele-
graph.co.uk/news/worldnews/europe/ukraine/11025137/Ukraine-crisis-
the-neo-Nazi-brigade-fighting-pro-Russian-separatists.html

232   "One million Ukrainian children now need aid as number doubles over
past year—UNICEF," UN News Centre (Feb. 17, 2017). Retrieved at:
http://www.un.org/apps/news/story.asp?NewsID=56193#.WLbuTdIrLcv

233   "More than 20 MILLION face starvation in worst humanitarian crisis since
WWII, UN boss warns," *The Sun* (March 11, 2017). Retrieved at: https://
www.google.com/amp/s/www.thesun.co.uk/news/3065143/20-million
-starvation-humanitarian-crisis-un-boss-warns/amp/

234   "What are the Minsk Agreements?" N.S., *The Economist* (Sept. 14, 2016).
Retrieved at: http://www.economist.com/blogs/economist-explains/2016/
09/economist-explains-7

235 "John Kerry admits defeat: The Ukraine story the media won't tell, and why US retreat is a good thing," Patrick L. Smith, *Salon* (May 19, 2015). Retrieved at: http://www.salon.com/2015/05/19/john_kerry_admits_ defeat_the_ukraine_story_the_media_wont_tell_and_why_u_s_ retreat_is_a_good_thing/

236 "Why Is Washington Still Pushing for War With Russia?" James Carden, *The Nation* (June 11, 2015). Retrieved at: https://www.thenation.com/ article/why-washington-still-pushing-war-russia/

237 "Joe Biden, His Son and the Case Against a Ukrainian Oligarch," James Risen, *New York Times* (Dec. 8, 2015). Retrieved at: https://www.nytimes. com/2015/12/09/world/europe/corruption-ukraine-joe-biden-son-hunt- er-biden-ties.html?_r=0

238 "In Hopelessly Corrupt Ukraine, Business Is Business for Joe Biden's Son," *Russia Insider* (Feb. 6, 2016). Retrieved at: http://russia-insider.com/en/ politics/hopelessly-corrupt-ukraine-business-business-joe-bidens-son/ri12650

239 Risen, ibid.

240 See generally, "To Understand Crimea, Take a Look at Its Complicated History," Adam Taylor, *Washington Post* (Feb. 27, 2014). Retrieved at: https://www.washingtonpost.com/news/worldviews/wp/2014/02/27/ to-understand-crimea-take-a-look-back-at-its-complicated-history/?utm_ term=.b1a40dd5bf92

241 Ibid.

242 "One Year After Russia Annexed Crimea, Locals Prefer Moscow To Kiev," Kenneth Rapoza, *Forbes* (March 20, 2015). Retrieved at: https://www. forbes.com/sites/kenrapoza/2015/03/20/one-year-after-russia-annexed- crimea-locals-prefer-moscow-to-kiev/#6322c7b510db

243 Vine, David, *Base Nation: How US Military Bases Abroad Harm America and The World* (Metropolitan Books Henry Holt & Company, LLC, 2015).

244 "Putin withdrawing Russian forces from Syria: why now and why it mat- ters," Max Fisher, *Vox* (March 14, 2016). Retrieved at: http://www.vox. com/2016/3/14/11224544/putin-syria-russia-withdraw

245 Vine, ibid.

246 "US Deploys Third Carrier Group In Asia To Boost 'Naval Air Forces' In Disputed South China Sea," Tyler Durden, *Zero Hedge* (Jan. 14, 2017). Retrieved at: http://www.zerohedge.com/news/2017-01-14/us-deploys- vinson-aircraft-carrier-group-asia-boost-naval-air-forces-disputed-south-

247 "CIA Admits Role in 1953 Iranian Coup," Saeed Kamali Dehghan and Rich-
     ard Norton-Taylor, *The Guardian* (Aug. 19, 2013). Accessed at: https://www.
     theguardian.com/world/2013/aug/19/cia-admits-role-1953-iranian-coup

248 Ibid.

249 "Torture's Teachers," A.J. Langguth, *New York Times* (June 11, 1979)
     https://msuweb.montclair.edu/~furrg/langguthleaf.html

250 "NYT's 'Tinfoil Hat' Conspiracy Theory," Robert Parry, *Consortium News*
     (March 20, 2017). Retrieved at: https://consortiumnews.com/2017/03/19/
     nyts-tinfoil-hat-conspiracy-theory/

251 "Frankenstein The CIA Created," Jason Burke, *The Guardian* (January 17,
     1990) at https://www.theguardian.com/world/1999/jan/17/yemen.islam

252 The Brzezinski Interview with Le Nouvel Observateur (1998). Translated
     from the French by William Blum and David N. Gibbs. This translation
     was published in Gibbs, "Afghanistan: The Soviet Invasion in Retro-
     spect," *International Politics* 37, no. 2, 2000, pp. 241-242. Quoted with per-
     mission from David N. Gibbs. Retrieved at http://dgibbs.faculty.arizona.
     edu/sites/dgibbs.faculty.arizona.edu/files/afghan-ip_3.pdf

253 Ibid.

254 "Russian soldier missing in Afghanistan for 33 years is found living as
     nomadic sheikh in remote Afghan province," *Daily Mail*. http://www.
     dailymail.co.uk/news/article-2288544/Russian-soldier-missing-Afghanistan
     -33-years-FOUND-living-nomadic-sheikh-remote-Afghan-province.html

255 Michael Parenti, "Afghanistan: Another Untold Story," *Common
     Dreams* (Dec. 2, 2008). Retrieved at: http://www.commondreams.org/
     views/2008/12/02/afghanistan-another-untold-story

256 "911 A Turning Point for Putin," CNN World Edition (Sept. 10, 2002).
     Retrieved at: http://www.edition.cnn.com/2002/WORLD/europe/09/10/
     ar911.russia.putin/index.html

257 "Bush and Putin: Best of Friends," Caroline Wyatt, BBC (June 16, 2001).
     Retrieved at: http://news.bbc.co.uk/2/hi/europe/1392791.stm

258 CNN, ibid.

259 Ibid.

260 "Empire Files: Post-Soviet Russia, Made in the USA.," Abby Mar-
     tin, Telesur (Jan. 23, 2017). Retrieved at: https://www.youtube.com/
     watch?v=e7HwvFyMg7A&sns=em

261   "The Source of The Trouble," *New York Magazine*, Retrieved at: http://
      nymag.com/nymetro/news/media/features/9226/

262   "Half-Million Iraqis Died in the War, New Study Says," Dan Vergano, Oct.
      16, 2013, *National Geographic*, (October 13, 2013) Retrieved at: http://news.
      nationalgeographic.com/news/2013/10/131015-iraq-war-deaths-survey-2013/

263   "Taliban's Ban on Poppy A Success, US Aides Say," Barbara Cros-
      sette, *New York Times* (May 20, 2001). Retrieved at: http://www.nytimes.
      com/2001/05/20/world/taliban-s-ban-on-poppy-a-success-us-aides-say.
      html

264   "The Real Afghanistan Surge Is in Heroin Production and Tripled Opium
      Cultivation since the US military arrived/ UN and US Government docu-
      ments," Meryl Nass, M.D., *Washington's Blog* (Sept. 13, 2015). Retrieved at:
      http://www.washingtonsblog.com/2015/09/the-real-afghanistan-surge-is-in-her-
      oin-production-and-tripled-opium-cultivation-since-the-us-military-arrived
      -un-and-us-government-documents.html

265   Valentine, Douglas, *The CIA As Organized Crime* (Clarity Press, Inc., 2017).

266   "Post-9/11 Wars Have Cost Nearly $5 Trillion (and Counting): Report,"
      Nadia Prupis, *Common Dreams* (Sept. 13, 2016). Retrieved at: http://www.
      commondreams.org/news/2016/09/13/post-911-wars-have-cost-nearly
      -5-trillion-and-counting-report

267   "The Redirection," Seymour M. Hersh, *New Yorker* (March 5, 2007).
      Retrieved   at: http://www.newyorker.com/magazine/2007/03/05/
      the-redirection

268   "Why the Arabs Don't Want Us in Syria," Robert Kennedy, Jr., *Polit-
      ico* (Feb. 22, 2016). Retrieved at: http://www.politico.com/magazine/
      story/2016/02/rfk-jr-why-arabs-dont-trust-america-213601

269   "In Syria, militias armed by the Pentagon fight those armed by the CIA,"
      Nabih Bulos, W.J. Hennigan and Brian Bennett, *LA Times* (March 27,
      2016). Retrieved at: http://www.latimes.com/world/middleeast/la-fg-cia-
      pentagon-isis-20160327-story.html

270   "There Is More Than One Terrible Truth To Tell In The Terrible Story
      of Aleppo," Robert Fisk, *Counterpunch* (Dec. 14, 2016). http://www.
      counterpunch.org/2016/12/14/there-is-more-than-one-truth-to-tell-
      in-the-terrible-story-of-aleppo/

271   "Banned By 119 Countries, US Cluster Bombs Continue to Orphan

Yemeni Children," Alex Emmons, Mohammed Ali Kalfood, *The Inter-cept* (Dec. 14, 2016). Retrieved at: https://theintercept.com/2016/12/14/banned-by-119-countries-u-s-cluster-bombs-continue-to-orphan-yemeni-children/

272 "Russia's Military Action In Syria—Timeline," Ben Quinn, *The Guard-ian* (March 14, 2016). Retrieved at: https://www.theguardian.com/world/2016/mar/14/russias-military-action-in-syria-timeline

273 "Islamic State Tightens Grip on Libyan Stronghold of Sirte," Tamer El-Ghobashy and Hassan Morajea, *Wall Street Journal* (Nov. 29, 2015). Retrieved at: https://www.wsj.com/articles/islamic-state-entrenches-in-sirte-libya-1448798153

274 "US Intervention in Libya Now Seen as a Cautionary Tale," Paul Richter and Christi Parsons, *LA Times* (June 27, 2014). Retrieved at: http://www.latimes.com/world/middleeast/la-fg-us-libya-20140627-story.html

275 "Wars and conflict likely to worsen in 2016," Jean-Marie Guéhenno, *Financial Review* (Jan. 7, 2016). Retrieved at: http://www.afr.com/news/world/wars-and-conflict-is-likely-to-worsen-in-2016-20160106-gm05nx#ix-zz4aUWt41Rn

276 Ibid.

277 Richter and Parson, ibid.

278 "Putin: Libya Coalition Has No Right To Kill Gaddafi," Gleb Bryanski, Reuters (April 26, 2011). Retrieved at: http://www.reuters.com/article/us-russia-putin-libya-idUSTRE73P4L920110426

279 "Putin Calls Killing of Gaddafi Repulsive and Accuses Opponents With Working With West To Destabilize Russia," Rebecca Seales, *Daily Mail Online* (Dec. 11, 2011). Retrieved at: http://www.dailymail.co.uk/news/article-2074537/Vladimir-Putin-says-killing-Gaddafi-repulsive.html

280 "Hillary Clinton on Gaddafi: We came, we saw, he died," CBS News (Oct. 20, 2011). Retrieved at: https://www.youtube.com/watch?v=Fgcd1ghag5Y

281 "Clinton Emails On Libya Expose The Lie of "Humanitarian Inter-vention," Daniel Kovalik, *Huffington Post* (Jan. 22, 2016). Retrieved at: http://www.huffingtonpost.com/dan-kovalik/clinton-emails-on-libya-e_b_9054182.html

282 "Libyan Rebels Appear to Take Leaf from Kaddafi's Playbook," David Zucchino, *LA Times* (Mar. 24, 2011). Retrieved at: http://articles.latimes.com/2011/mar/24/world/la-fg-libya-prisoners-20110324

283 "Libya's spectacular revolution has been disgraced by racism," Richard Seymour, *The Guardian* (Aug. 30, 2011). Retrieved at: https://www.theguardian.com/commentisfree/2011/aug/30/libya-spectacular-revolution-disgraced-racism

284 "What Are We Doing in Libya," Doug Bandow, *American Spectator* (June 28, 2011). Retrieved at: https://spectator.org/26545_what-are-we-doing-libya/

285 See, e.g., Maximillian Forte, *Slouching Towards Sirte*.

286 "Libya's Economy Faces New Tests After Gadhafi Era," Peter Kenyon, NPR (Nov. 14, 2011). Retrieved at: http://www.npr.org/2011/11/14/142289603/libyas-economy-faces-new-tests-after-gadhafi-era

287 "US blocks Russia's draft statement in UN on peaceful resolution of Bani Walid violence," *RT News* (Oct. 23, 2012) (https://www.rt.com/news/us-russia-libya-statement-068/

288 Quoted by me in my article, "Libya and the West's Human Rights Hypocrisy," *Huffington Post*. Retrieved at: http://www.huffingtonpost.com/dan-kovalik/human-rights-libya_b_2001880.html The original AI link appears to be dead.

289 "Libya: new testimonies reveal horrors inflicted on refugees and migrants by traffickers," Amnesty International (July 1, 2016). Retrieved at: https://www.amnesty.org.uk/press-releases/libya-new-testimonies-reveal-horrors-inflicted-refugees-and-migrants-traffickers

290 "Libya: Stop Revenge Crimes Against Displaced Persons," Human Rights Watch (March 20, 2013). Retrieved at: https://www.hrw.org/news/2013/03/20/libya-stop-revenge-crimes-against-displaced-persons

291 Forte, ibid.

292 "Pres Obama on Fareed Zakaria GPS," CNN (Feb. 1, 2015). Retrieved at: http://cnnpressroom.blogs.cnn.com/2015/02/01/pres-obama-on-fareed-zakaria-gps-cnn-exclusive/

293 "Putin's chemical weapons scheme could save Obama from Syrian mess," David Horsey, *LA Times* (Sep. 12, 2013). Retrieved at: http://articles.latimes.com/2013/sep/12/nation/la-na-tt-putins-weapons-scheme-20130911

294 Ibid.

295 "Obama Thanks Putin for Russia's Role in Iran Nuclear Deal," Reuters (July 16, 2015). Retrieved at: http://www.nbcnews.com/storyline/iran-nuclear-talks/obama-thanks-putin-russias-role-iran-nuclear-deal-n392976

296   US strikes on Syrian troops: Report data contradicts 'mistake' claims,"
      Gareth Porter, *Middle East Eye* (Dec. 6, 2016). Retrieved at: http://www.
      middleeasteye.net/news/us-strike-syrian-troops-report-data-contradicts-
      mistake-claims-1291258286

297   "US admits carrying out airstrike that Russia says killed 62 Syrian sol-
      diers," Karen DeYoung and Thomas Gibbons-Neff, *Washington Post* (Sept.
      17, 2016) Retrieved at: https://www.washingtonpost.com/world/mid-
      dle_east/russia-and-syria-blame-us-led-coalition-for-deadly-strike-on-syr-
      ian-troops/2016/09/17/8dabf5d6-7d03-11e6-8064-c1ddc8a724bb_story.
      html?utm_term=.b52166ac3126

298   Ibid.

299   "Jimmy Carter Is Correct that the US Is No Longer a Democracy," Eric
      Zeusse, *Huffington Post* (Aug. 3, 2015). Retrieved at: http://www.huffing-
      tonpost.com/eric-zuesse/jimmy-carter-is-correct-t_b_7922788.html

300   "US Elections Ranked Worst Among Western Democracies. Here's Why,"
      Pippa Norris, *Washington Post*, (March 29, 2016). Retrieved at: https://
      www.washingtonpost.com/posteverything/wp/2016/03/29/u-s-elec-
      tions-ranked-worst-among-western-democracies-heres-why/?utm_term=.
      f3ddb767e5f7

301   "US Prisons House More Inmates Than Stalin's Gulags," RI Staff, *Rus-
      sian Insider* (May 1, 2015). Retrieved at: http://russia-insider.com/en/
      more-people-rotting-us-prisons-height-stalins-gulags/6319

302   Ibid.

303   "Comey Confirms F.B.I. Inquiry on Russia; Sees No Evidence of Wire-
      tapping," Matthew Rosenberg, Emmarie Huetteman, and Michael S.
      Schmidt, *New York Times* (March 21, 2017). Retrieved at: https://www.
      nytimes.com/2017/03/20/us/politics/intelligence-committee-russia-don-
      ald-trump.html

304   "Trump, Putin & The New Cold War," Evan Osnos, David Remnick, and
      Joshua Yaffa, *New Yorker* (March 6, 2017). Retrieved at: http://www.newyo-
      rker.com/magazine/2017/03/06/trump-putin-and-the-new-cold-war

305   "IMF says Western sanctions could cut 9 pct off Russia's GDP," Jason
      Bush, Reuters (Aug. 3, 2015). Retrieved at: http://www.reuters.com/
      article/russia-economy-imf-idUSL9N0OK04620150803

306   Osnos, Remnick, and Yaffa, Ibid.

307   Ibid.

308 "New evidence Sony hack was 'inside' job, not North Korea," Post Staff Report, *New York Post* (Dec. 30, 2014). Retrieved at: http://nypost.com/2014/12/30/new-evidence-sony-hack-was-inside-job-cyber-experts/

309 "John McAfee: 'I Can Promise You It Wasn't Russia Who Hacked the DNC,'" *Sputnik News* (March 21, 2017). Retrieved at: https://sputniknews.com/science/201703211051795848-mcafee-russia-dnc-hack/

310 Of course, the Department of Homeland Security, quite tellingly, made it clear that it "does not provide any warranties of any kind regarding any information contained within" the report purporting to pin the alleged hack on the Russians.

311 (For more on this, see Valentine, Douglas, Ibid. and my friend Douglas Valentine's book, *The CIA As a Criminal Organization*).

312 "Kennedy vs. the Military," Robert Dallek, *The Atlantic*. Retrieved at: https://www.theatlantic.com/magazine/archive/2013/08/jfk-vs-the-military/309496/

313 Ibid.

314 "Lie by Lie: A Timeline of How We Got Into Iraq," Jonathan Stein and Tim Dickinson, *Mother Jones* (Sept./Oct. 2006 issue). Retrieved at: http://m.motherjones.com/politics/2011/12/leadup-iraq-war-timeline

315 "US Intel Vets Dispute Russia Hacking Claims," Veterans Intelligence Professionals for Sanity, *Consortium News* (Dec. 12, 2016). Retrieved at: https://consortiumnews.com/2016/12/12/us-intel-vets-dispute-russia-hacking-claims/; and, "The Dubious Case on Russian 'Hacking,'" William Binney and Ray McGovern, *Consortium News* (Jan. 6, 2017). Retrieved at: https://consortiumnews.com/2017/01/06/the-dubious-case-on-russian-hacking/

316 "How 'New Cold Warriors' Cornered Trump," Gareth Porter, *Consortium News* (Feb. 25, 2017). Retrieved at: https://consortiumnews.com/2017/02/25/how-new-cold-warriors-cornered-trump/

317 "Seymour Hersh Blasts Media for Uncritically Promoting Russian Hacking Story," Jeremy Scahill, *The Intercept* (Jan. 25, 2017). Retrieved at: https://theintercept.com/2017/01/25/seymour-hersh-blasts-media-for-uncritically-promoting-russian-hacking-story/

318 Ibid.

319 "WikiLeaks Releases Trove of Alleged C.I.A. Hacking Documents," Scott Shane, Matthew Rosenberg, and Andrew W. Lehren, *New York Times* (March 7, 2017). Retrieved at: https://www.nytimes.com/2017/03/07/world/europe/wikileaks-cia-hacking.html?_r=0

320 Ibid.

321 "WikiLeaks' Latest CIA Data Dump Undermines Case Against Russia Election Hack," Dave Lindorff, *Counterpunch* (March 10, 2017). Retrieved at: http://www.counterpunch.org/2017/03/10/wikileaks-latest-cia-data-dump-undermines-case-against-russia-election-hack/;

322 "Kucinich Pins Flynn Leak on Intelligence Community—Warns of Another Cold War," Fox News (Feb. 14, 2017). Retrieved at: http://www.foxbusiness.com/politics/2017/02/14/kucinich-pins-flynn-leak-on-intel-community-warns-another-cold-war.html

323 Gareth Porter, ibid.

324 "The Missing Logic of Russia-Gate," Robert Parry, *Consortium News* (March 20, 2017). Retrieved at: https://consortiumnews.com/2017/03/20/the-missing-logic-of-russia-gate/

325 "Why Did the Saudi Regime and Other Gulf Tyrannies Donate Millions to the Clinton Foundation?" Glenn Greenwald, *The Intercept* (Aug. 25, 2016). Retrieved at: https://theintercept.com/2016/08/25/why-did-the-saudi-regime-and-other-gulf-tyrannies-donate-millions-to-the-clinton-foundation/

326 "In Hopelessly Corrupt Ukraine, Business Is Business for Joe Biden's Son," *Russia Insider* (Feb. 6, 2016). Retrieved at: http://russia-insider.com/en/politics/hopelessly-corrupt-ukraine-business-business-joe-bidens-son/ri12650

327 "Russia, Trump, and a New Détente," Robert David English, *Foreign Affairs* (March 15, 2017). Retrieved at: http://us-russia.org/4692-russia-trump-and-a-new-dtente.html

328 Greg Jaffe and Adam Entous, "Trump ends covert CIA program to arm anti-Assad rebels in Syria, a move sought by Moscow." *The Washington Post,* July 19, 2017. Retrieved at https://www.washingtonpost.com/world/national-security/trump-ends-covert-cia-program-to-arm-anti-assad-rebels-in-syria-a-move-sought-by-moscow/2017/07/19/b6821a62-6beb-11e7-96ab-5f38140b38cc_story.html?pushid=596fab4ff-1dad71d00000034&tid=notifi_push_breaking-news&utm_term=.ba88d2966e95.

329 Robert Fisk, "Syria's 'moderates' have disappeared and there are no good guys." *Independent*, Oct. 4, 2015. Retrieved at http://www.independent.

co.uk/voices/syria-s-moderates-have-disappeared-and-there-are-no-good-guys-a6679406.html.

330 Norman Solomon, "How the Russia Spin Got So Much Torque." *Common Dreams,* May 1, 2017. Retrieved at https://www.commondreams.org/views/2017/05/01/how-russia-spin-got-so-much-torque.

331 Norman Solomon, "Democrats Face Failing Russia-gate Scheme." *Consortium News,* June 26, 2017. Retrieved at https://consortiumnews.com/2017/06/26/democrats-face-failing-russia-gate-scheme/.

332 Philip Weiss, "Clinton lost because PA, WI, and MI have high casualty rates and saw her as pro-war, study says." *Mondoweiss,* July 6, 2017. Retrieved at http://mondoweiss.net/2017/07/clinton-because-communities/.

333 Katie Reilly, "Hillary Clinton is Less Popular Than President Trump, Poll Finds." *Time,* July 19, 2017. Retrieved at: http://time.com/4864023/hillary-clinton-donald-trump-less-popular-poll/

334 Greg Palast, "The Election was Stolen – Here's How...." *Gregpalast.com,* November 11, 2016. Available at http://www.gregpalast.com/election-stolen-heres/.

335 Erik Sherman, "60% Of House Democrats Vote For A Defense Budget Even Bigger Than Trump's." *Forbes,* July 14, 2017. Available at https://www.forbes.com/sites/eriksherman/2017/07/14/most-house-democrats-just-voted-for-a-defense-budget-far-bigger-than-trumps/#12d268b36ea0.

336 Ibid.

337 Ibid.

338 Glenn Greenwald, "With New D.C. Policy Group, Dems Continue to Rehabilitate and Unify With Bush-Era Neocons." *The Intercept,* July 17 2017. Available at https://theintercept.com/2017/07/17/with-new-d-c-policy-group-dems-continue-to-rehabilitate-and-unify-with-bush-era-neocons/.

339 Jeff Darcy, "The Undeniable Pattern Of Russian Hacking." *Moon of Alabama,* July 6, 2017. Available at http://www.moonofalabama.org/2017/07/the-undeniable-pattern-of-russian-hacking.html#more.

340 Molly Hennessy-Fiske, "Nearly 300 died in Mosul airstrike, making it one of the deadliest attacks on civilians in recent memory." *The Los Angeles Times,* April 5, 2017. Available at http://www.latimes.com/world/middlee-ast/la-fg-iraq-mosul-casualties-20170405-story.html.

341 Jason Le Miere, "Under Trump, U.S. Military Has Allegedly Killed Over

1,000 Civilians In Iraq, Syria In March." *Newsweek*, March 31, 2017. Available at http://www.newsweek.com/trumps-war-civilian-deaths-syria-577353.

342   Seymour M. Hersh, "Trump's Red Line." *Welt*. June 25, 2017. Available at https://www.welt.de/politik/ausland/article165905578/Trump-s-Red-Line.html.

342   David Rutz, "New York Times, Associated Press Correct Claims That All 17 Intelligence Agencies Agreed on Russian Interference." *The Washington Free Beacon*, July 5, 2017. Retrieved at: http://freebeacon.com/national-security/new-york-times-associated-press-correct-claims-that-all-17-intelligence-agencies-agreed-on-russian-interference/.

343   Josephine Wolff, "The FBI Is Harder To Trust on The DNC Hack Because It Relied on Crowd Strike." *Slate*, May 9, 2017. Retrieved at: http://www.slate.com/blogs/future_tense/2017/05/09/the_fbi_is_harder_to_trust_on_the_dnc_hack_because_it_relied_on_crowdstrike.html

344   "Intel Veterans Challenge 'Russia Hack' Evidence." *Consortium News,* July 24, 2017. Retrieved at: https://consortiumnews.com/2017/07/24/intel-vets-challenge-russia-hack-evidence/.

345   Robert Parry, "How Russia-gate Met the Magnitsky Myth." *Consortium News,* July 13, 2017. Available at https://consortiumnews.com/2017/07/13/how-russia-gate-met-the-magnitsky-myth/.

346   Ellen Nakashima, Adam Entous, and Greg Miller, "Russian ambassador told Moscow that Kushner wanted secret communications channel with Kremlin." *The Washington Post,* May 26, 2017. Available at https://www.washingtonpost.com/world/national-security/russian-ambassador-told-moscow-that-kushner-wanted-secret-communications-channel-with-kremlin/2017/05/26/520a14b4-422d-11e7-9869-bac8b446820a_story.html?utm_term=.77ddcf4bde6a.

347   Parry, "How Russia-gate Met the Magnitsky Myth."

348   Michael Sainato, "Russian Lawyer Was Lobbying Against Sanctions Clinton Opposed After Paid Speech Gig," *The Observer*, July 13, 2017. Available at http://observer.com/2017/07/natalia-veselnitskaya-hillary-clinton-magnitsky-act/.

349   Jeffrey Lord, "Special Report--Dick Morris: Bill Clinton Meddled in Russian Election for Yeltsin," *American Spectator,* July 11, 2017. Retrieved at: https://spectator.org/dick-morris-bill-clinton-meddled-in-russian-election-for-yeltsin/.

THE PLOT TO
SCAPEGOAT
RUSSIA